PROPHETS
WITHOUT HONOR

Howard Box
112 Providence Rd
Oak Ridge TN 37830
howardbox@webtv.net
(865) 482-2311

PROPHETS WITHOUT HONOR

Public Policy and the Selective Conscientious Objector

studies in christian ethics series

JOHN A. ROHR

Nashville   ABINGDON PRESS   New York

PROPHETS WITHOUT HONOR

Copyright © 1971 by Abingdon Press

ISBN 0-687-34465-4

Library of Congress Catalog Card Number: 77–148860

SET UP, PRINTED, AND BOUND BY THE
PARTHENON PRESS, AT NASHVILLE,
TENNESSEE, UNITED STATES OF AMERICA

Amen, amen, I say unto you,
no prophet is without honor
except in his own country.

Luke 4: 24

to those who know
they are my brothers
gratefully

PREFACE

This essay is a "study in public policy" because it treats selective conscientious objection in terms of whether or not it should be the law of the land. Thus, the focus of my study is selective objection as a substantive political issue. Needless to say, this is not the only way a political scientist may approach this issue. An interesting behavioral study could be done on what sorts of persons become selective objectors. Their familial, religious, and economic backgrounds could be traced to see if it is possible to typify selective conscientious objectors in some meaningful way. A biographical approach would also be of interest. Here one might rehearse the salient political values considered by a young man in his painful decision to refuse to serve in a particular war.[1]

I have chosen the public policy approach because I believe a political scientist can make a distinctive contribution to public debate by asking pertinent questions and offering relevant guidelines for discussion. The scholar's role differs from that of the advocate, but this difference does not absolve the scholar from his responsibility to clarify issues by discussing them in the same terms as the participants in public argument. In this way the political scientist can bridge the relevance gap by speaking to the issues of the day without reducing his expertise to special pleading. Hopefully, he can elevate the level of public discourse so a given policy proposal will be accepted or rejected for only the best of reasons.

My original plan was to divide this study into three areas—constitutional,

[1] For a psychiatrist's account of the prison problems of war resisters, see Willard Gaylin, *In Service of Their Country: War Resisters in Prison* (New York: Viking Press, 1970).

theoretical, and administrative. I soon discovered, however, the wisdom of Woodrow Wilson's observation that "administration is the heart of modern government." I found it increasingly difficult to discuss constitutional and theoretical questions without getting into administrative questions as well. Massive constitutional and theoretical questions arose as soon as I pondered just how selective conscientious objection would work in practice. For this reason I incorporated the administrative considerations into the two sections that comprise this book.

The first section takes up the constitutional question: Is there a constitutional right to selective conscientious objection? Here the focus of inquiry is whether the principles underlying recent Supreme Court interpretations of the first amendment have implicitly committed our society to include in its fundamental law the right to refuse military service in a particular war on grounds of conscience. My conclusion is that they have not. The absence of a *constitutional* right to selective conscientious objection, however, leaves open the question of whether selective objection should become law by Act of Congress. In Part II—The Policy Question—I address this problem. Despite the absence of a constitutional *mandate* for selective conscientious objection, are there sound theoretical and practical considerations that may prompt Congress to adopt such a measure anyway?

Although the debate over conscientious objection to particular wars raises certain perennial issues of "man and the state," the timeliness of the question has presented some practical problems in writing this book. One of these is simply keeping up-to-date with recent court decisions touching this topic. In *U.S.* v. *Sisson*[2] (a case explored at some length in chapter four) the Supreme Court had an opportunity to decide the constitutional standing of the case for selective objectors, but chose to dispose of it on technical grounds without reaching the constitutional issues. There are several similar cases at various steps in the federal appellate process, but there is no way of knowing when, if ever, the Supreme Court will actually address the constitutional question.[3] The issue of selective conscientious objection may be of such high political visibility that the Court will sidestep it by employing the technical procedures Alexander Bickel has aptly called "the passive virtues." [4]

It is possible, however, that the constitutional issue will be settled before this book is published. If it is and if the Court should reject the case for

[2] 399 *U.S.* 367 (1970).

[3] The Court has agreed to hear oral arguments in *U.S.* v. *Gillette* (420 F 2d 298) and *Negre* v. *Larsen* (418 F 2d 908). Although these cases involve selective conscientious objectors, the Court may dispose of them without reaching the constitutional question. See *New York Times*, June 30, 1970, p. 1.

[4] Alexander M. Bickel, *The Least Dangerous Branch* (Indianapolis: Bobbs-Merrill, 1962), pp. 113-99.

selective objection, the argument of the first section of this book would be sustained. The book's second part would then acquire a new urgency, for a Supreme Court decision rejecting the constitutional case for selective objection would mean that selective objection could become public policy only by an Act of Congress.

Should the Court uphold a constitutional right to selective objection, the reader might look upon the first section of this study as an "instant criticism" of such a decision. In the pages that follow I try to show that a favorable verdict on selective objection would be inconsistent with previous decisions of the Court. Should the Supreme Court, then, uphold selective objectors, I could only invite the careful reader to compare the reasons for my prediction that the Court would not do this with whatever reasons the Court might offer for doing it.

A Supreme Court decision favorable to selective objection would not render moot the problem of whether Congress should support such a policy. As I shall show in chapter two, the strongest constitutional case for selective objection rests on the manner in which the Selective Service Act presently discriminates against objectors to the advantage of the complete pacifist. That is, if the Court should affirm a constitutional right to selective objection, it is not likely to do so by reading selective objection directly into the first amendment. The Court is more likely to proceed indirectly by disallowing the present favoritism shown to pacifists. In effect the Court would tell Congress that whatever it does for total objectors it must do for selective objectors. Congress would then be faced with a choice between excluding all forms of conscientious objection on the one hand or including selective along with total pacifism on the other.[5] The policy (as opposed to constitutional) arguments for and against selective objection in the second part of this book would, hopefully, contribute to an informed public opinion while this issue was being debated in Congress.

Throughout this study I use the letters SCO to stand for selective conscientious objector(s) and/or objection. CO stands for total (i.e., all wars) conscientious objector(s) and/or objection.

I wish to express my gratitude in the first place to those Jesuits who have encouraged me in my interest in the sort of question this book addresses. Over the past eighteen years they have given me the support—intellectual, spiritual, and financial—that has made this work possible. Special thanks are due to the members of the Faber Hall Community for their unfailing patience and kindness during the years in which this volume was composed.

[5] For a judicial attempt to declare the present provision for conscientious objectors unconstitutional without doing away with the exemption, see the concurring opinion of Mr. Justice Harlan in *U.S.* v. *Welsh*, 399 *U.S.* 333 (1970).

Prophets Without Honor is a slightly revised version of the dissertation I submitted to the Political Science Department of the University of Chicago in March, 1970. I am most grateful to the faculty, staff, and students of that fine department for the stimulating years I spent with them. I am grateful, too, to the University for the considerable financial assistance I received during those years. I wish to express special appreciation to Professors C. Herman Pritchett and Joseph Cropsey for their many helpful suggestions in completing my research. I can never express adequately my gratitude to Professor Herbert J. Storing, the chairman of my research committee. He combines depth of insight, clarity of expression, and dedication to his students in a most remarkable manner.

I received considerable assistance from many members of the legal profession in securing the information and materials necessary for this study. Among the men to whom I am indebted are Professors Gerhard Casper and Robert A. Burt of the law faculty of the University of Chicago; Melvin L. Wulf and M. M. Karpatkin of the American Civil Liberties Union; Francis X. Beytagh, David M. Hartigan, and Samuel K. Skinner of the Justice Department; Lt. Robert Teaff of the Judge Advocate's Group, United States Navy; and the following attorneys who have defended selective conscientious objectors: Richard Harrington, George Pontikes, Anthony J. Murray, Harry F. Peck, and Harold P. Southerland.

I am most grateful to Richard A. McCormick, Paul Ramsey and Roger L. Shinn for their thoughtful suggestions in editing this volume. Finally, my thanks to those good friends who helped in preparing and proofreading the manuscript—especially Maureen Hallinan, Michael Czerny, and Robert Burns.

J.A.R.
October, 1970

CONTENTS

PART I
THE CONSTITUTIONAL QUESTION

Roper: So now you'd give the Devil benefit of law!

More: Yes. What would you do? Cut a great road through the law to get after the Devil?

Roper: I'd cut down every law in England to do that!

More: (*Roused and excited*) Oh? (*Advances on Roper*) And when the last law was down, and the Devil turned round on you—where would you hide, Roper, the laws all being flat? This country's planted thick with laws from coast to coast—man's laws, not God's—and if you cut them down—and you're just the man to do it—do you really think you could stand upright in the winds that would blow then? (*Quietly*) Yes, I'd give the Devil benefit of law, for my own safety's sake.

A Man for All Seasons
Act I

I
The Conscientious Objector

The story of the total pacifist, the traditional CO, is the most likely starting point for this study of the questions raised by the selective objector. This is not because their problems are the same. Indeed, a major theme in this book is that the case for selective objection rests on grounds quite different from those that have traditionally supported the total objector. Nevertheless, the total objector is a fixed star in our legislative constellation and, as such, is constantly referred to for *a pari* arguments in support of SCO. This opening chapter will follow the lead of the SCO literature by reviewing the role of the CO in the history and the courts of the United States.

A Historical Survey

The historical survey of total objection will be brief and selective; brief because it has been handled thoroughly elsewhere[1] and selective because I shall consider only those aspects of CO which relate to my topic. Specifically, I shall consider the main outlines of the provisions made for CO's when Americans have gone to war and then point out several recurring themes that are salient in the SCO question.

MAIN PROVISIONS FOR CO. A full year before the Declaration of Inde-

[1] John H. Mansfield, "Conscientious Objection, 1964 Term," *Religion and the Public Order*, ed. Donald A. Giannella (Chicago: University of Chicago Press, 1965), pp. 3-81; Mulford Q. Sibley and Philip E. Jacob, *Conscription of Conscience: The American State and the Conscientious Objector, 1940-47* (Ithaca, N.Y.: Cornell University Press, 1952); Jack F. Leach, *Conscription in the U.S.: Historical Background* (Rutland, Vt.: C. E. Tuttle, 1952).

pendence the Continental Congress, recognizing that "there are some people who from Religious Principles cannot bear Arms in any case," declared that "this Congress intend no violence to their Consciences." [2] The Congress urged such persons to *"contribute liberally,* in this time of universal calamity, to the relief of their distressed brethren in the several colonies, and to do all other services to their oppressed country, which they can consistently with their Religious Principles." [3] Thus, at the very outset we observe a striking similarity between the policy of the First Continental Congress and the present handling of CO's—restricting the exemption to those who by "religious training and belief" are conscientiously opposed to "participation in war in any form." [4] While the present law *requires* some form of alternative service, the Continental Congress, in accordance with its limited powers, *recommended* liberal contributions to meet the needs of their distressed countrymen. In both cases, however, the supposition is that the objector will support the government action in any way he can.

During the Revolution the effective power to conscript lay, of course, with the colonies. The most common method of accommodating CO's was a provision excusing from military service those who hired a substitute or paid a "commutation fee," but this privilege was not restricted to those unwilling to serve for reasons of conscience. At least five colonies, however, had special arrangements for CO's, the most common of which was a provision for military service not directly connected with the bearing of arms.[5]

There was no conscription in either the War of 1812 or the Mexican War, although the House version of the ill-fated Federal Draft Bill of 1814 contained an exemption for CO's.

For the first two years of the Civil War the ranks of the Confederate and Union armies were filled with men conscripted by the states. In March, 1863 the first national draft act was passed. It contained no explicit provisions for CO's, but excused from military service those who could either provide a substitute themselves or pay the War Department $300. The Draft Act of 1864 recognized the rights of CO's already in uniform. They were to be considered noncombatants under the jurisdiction of the Secretary of War whose responsibility it was to assign them "to duty in the hospitals, or to the care of freedmen." [6] The same act provided that the CO could stay out of the army by paying $300 to the Secretary of War. This sum could be applied only to the care of sick and wounded soldiers.[7]

[2] *Conscientious Objection,* Selective Service Monograph No. 11 (Washington, D.C.: Government Printing Office, 1950), p. 33. Hereafter referred to as *SSM* 11.
[3] *Ibid.,* p. 34.
[4] 50 U.S.C.A. App. § 456 (j).
[5] *SSM* 11, pp. 29-37.
[6] *Ibid.,* p. 42.
[7] *Ibid.*

There was no need for conscription during the Spanish-American War. In World War I the United States adopted a new policy toward CO's. There was no provision for hiring a substitute or paying a commutation fee. All able-bodied men within specified age limits, CO's included, were liable for military service. Section four of the Selective Service Act of May 18, 1917 exempted from combatant status members "of any well-recognized religious sect or organization . . . whose existing creed or principles forbid its members to participate in war in any form."[8] Such men, however, were considered military personnel because the same section provided that "no person so exempted shall be exempted from service in any capacity the President shall declare to be non-combatant."[9] Among the military activities declared to be noncombatant were the Medical Corps, the Quartermaster Corps, and the Corps of Engineers.

Two administrative regulations liberalized the provisions of the Selective Service Act. The first was an order from the Adjutant General of the Army expanding the area of conscience to include those with "personal scruples" against war as well as members of historic peace churches.[10] The second was based on an opinion of the Judge Advocate General advising the Secretary of War that he could grant "furloughs" for agricultural, industrial, and hospital work.[11] This satisfied the consciences of many who were opposed to being "in the army," though they were still under the jurisdiction of the Secretary of War.

These administrative regulations found their way into the Congressional provisions for CO's in the Draft Act of 1940. CO status was no longer connected with sectarian membership, but instead was based on "religious training and belief." Those who objected to noncombatant roles in the Army were assigned to civilian work of national importance under civilian direction.[12] An elaborate appeals system was established whereby a CO whose claim was rejected by his local board could appear before an appellate draft board. When such appeals were made, the Justice Department would investigate the claim and advise the appellate board.[13]

The only significant change in the Selective Service Act of 1948 was its attempt to define religious training and belief more closely. A CO had to believe in a relation to a Supreme Being involving duties superior to those arising from any human relation. The law explicitly excluded beliefs that were essentially political, sociological, or philosophical as well as a "merely

[8] *Ibid.*, p. 49.
[9] *Ibid.*
[10] *Ibid.*, pp. 54-55.
[11] *Ibid.*, p. 59.
[12] *Ibid.*, p. 89.
[13] *Ibid.*

personal code." [14] The 1967 Act omitted the Supreme Being clause and the investigation by the Justice Department upon appeal from a local board's denial of a CO claim.[15]

MAIN THEMES. The novelty of SCO is apparent when one reads through the debates over CO in American history. Whenever the issue appears it is in terms of objection to *all* wars. The only exception is Senator Robert M. La Follette's amendment to the Draft Act of 1917. He would have exempted from military service those who had "a conscientious objection to the undertaking of combatant service in the *present* war." [16] La Follette and Senator Charles S. Thomas of Colorado had been unhappy with the Act's provision for CO's. Thomas had little enthusiasm for the CO exemption, but if it had to be granted he insisted that it not be restricted to members of historic peace churches. The exemption should reach all who were opposed to war on grounds of conscience.[17] The amendments of La Follette and Thomas had been discussed together until Senator James W. Wadsworth of New York pointed out the significant difference between the two positions and thereby introduced the first "great debate" on SCO:

[The present war position] is very different from the contention which the Senator from Colorado has been making. The Senator from Colorado has been contending, and he, of course, is entitled to his conviction and his contention, that a person who has a conscientious conviction against war in the abstract, against bearing arms in any war as a matter of principle, should be exempted, but the provision in the amendment of the Senator from Wisconsin would go to the extent of saying that any man in the United States who has a conscientious conviction against taking part in *this* war shall be exempt. I call that to the careful consideration of the Senate.[18]

The ensuing debate was spirited, but short-lived. La Follette defended his amendment on the grounds that many Americans of German ancestry would have conscientious objections against fighting Germany and Austria. His argument was buried in an avalanche of outrage.[19] For our purposes the most interesting aspect of the ill-fated amendment is its overtly *political* character. One of the major problems in the current SCO debate is the question (sometimes substantive, but often semantic) of whether a

[14] 50 U.S.C.A. App. § 456 (j), 1951 edition. The reasons for this change are given in some detail below. Cf. pp. 33-35.

[15] 50 U.S.C.A. App. § 456 (j), 1968 edition.

[16] *Congressional Record*, 65th Congress, 1st Session, 1917, LV, 1474, col. b (April 28, 1917).

[17] *Ibid.*, p. 1004, col. b (April 24, 1971). As we saw above (p. 19), the Adjutant General accomplished by administrative regulation what Senator Thomas would have achieved by statute.

[18] *Ibid.*, p. 1475, col. b (April 28, 1917). Emphasis added.

[19] *Ibid.*, pp. 1476-1478 (April 28, 1917).

"conscientious" objection can also be "political" or whether it must rest on "religious" grounds.

A second theme in the history of the American response to CO is the widespread recognition of the patriotism of the objectors. In Pennsylvania, it is true, the Quakers were often severely criticized for failing to do their share in fighting against the Indians and the French. This may have been due to the large numbers of Quakers in that colony. The practical consequences of their refusal to take up arms would be felt more keenly in Pennsylvania than elsewhere. In general, however, the Quakers and other pacifist groups usually won high marks for patriotism when the nation debated CO. Thus, when Congress was discussing a Federal Draft during the War of 1812, Mr. Lewis of Virginia rose to argue for exemptions for CO's. For him they were "a class of industrious, respectable, and highly meritorious citizens." [20] During the Civil War Senator Henry B. Anthony defended the CO provision for Quakers on the grounds that "even in the slave-holding states they have not been slaveholders," and "even now this class of people in the rebel states are mostly Union men, and have suffered greatly for their attachment to the Union." [21] Anthony went on to say that the Quakers hold opinions

that have been entertained for two hundred years by as intelligent men as have ever spoken the English language, and [they] have borne every persecution that the old martyrs ever bore in defense of these principles—educated intelligent men; and I think we ought to respect them.[22]

Even Senator John Conness, who opposed the CO exemptions, had nothing but praise for the character of the Quakers. They are "the truest, the noblest, and the sternest patriots that I have met in the country." [23]

In more recent times Senator Wayne Morse confessed that he was "at a loss to understand the psychology of conscientious objectors." [24] "They perplex me," he said.[25] His own personal advice to a CO was, "You should recognize that you have control over your body, and you ought to offer your body to your country and your conscience to your God." [26] It would be difficult to imagine a more insensitive statement, yet the very next day Morse acknowledged that we have "no finer citizenry" than some of those

[20] *Annals of Congress,* 13th Congress, 2nd Session, XXVIII, 772 (December 8, 1814).
[21] *Congressional Globe,* 38th Congress, 1st Session, p. 205, col. a (January 14, 1864).
[22] *Ibid.,* p. 205, col. b (January 14, 1864).
[23] *Ibid.,* p. 206, col. a (January 14, 1864).
[24] *Congressional Record,* 80th Congress, 2nd Session, 1948, XCIV, 7277, col. b (June 7, 1948).
[25] *Ibid.*
[26] *Ibid.*

who "hold convictions of conscientious objection insofar as military service is concerned." [27]

Similar statements praising the patriotism and civic virtue of members of the peace churches could easily be presented. They are relevant because they show that SCO is not merely an extension of the CO question. When Congress was granting CO exemptions at different points in our history, there was never any question of the loyalty or patriotism of the objectors. Senator Morse's advice to the CO is instructive. The statement that the young man has control over his body seems to suggest that he does not have control over his conscience. For Morse the CO's conscience is, perhaps, what Justice Holmes would call a "can't help." It is no embarrassment to the government to indulge a "can't help," especially if the person so afflicted is otherwise a good citizen. The SCO presents an entirely different case. His position is not a "can't help," but is based on arguments that are constitutional, political, and historical—as well as moral or religious. Frequently he takes to the streets to protest his opposition to the government's policy and may even be openly sympathetic to the enemy. History may show that the dissenters were the true patriots of our time, but at present it is not surprising if the Justice Department, Congress, and perhaps even the Courts may not see it that way. The SCO raises his claim in a political accent different from that of the total CO of the past. He is not a tame irrelevancy whose eccentricities a liberal society can easily indulge.

Another theme in the history of the American CO is the question of sincerity—how to protect the conscience of the individual without letting cowards and slackers get by. The problem has been more acute since 1940 when Congress substituted "religious training and belief" for membership in a peace church as the guiding norm. It was the problem of sincerity that led Senator James D. Phelan to oppose Senator Thomas' amendment to the 1917 Draft Act. Thomas' amendment, as has been noted, would have extended the exemption to all who were conscientiously opposed to war instead of restricting it to members of the peace churches. If Congress accepted the Thomas amendment, Phelan feared it meant "opening the doors to every slacker who, without any sincere and long established convictions might declare his so-called 'conscientious scruples' in order to avoid service." [28]

The Revolutionary Period showed that even when the exemption was restricted to members of specified churches, the sincerity problem still appeared. The Military Association for the City and Liberties of Philadelphia complained in a memorial of September 27, 1775 "that People sincerely and

[27] *Ibid.*, p. 7303, col. b (June 8, 1948).
[28] *Ibid.*, 65th Congress, 1st Session, LV, 1479 (April 28, 1917).

22

religiously scrupulous are but few in comparison to those who upon this Occasion as well as others, make conscience a convenience." [29]

The question of how sincerity should be tested was brought up by Senator Anthony in the Civil War Draft debate. He felt that there were many Quakers who did not have conscientious scruples against military service despite their religious affiliation. Rather than look to church membership alone, Anthony would have the objectors appear before some tribunal or officer to prove that "their walk and conversation has been in accordance with their religious profession." [30]

In 1917 Congress rejected a proposal that would let a man's uncontradicted oath suffice to prove his sincerity.[31] In 1940 Congressman Voorhis complained bitterly that the House changed the original wording of the draft bill to let the local board, not the Justice Department, determine sincerity. He felt the Justice Department would be more likely to develop uniform national standards for judging CO claims.[32] For similar reasons Senator Morse proposed a National Commission on CO to accompany the Draft Act of 1948.[33]

These examples will suffice to show the perennial concern with sincerity in the administration of the CO exemption. If sincerity has been a problem for the traditional CO, it would be even more of a problem for the SCO. The total objector can point to lifelong membership in a peace church or, if he is not a church-goer, he can offer as proof of his sincerity the fact that he was associated with pacifist groups long before the government tried to draft him. It is easier for him to establish his sincerity than it is for the SCO. The very fact that the SCO objects to a *particular* war means that he cannot point as readily as the total objector to lifelong patterns of behavior consistent with his belief.

A fourth theme is the coincidence of national interest and respect for the individual's conscience. While the latter has always been the primary motive for exempting CO's, the consideration that it is in the government's best interest to do so has never been far from the surface. Thus, President Lincoln rejected the suggestion that he conscript Quakers and Mennonites. "People who do not believe in war," he said, "make poor soldiers." [34] He added further, "They are excellent farmers" and "this country needs good farmers fully as much as it needs good soldiers." [35]

Senator La Follette followed the same reasoning in his unsuccessful attempt

[29] SSM 11, p. 34.
[30] Congressional Globe, 38th Congress, 1st Session, p. 204, col. b (January 14, 1864).
[31] Congressional Record, 65th Congress, 1st Session, 1917, LV, 1476 (April 28, 1917).
[32] Ibid., 76th Congress, 3rd Session, 1940, LXXXVI, 11694, col. a (September 7, 1940).
[33] Ibid., 80th Congress, 2nd Session, 1948, XCIV, 7278 (June 7, 1948).
[34] SSM 11, p. 42
[35] Ibid.

to exempt German-Americans with conscientious scruples against fighting the Central Powers in World War I:

It seemed to me that, just as a practical question, they ought not to be required to go into the service to fight against their kith and kin, provided they have conscientious objections to so doing. We want soldiers whose hearts are in the work that is assigned to them, soldiers who have no reservations whatever. If we are to make an army effective, it ought to be an army that has no scruples against shooting the people with whom we are at war.[36]

Frequent examples of national interest arguments on behalf of CO occurred during the debate on the Civil War Draft. Senator Daniel Clark pointed out that Quakers and Shakers would bitterly resent any attempt to make them fight, "but if you excuse them from military service they will pour out of their substance to aid the country, and their blessings to help your cause." [37]

Perhaps the clearest statement of making the best of both worlds came from Senator Anthony:

The object of this bill is to amend the defects which experience has found in the working of the enrollment act and I submit to the Senate that the invasion of the rights of conscience is one of the most serious of those defects. There has not been a single man added to the Army who was worth the rations that he ate by the refusal to exempt persons conscientiously scrupulous as to bearing arms. I might tell you, Mr. President, the most piteous stories of the sufferings and persecutions of this class of people. . . . But I cannot show you and you cannot show me one single efficient man that has been added to the Army by the impressment of men conscientiously scrupulous against bearing arms.[38]

The proponents of SCO might borrow a page from CO history and structure their arguments for SCO along national interest lines. Usually the case for SCO is couched in terms of man *versus* the state. Two lines of argument then follow. The first is a strident claim for the absolute value of conscience; the second is a measured appeal to balance the considerable benefits SCO would bring to the individual against the insignificant harm it would do to the state. History suggests a more fruitful argument might come from emphasizing the harmony rather than the clash of personal and governmental interests that could result from SCO.[39]

[36] *Congressional Record,* 65th Congress, 1st Session, 1917, LV, 1476, col. b (April 28, 1917).
[37] *Congressional Globe,* 37th Congress, 3rd Session, p. 994, col. b (February 16, 1863).
[38] *Ibid.,* 38th Congress, 1st Session, p. 204, col. b and p. 205, col. a (January 14, 1864).
[39] Cf. below, Chapter VII, pp. 156 ff.

The CO in Court

We have seen the main outlines of CO in American history. It would be helpful to turn to the courts to see how they have handled this question. Again, the scope of my investigation is limited only to those aspects of the CO cases that will contribute to an analysis of SCO.

THE SELECTIVE DRAFT LAW CASES. In the *Selective Draft Law Cases*[40] of 1918, CO played a very minor role. The main point in the opinion of Chief Justice White was to uphold the constitutionality of the Draft on the basis of Congress' power to raise and support armies, to declare war, to make rules for the land and naval forces, and to make all laws necessary and proper for executing these granted powers. The only reference to CO came in response to the contention that the exemption of ministers, theological students, and members of pacifist sects constituted an "establishment of a religion or an interference with the free exercise thereof." [41]

The Court felt that it need only state the argument without comment, "because we think its unsoundness is too apparent to require us to do more." [42]

THE NATURALIZATION CASES. Three naturalization cases in the years 1929-31 raised the CO question more directly. In *U.S.* v. *Schwimmer*[43] the Supreme Court upheld the District Court for the Northern District of Illinois in its denial of citizenship to a forty-nine-year-old woman who described herself as an "uncompromising pacifist." The fact that Congress had exempted CO's in World War I did not exempt Miss Schwimmer from the provisions of the Naturalization Act of 1906. Among these provisions is the requirement of an oath that the applicant will "support and defend the Constitution and laws of the United States against all enemies foreign and domestic." [44] The Court interpreted this oath to mean the applicant must be willing to defend the Constitution *by force of arms* if necessary. Her sex and age were irrelevant because the "influence of conscientious objectors against the use of military force in defense of the principles of our Government is apt to be more detrimental than their mere refusal to bear arms." [45] She is likely to influence others along the same line; anything "that tends to lessen the willingness of citizens to discharge their duty to bear arms in the country's defense detracts from the strength and safety of the Government." [46]

The second and third naturalization cases touching on CO were *U.S.* v.

---

[40] 245 U.S. 366 (1918).
[42] *Ibid.*
[44] *Ibid.*, at 646.
[46] *Ibid.*, at 650.

[41] *Ibid.*, at 390.
[43] 279 U.S. 644.
[45] *Ibid.*, at 651.

Macintosh [47] and its companion case, *U.S.* v *Bland*.[48] The applications for citizenship were denied on the grounds that naturalization is a privilege "to be given, qualified, or withheld as Congress may determine." [49] Congress had determined that naturalization be given only to those who swear they are willing to bear arms in defense of the nation—a condition Macintosh and Bland failed to meet. Miss Bland qualified her oath with the words, "as far as my conscience as a Christian will allow." [50] Upon investigation it became apparent that Miss Bland, like Miss Schwimmer, was an "uncompromising pacifist."

Macintosh's position is more interesting because he qualified his oath to defend the Constitution by force of arms with the proviso "that the war was morally justified." [51] Thus he was the first SCO to appeal before the Supreme Court. He was a Baptist minister and a professor of theology at Yale University Divinity School. During World War I he had served as a chaplain in the Canadian Army. Since naturalization was the point at issue, the nature of Macintosh's objection, selective or total, made little difference. In either case he failed to meet the statutory provisions requiring the oath Macintosh could take only with qualification. Nevertheless, we have as dictum on SCO this statement of Justice Sutherland:

He is unwilling to leave the question of his future military service to the wisdom of Congress where it belongs, and where every native-born or admitted citizen is obliged to leave it. In effect, he offers to take the oath of allegiance only with the qualification that the question whether the war is necessary or morally justified must, so far as his support is concerned, be conclusively determined by reference to his opinion.

When he speaks of putting his allegiance to the will of God above his allegiance to the government, it is evident, in the light of his entire statement that he means to make *his own interpretation* of the will of God the decisive test which shall conclude the government and stay its hand.

We are a Christian people (*Holy Trinity Church* v. *U.S.* 143 U.S. 457, 470-71), according to one another the equal right of religious freedom and acknowledging with reverence the duty of the obedience to the will of God. But also, we are a nation with the duty to survive; a Nation whose Constitution contemplates war as well as peace; whose government must go forward upon the assumption, and safely can proceed on no other, that unqualified allegiance to the Nation and submission and obedience to the laws of the land, as well those made for war as those made for peace, are not inconsistent with the will of God.[52]

[47] 283 U.S. 605 (1931).
[49] *Ibid.*, at 605.
[51] *Ibid.*, at 608.
[48] 283 U.S. 636 (1931).
[50] *Ibid.*, at 636.

[52] *Ibid.*, at 624-25. The government brief made the following attack on SCO: "The assumption in the opinion of the Court below that the respondent refused to bear arms in defense of this country because of conscientious or religious scruples, is hardly justified by the record. The stipulated facts and his answers to questions disclose a willingness

Macintosh could not make an absolute promise that he would refrain from criticism of the government in its prosecution of a war he considered unjust, because such a decision could not be made before all the circumstances were known. Unlike contemporary SCO's however, Macintosh "did not question that the government under certain conditions could regulate and restrain the conduct of the individual citizen, even to the extent of imprisonment." [53]

Although Macintosh lost his case, he had the consolation of seeing his side taken by a distinguished dissenting foursome—Hughes, Holmes, Brandeis, and Stone. The dissenting opinion of Chief Justice Hughes dealt primarily with the majority's interpretation of the Naturalization Act. He thought the Court erred in following the *Schwimmer* doctrine that the oath to defend the Constitution meant defense by force of arms. On the issue of selective objection Hughes' dicta were somewhat disappointing. Having argued that opposition to all wars should not be a bar to citizenship, he concluded, "there would seem to be no reason why a reservation of religious or conscientious objection to participation in wars believed to be unjust should constitute such a disqualification." [54] In equating the implications for citizenship of total and selective objection, the Chief Justice seemed to overlook the tremendous political difference between the two positions. Sutherland's opinion, as we shall see, is totally discredited today while Hughes and his distinguished colleagues have been vindicated. But in the first judicial skirmish over SCO it was the majority opinion and the government's brief [55] that proved more alert to the far-reaching implications of SCO.

HAMILTON v. *REGENTS OF THE UNIVERSITY OF CALIFORNIA* (1934). In *Hamilton*[56] the Court continued its hard line on CO's. Justice Butler rejected petitioner's argument that the University's requirement of compulsory training in military science infringed upon the "liberty" guaranteed by the

---

to bear arms if he is able to satisfy himself 'that the war was morally justified.' But he insists upon the reserved right to determine that matter for himself. Thus he is not opposed to all war or combatant service on the ground of conscientious or religious scruples. The position of respondent is merely that of a highly educated man with that deep sense of right and wrong which every applicant for citizenship is presumed to possess, seeking to transfer from Congress to himself, the right to determine whether the defense of this country requires him to bear arms. According to his own record statements, there is no claim of conscientious or religious views that sets him apart from any other applicant for citizenship; and the gravity of the right he claims would seem to require that such right be accorded every other otherwise qualified applicant. If this were done, the Constitutional power of Congress to declare war and raise and support armies would be seriously affected" (*ibid.*, at 607-608).

[53] *Ibid.*, at 619.
[55] See note 52.
[54] *Ibid.*, at 635.
[56] 293 U.S. 245 (1934).

27

Fourteenth Amendment. The concurring opinion of Justice Cardozo is more relevant to our inquiry because its legal basis is closer to contemporary constitutional doctrine than that of the majority opinion. Justice Butler saw no need "to enumerate or comprehensively define what is included in the 'liberty' protected by the due process clause," [57] whereas Cardozo, anticipating future constitutional developments, "assumes for present purposes that the religious liberty protected by the First Amendment against invasion by the nation is protected by the Fourteenth Amendment against invasion by the states." [58]

Thus, Cardozo puts the question the way it would be put today. The fact, too, that Cardozo was joined by Brandeis and Stone, two dissenters to the discredited *Macintosh* doctrine, lends a more contemporary flavor to the concurring opinion.

Instead of relying on *Macintosh,* Cardozo defends the University's requirement by analyzing the traditional American response to CO's. This response has been twofold: respect for conscience joined with a requirement of support for the war effort by "supplying the army with a substitute or with the money necessary to hire one." [59] The military science requirement, he argues, imposes a lighter burden on conscience than providing men and money to wage a war already underway and therefore cannot be considered a violation of our traditional understanding of religious liberty.

An interesting point in Cardozo's opinion is his candid recognition that the traditional method of accommodating CO's—providing a substitute or the monetary equivalent—did not shrink from imposing a burden on the consciences of those it would accommodate. An "affront to conscience" is the way he puts it. He seems to see the need for *some* burden or "affront to conscience" as part of the very process that recognizes the demands of conscience. Thus, Cardozo's opinion suggests that the American understanding of political life implies a readiness to suffer some limitation upon the claims of one's conscience.

GIROUARD v. *U.S. (1944). In re Summers*[60] was the last CO case to apply *Macintosh*. Mr. Justice Reed, speaking for a closely divided Court, found that if it is no abridgment of the first amendment for Congress to deny citizenship to aliens who refuse to pledge military service, then surely Illinois can deny admission to the bar to a CO without violating "the principles of religious freedom which the Fourteenth Amendment secures against state action." [61] Black, Douglas, Murphy, and Rutledge dissented.

Before the beginning of the 1945 October term Justice Burton replaced

[57] *Ibid.,* at 262.
[59] *Ibid.,* 266.
[61] *Ibid.,* at 573.

[58] *Ibid.*
[60] 325 U.S. 561 (1944).

28

Justice Roberts and joined the four dissenters in *Summers* to overrule *Macintosh*. The case was *Girouard* v. *U.S.*[62] Interestingly, Chief Justice Stone dissented from the majority opinion, even though as an Associate Justice he had dissented from the majority opinion in *Macintosh* some fourteen years earlier. His reason was that Congress had ample opportunity to change the *Macintosh* rule in its three revisions of the Naturalization Act subsequent to that case. It failure to do so could only mean that Congress accepted the Court's interpretation of its intentions.

Justice Douglas' majority opinion thought it was "at best treacherous to find in congressional silence alone the adoption of a controlling rule of law." [63] He did not think the Court could "properly place on the shoulders of Congress the burden of the Court's own error." [64]

In describing the role of CO's in times of national peril, Douglas dwelt at great length on the contributions such persons make to the war effort. He singled out the services of such noncombatants as the "nuclear physicists who developed the atomic bomb, the worker at this lathe, the seamen on cargo vessels. . . . These, too, made essential contributions." [65] He continued:

And the annals of the recent war show that many whose religious scruples prevented them from bearing arms, nevertheless, were unselfish participants in the war effort. Refusal to bear arms is not necessarily a sign of disloyalty or a lack of attachment to our institutions. One may serve his country faithfully and devotedly, though his religious scruples make it impossible for him to shoulder a rifle. Devotion to one's country can be as real and as enduring among noncombatants as among combatants. One may adhere to what he deems to be his obligation to God and yet assume all military risks to secure victory. The effort of war is indivisible; and those whose religious scruples prevent them from killing are no less patriots than those whose special traits or handicaps result in their assignment to duties far behind the fighting front. Each is making the utmost contribution according to his capacity. The fact that his role may be limited by religious convictions rather than by physical characteristics has no necessary bearing on his attachment to his country or on his willingness to support it to his utmost.[66]

Douglas' image of the CO is instructive for our purposes. There are precious few CO's who would be consoled by the thought that "the effort of war is indivisible." Their willingness to accept alternative service would seem to rest precisely on the denial of this assertion. The comparison of the CO's religious scruples to physical handicaps is redolent of the Holmes-Morse "can't helps" discussed above. The idea that the CO "is making the utmost contribution according to his capacity" ignores the moral dimension of the

[62] 328 U.S. 61 (1946).   [63] *Ibid.*, at 69.
[64] *Ibid.*, at 69-70.   [65] *Ibid.*, at 64.
[66] *Ibid.*

objector's position. The dignity of the CO's position is based on his freedom to do otherwise. He is not doing his utmost. His choice deserves our respect only because it is moral and it is moral only because it is free. He *could* fight, but chooses not to.

It is interesting that Douglas, despite his impeccable libertarian credentials, disregards the free choice basis of the CO position. This cannot be done, of course, in the case of the SCO because his freedom of choice is all too visible in his claim to "select" the wars to which he will object. It would be unfair to total objectors if we drew the distinction between CO's and SCO's along the lines of compulsion and free choice. Both choose freely. The difference is that the total objector *makes no special condemnation of his own government.* His refusal to fight condemns all men for their participation in the sinful folly of war. The SCO attacks the policies of his own government in an immediate concrete setting. The SCO could never give the support to the nation's war effort that Douglas praises in the CO's of World War II. The total objector can give some support to the nation in arms because it is *his* nation and he may wish to further the values for which it stands within his self-imposed limits. Since the SCO objects precisely to *this* war, it is hard to see how his conscience could permit him to do anything to support it.[67] Thus, the SCO is politically in a more vulnerable spot because he could seldom enjoy the favorable image of the total objector without violating his conscience. Douglas' opinion in *Girouard* is instructive, then, because, despite its misunderstanding of the CO position, it brings out the political problem the SCO will present when his case is compared with the traditionally favorable image of the CO.

THEOCRATIC WARS. *Sicurella* v. *U.S.*[68] involved a Jehovah's Witness who appealed his conviction for refusing to report for induction after his draft board had denied his CO claim. The appeal board had upheld the denial, relying on a recommendation of the Justice Department that Sicurella failed to qualify because of his willingness to fight in defense of "his ministry, Kingdom interests and . . . his fellow brethren." The Court reversed the conviction on the grounds that the Justice Department had committed an error of law in its recommendation. A Jehovah's Witness should not be denied a CO exemption because he would fight with spiritual weapons in theocratic wars. In giving the opinion of the Court, Justice Clark asserted:

We believe that Congress had in mind real shooting wars when it referred to participation in war in any form—actual military conflicts between nations of the

---

[67] I know of no SCO who has expressed a willingness to accept noncombatant status. For a discussion of SCO and non combat status, cf. Chapter IV, pp. 79-82.

[68] 348 U.S. 385.

earth in our time—wars with bombs and bullets, tanks, planes and rockets. We believe the reasoning of the Government in denying petitioner's claim is so far removed from any possible congressional intent that it is erroneous as a matter of law.[69]

This case is important for our purposes, since Sicurella's willingness to fight at Armageddon suggests that his objection to war is, at least in principle, selective. Indeed, this was one of the reasons that Justice Minton in dissent would have upheld Sicurella's conviction—"he reserves the right to choose the wars in which he will fight." [70]

The majority opinion is less than a model of clarity. This is not entirely the fault of Justice Clark. Sicurella's CO form contains several bewildering statements. He denies that he would use "carnal weapons" or "weapons of warfare" in defending himself or "the Kingdom interests." But in reply to the question, "Under what circumstances, if any, do you believe in the use of force?" he answered:

Only in the interests of defending Kingdom interests, our preaching work, our meetings, our fellow brethren and sisters and our property against attack. I (as well as all Jehovah's Witnesses) defend those when they are attacked and are forced to protect such interests and scripturally so.[71]

He qualified this statement by saying his resort to force would take place only if he were attacked in his own home or meeting places.

A CO claim need only show that the registrant is opposed to *war*, not to *force*.[72] For this reason the government did not press Sicurella's willingness to defend his home and his associates. It was his readiness to defend "Kingdom interests" that attracted the government's attention. Clark maintained that whatever Kingdom interests may be, they would not be defended by carnal weapons. This was not entirely accurate, for, although this is precisely what Sicurella said,[73] we have already seen that he mentioned the defense of "Kingdom interests" in reply to the question of when he would use *force*.

The government submitted a copy of the *Watchtower* magazine to show that Jehovah's Witnesses extolled the ancient wars of Israel and were willing to participate in theocratic wars again. Since, as Justice Reed pointed out in dissent, the Bible recounts "blood and flesh wars," Clark had to retreat from his carnal-spiritual distinction. His reply was the following unadorned assertion: "The test is not whether the registrant is opposed to all wars, but

[69] *Ibid.*, at 391.   [70] *Ibid.*, at 395.
[71] *Ibid.*, at 387.
[72] *Annett* v. *U.S.* 205 F 2d 689 (1953) and *Pekarski* v. *U.S.* 207 F 2d 930 (1953).
[73] 348 U.S., at 387.

whether he is opposed, on religious grounds, to *participation* in war." [74] The statute exempts anyone "who, by reason of religious training and belief, is conscientiously opposed to participation in war in any form." Clark maintains "in any form" modifies "participation" rather than "war." This interpretation plays havoc with the 1-A-O category which was established for those who serve in the armed forces in a noncombatant role. This role is a "form" of "participation" in war which is compatible with the consciences of men who have already qualified as CO's. Under Clark's interpretation the 1-A-O category would be a contradiction in terms. One could become a CO only by refusing to participate *in any form* in war. By the very act of accepting alternate military service, he would lose his CO status.[75] The only way out of this embarrassment would be to say that alternate military service is not participation in any form. This would be sheer nominalism since noncombatants are considered military personnel, wear the uniform of their nation, and have their task defined in terms of supporting the objectives of the command to which they are attached.

Nor would Clark's interpretation really solve the problem he addresses. If the statute means that the exemption goes to those opposed to any form of participation in war, the theocratic warrior is still in trouble unless the Court simply defines the problem out of existence by saying theocratic wars are not wars. Sicurella's reference to spiritual weapons sufficiently obfuscates the issue to enable the Court to say in this case that theocratic wars are not real wars. Had *Hartman*[76] been before the Court, there would have been no talk of spiritual weapons and the Court would have had to face squarely the difficulty of saying the biblical wars were not wars. Even though such a definition might be arbitrary it would have been better for the Court to have taken this step rather than rely on its tortuous interpretation of "in any form." For in either case the Court must live with the assertion—to

---

[74] *Ibid.*, at 390 (italics in text). Clark offers no citation to support his interpretation. In an Eighth Circuit case involving a Jehovah's Witness, Judge Woodrough said, "The words 'in any form' obviously relate not to 'war' but to 'participation' in war. War, generally speaking, has only one form, a clash of opposing forces. But a person's participation therein may be in a variety of forms." *Taffs* v. *U.S.*, 208 F 2d 329. Woodrough's statement does not address the problem of selective objection. For the SCO war has at least two "forms"—just and unjust—even though in both cases a clash of opposing forces is involved. Cf. *U.S.* v. *Hartman*, 209 F 2d 366 where Judge Medina follows *Taffs*. In *Jessen* v. *U.S.*, 212 F 2d 897, Chief Judge Phillips does not attempt to interpret "in any form." He simply states that Congress did not intend theocratic wars to be included in the statute. He cites *Taffs*. Cf. also *Hinkle* v. *U.S.*, 216 F 2d 8 (1954) and *Shepherd* v. *U.S.*, 217 F 2d 942 (1954). Clark's interpretation was followed in *Mayfield* v. *U.S.*, 220 F 2d 729 and *U.S.* v. *Lauing*, 221 F 2d 425.

[75] CO's are classified 1-0 if they refuse to serve in the armed forces in any capacity. They are usually given some form of civilian service which is "in the national interest." Category 1-A-0 involves alternate military service, i.e., noncombat. 37 *CFR* 1622.11 and 1622.14.

[76] 209 F 2d 366.

be sure, not unreasonable—that Congress simply was not thinking of theocratic wars when it passed this statute.

SEEGER AND WELSH. *U.S.* v. *Seeger*[77] and *U.S.* v. *Welsh* [78] are the last CO cases to be considered in this chapter. The Court's mighty effort in *Seeger* to defend the constitutionality of the "religious training and belief" and "Supreme Being" clauses has attracted considerable attention.[79] Similar attention will undoubtedly be lavished on *Welsh*. Since our interest focuses on the second qualification for CO status—objection to war in any form—the central issue of *Seeger* and *Welsh* is not directly related to our question. We cannot ignore these cases, however, because many proponents of SCO see a hopeful parallel between what the Court has done in *Seeger* and what it might do for SCO. An elementary knowledge of these cases is necessary to understand part of the constitutional case for SCO.

The "religious training and belief" clause of the 1940 Draft Act was interpreted in different ways in the Second and Ninth Circuits. In *U.S.* v. *Kauten*[80] the Second Circuit suggested a broad interpretation of "religious" that equated religion with conscience. The Ninth Circuit in *Berman* v. *U.S.*[81] offered a more traditional interpretation that associated a relation to a Supreme Being with religion. Neither case came to the Supreme Court.

In the 1948 Act "Congress amended the language of the statute and declared that 'religious training and belief' was to be defined as 'an individual's belief in a relation to a Supreme Being involving duties superior to those arising from any human relation, but not including essentially political, sociological, or philosophical views or a merely personal moral code.' " [82] At the time it was commonly thought that Congress had favored the Berman interpretation of religious training and belief over that of *Kauten*.

Seeger was convicted in the District Court for the Southern District of New York of having refused to submit to induction in the armed forces. The District Court upheld the Draft Board's decision that Seeger's religious beliefs did not satisfy the 1948 Congressional definition. Seeger had "a belief in and devotion to goodness and virtue for their own sakes, and a religious faith in a purely ethical creed." [83] The Court of Appeals for the Second District reversed the conviction on constitutional grounds holding that the Supreme Being definition of religion distinguished "between internally derived and externally compelled beliefs" and was, therefore, an

[77] 380 U.S. 163 (1965). [78] 399 U.S. 333 (1970).
[79] The most perceptive comment on *Seeger* is Mansfield, pp. 3-81.
[80] 133 F 2d 703.
[81] 156 F 2d 377.
[82] *U.S.* v. *Seeger* 380 U.S., at 163.
[83] *Ibid.*, at 166.

"impermissible classification under the due process clause of the Fifth Amendment." [84]

The Supreme Court upheld the constitutionality of the Supreme Being clause, but interpreted it in such a way as to save Seeger. In his concurring opinion Justice Douglas said he did not think the Court's opinion was a *tour de force,* but if it were, "it is no more so than other instances where we have gone to extremes to construe an Act of Congress to save it from demise on constitutional grounds." [85]

In the majority opinion Justice Clark said religious training and belief would include

all sincere religious beliefs which are based upon a power or being, or upon a faith, to which all else is subordinate or upon which all else is ultimately dependent. The test might be stated in these words: A sincere and meaningful belief which occupies in the life of the possessor a place parallel to that filled by the God of those admittedly qualifying for the exemption comes within the statutory definition. [86]

While the *Seeger* case shows a generous disposition toward CO's on the part of the Court, there are several cautions we should observe before making any applications to SCO.

In commenting on the statute's distinction between religious beliefs and those that are political, sociological, or economic, [87] Justic Clark states:

These judgments [political, sociological and economic] have historically been reserved for the Government, and in matters which can be said to fall within these areas the conviction of the individual has never been permitted to override that of the State. [88]

More significant for SCO is the fact that in upholding Seeger's sincerity, Clark relies on the *universal* character of his objection to war. He had studied the beliefs of the Quakers and shared "their opposition to war in any form." [89] It is not an encouraging sign for SCO if the Court takes the universal nature of objection to war as an index of the sincerity of a "religious" belief. It was not by accident that Clark saw a connection between universal objection and the sincerity required for "religious" belief. As we have seen above, it was *U.S.* v. *Kauten*[90] that first suggested the broad interpretation

[84] 326 F 2d 846.   [85] 380 U.S., at 188.
[86] *Ibid.,* at 176.
[87] "Economic" is Clark's word. The statute says "essentially political, sociological, or philosophical views." This may have been inadvertent on Clark's part. The difference is important for our purposes, because, as we shall see, the just war theory, which is so important for SCO, could possibly be considered "essentially philosophical," whereas it would take vigorous Marxian presuppositions to call it "essentially economic."
[88] 380 *U.S.,* at 173.   [89] *Ibid.,* at 186.
[90] 133 F 2d 703.

of "religion" that the Supreme Court adopted in *Seeger*. Augustus Hand identified religion with conscience in *Kauten*—a step the Supreme Court was unwilling to take in *Seeger*, though it certainly moved far in that direction. To determine what sort of decisions were truly conscientious (and therefore "religious" in *Kauten*) Judge Hand offered the following test:

There is a distinction between a course of reasoning resulting in a conviction that a particular war is inexpedient or disastrous and a conscientious objection to participation in any war under any circumstances. The latter, and not the former, may be the basis of exemption under the Act. The former is usually a political objective, while the latter, we think, may justly be regarded as a response of the individual to an inward mentor, call it conscience or God, that is for many persons at the present time the equivalent of what has always been thought a religious impulse.[91]

Congress' response to the *Seeger* case was to omit the Supreme Being clause from the 1967 Draft Act. Section 6 (j) now reads:

Nothing contained in this title shall be construed to require any person to be subject to combatant training and service in the armed forces of the U.S. who, by reason of religious training and belief, is conscientiously opposed to participation in war in any form. As used in this subsection, the term "religious training and belief" does not include essentially political, sociological or philosophical views, or a merely personal moral code.[92]

If Congress intended to weaken the force of *Seeger* it chose a singularly inept means. In omitting the Supreme Being clause it simply removed one of the hurdles the Court had already cleared on its way to a broader understanding of religious training and belief.

In *U.S.* v. *Welsh* [93] the Court extended the principles of *Seeger* to include as "religious" certain beliefs even further removed from conventional religion. The government attempted to distinguish *Welsh* from *Seeger* on the grounds that Welsh's views were "essentially political, sociological or philosophical or a merely personal moral code." [94] The government based its contention upon the following excerpt from a letter Welsh had written to his draft board:

I can only act according to what I am and what I see. And I see that the military complex wastes both human and material resources, that it fosters

[91] *Ibid.*, at 708.
[92] 50 *USCA*, App. 456 (j).
[93] 399 U.S. 333 (1970). For an account of the interpretation of Welsh given to Selective Service Boards by Curtis W. Tarr, see *New York Times,* July 7, 1970, p. 1.
[94] *Ibid.*

disregard for (what I consider a paramount concern) human needs and ends; I see that the means we employ to "defend" our "way of life" profoundly change that way of life. I see that in our failure to recognize the political, social, and economic realities of the world, we, as a *nation,* fail our responsibility *as a nation.*[95]

Mr. Justice Black acknowledged the political character of Welsh's beliefs, but maintained they were not "essentially" political because they do not rest *"solely* upon considerations of policy, pragmatism or expediency." [96] Thus, for Black, "essentially" political means exclusively political. Religious and political beliefs are mutually exclusive. Once a belief is declared "religious" (with the *Seeger* understanding of "religion") it cannot be essentially political; nor can it be a merely personal moral code.[97] Black concluded his opinion with the statement that Welsh was entitled to a CO exemption simply because of the depth of his conviction. He interpreted section 6 (j) as exempting "from military service all those whose consciences, spurred by deeply held *moral, ethical* or religious beliefs, would give them no rest or peace if they allowed themselves to become a part of an instrument of war." [98]

Black's interpretation is noteworthy in that it equates moral, ethical, and religious beliefs whereas the statute he interprets distinguishes the spheres of religion and morality. Congress seems to have taken the distinction rather seriously since a "merely personal moral code" excludes a registrant from CO status. The only way to reconcile Black's interpretation with the wording of the statute is to maintain that Welsh's beliefs are moral, but not "merely personal." This is not very convincing, however, because the reason Welsh's views are considered religious is that they are "deeply held." A moral code can be "deeply held" without being "merely personal" if one accepts the moral teachings of a church or a comparable secular association. Clearly, this is not the case with Welsh. In matters moral Welsh is his own man. If his views are "religious" because they are "deeply held," they do not cease to be "merely personal" as well, unless one chooses to look upon "religion" as an incantation which a defendant may invoke to purge his beliefs of their obvious personal moral character.

[95] *Ibid.*   [96] *Ibid.* at 343.

[97] *Ibid.* It is interesting to note that Black excludes merely personal moral codes from the sphere of "religion." This is somewhat remarkable because of the Court's tendency to interpret religion in personal (not organizational) terms. According to Black, once a belief is declared "religious" it cannot be a personal moral code. But a "religious" belief is a belief that is "deeply held." Does this suggest that a moral code is a belief that is not "deeply held"?

[98] Ibid. at 344 (emphasis added). Selective Service Director, Curtis W. Tarr, may have been trying to limit Black's holdings when the guidelines he sent to the local boards stressed—even after *Welsh*—the need for "some kind of training" and "a system of belief." Black's opinion does not seem to warrant this interpretation. *Providence Sunday Journal,* July 26, 1970, p. N30; citing *New York Times News Service.*

It seems clear that Black was willing to make words mean whatever they had to mean to protect the constitutionality of the present wording of the CO provision. Three Justices (Douglas, Brennan, and Marshall) went along with Black. Mr. Justice Harlan concurred in the result—that Welsh's conviction should be reversed—but rejected Black's reasoning. Harlan felt that the only reasonable interpretation of the statute is that Congress intended to restrict the CO privilege to those with more traditional religious beliefs and that therefore the statute is unconstitutional.[99] Harlan complained that Black's opinion revealed an "Alice in Wonderland" world where words have no meaning. He acknowledged that *Seeger,* in removing the theistic requirement of 6 (j), had accomplished "a feat of remarkable judicial surgery." In *Welsh,* however, he protested that the Court "in the name of interpreting the will of Congress, has performed a lobotomy and completely transformed the statute by reading out of it any distinction between religiously acquired beliefs and those deriving from 'essentially political, sociological, or philosophical views or a merely personal code.' " [100]

The relevance of the *Welsh* case for the purpose of our inquiry lies in Black's willingness to go beyond *Seeger* by simply identifying conscientious beliefs with "religion." As we shall see in the following chapter, this is an important step in the constitutional argument for SCO. The significance of *Welsh as precedent,* however, is limited by its failure to rally a majority of the Court to one opinion. In the absence of an "opinion of the Court," the importance of *Welsh* for SCO is problematic.

[99] Ibid. at 345. Even though Harlan found the "religious" requirement unconstitutional, he maintained the CO exemption could still be preserved. When a statute is constitutionally defective "because of underinclusion," a court may extend "the coverage of the statute to include those who are aggrieved by exclusion." See *Skinner* v. *Okla.* 316 *U.S.* 535 (1942); *Iowa Des Moines National Bank* v. *Bennett,* 284 *U.S.* 239 (1931).

[100] *Ibid.* at 351.

II
Rights, Privileges, and Compelling Interests

Before turning to the SCO cases, it would be helpful to establish a frame of reference for evaluating the constitutional arguments these cases present by considering three questions: (1) Is the present CO exemption a constitutional right or a privilege conferred by Congress? (2) If it is a privilege, what tests may the Court impose to justify (or overturn) the favoritism shown to one class of objector (the CO) over another (the SCO)? (3) Could the Court impose the demanding test of *Sherbert* v. *Verner* [1]— "compelling state interest"—and, if so, how would this affect SCO?

CO—A Constitutional Right?

There are two main lines of argument to support a constitutional case for SCO. The first is a "direct" argument, i.e., that SCO is a first amendment right. The second is "indirect," i.e., that, although the present exemption is a privilege, congressional discrimination in favor of CO's over SCO's is arbitrary and therefore unconstitutional.

The constitutional status of the present CO exemption has a profound influence on the "direct" argument for SCO. A constitutional right to CO, combined with the Court's tendency to equate religion and conscience,[2]

[1] 374 U.S. 398.

[2] The second circuit equated religion and conscience in *Kauten* v. *U.S.*, 133 F 2d 703. The Supreme Court did not go quite so far in *Seeger* (380 U.S. 163). Justice Clark upheld the distinction between religion and a "merely personal moral code" (380 U.S. 186). Presumably, this moral code would be considered "conscientious." Although the

could be parlayed into a constitutional right to SCO. If CO's are *constitutionally* entitled to their exemption, the basis of this right would seem to be the free exercise clause of the first amendment. The only possible reason, then, for not exempting SCO's is that their type of objection is not "religious." If, however, conscience and religion are one, the SCO's objection is surely religious. There is no good reason why the constitutionally protected religious objection of the total objector should be respected, while that of his selective counterpart is ignored.[3]

This argument for SCO requires that two conditions be fulfilled: (1) religion is equated with conscience and (2) CO is a constitutional right. Neither condition taken alone can sustain an SCO argument. Thus, even if conscience is "religion," it is not entitled to constitutional exemptions for all its actions.[4] The free exercise of religion can be curtailed if the public order or a compelling state interest so demand. On the other hand, if not all conscientious judgments are "religious," a constitutional right for CO's could be denied to SCO's on the grounds that the former are religious and the latter are not.[5]

Since the "direct" argument for a constitutional right to SCO has *two* essential preconditions, the argument can be refuted if *either* of these conditions is successfully challenged. The precise meaning of "conscience" and

distinction is clear in principle, Clark's broad understanding of "religion" and "Supreme Being" challenges the imagination to provide a practical example of a decision based on a "merely personal moral code" that will not also be religious. Cf. *Torcaso* v. *Watkins,* 367 U.S. 488. As we saw at the end of the first chapter, four Justices in *Welsh* (399 U.S. 333) were willing to go beyond *Seeger* in identifying "religion" and "conscience." For a thorough discussion of the Supreme Court's understanding of conscience, see Alfred Killelea, "Judicial Accommodation of Conscience and Law" (unpublished Ph. D. dissertation, Department of Political Science, University of Chicago, 1969). For our purposes it will suffice to note that in the CO cases the Court has stopped short of simply equating religion and conscience. Cf. Marc Galanter, "Religious Freedom in the U.S.: A Turning Point," *Wisconsin Law Review,* II (1966), 238-43 and 255-264. He sees the "erosion" of an objective meaning of religion developing along two lines—belief and behavior. *Torcaso* and *Seeger* are the leading cases weakening an objective religion along lines of belief. *Murdock* v. *Pennsylvania,* 319 U.S. 105, is the leading case weakening an objective meaning along behavioral lines. This case broadened the understanding of religious activity to include selling religious pamphlets as well as the traditional religious activity of preaching and worshiping.

[3] If the CO exemption were a matter of legislative grace, the discrimination against the SCO could be justified on grounds of "reasonable relation" or "compelling state interest." This point is discussed at some length in the second and third sections of this chapter. No such condition can be imposed on a constitutionally guaranteed right unless, of course, the Constitution itself invites it. See the fourth amendment's guarantee against *unreasonable* search and seizure.

[4] *U.S.* v. *Reynolds,* 98 U.S. 145; *Jacobsen* v. *Mass.,* 197 U.S. 11; *Cantwell* v. *Conn.,* 310 U.S. 296; *Sherbert* v. *Verner,* 274 U.S. 398.

[5] In the CO literature there is a constant theme suggesting that it is the a priori and absolute character of the CO position that make it "really" religious. Cf. Chapter I, pp. 34-35.

"religion" in *Seeger* is, as we have seen,[6] somewhat obscure. For this reason the simplest way to test the "direct" argument is to analyze the merits of the case for CO as a constitutional right. If this case cannot be made, the "direct" argument for a constitutional right to SCO is deprived of one of its necessary conditions. Let us turn, once again, to the history and the courts of the American people to see what evidence can be gathered on the constitutional status of the CO exemption.

The simple fact that Congress has always debated whether or not it would grant the exemption suggests that Congress considers it within its discretion to recognize or reject the claims of CO's. Indeed, the Senate Armed Services Committee, in reporting the draft Act of 1948, stated unequivocally, "the exemption is viewed as a privilege." [7]

The major historical argument for this opinion is the failure of the First Congress to adopt a proposed amendment on CO in the Bill of Rights. The original text of what is now the Second Amendment reads as follows:

A well regulated militia, composed of the body of the people, being the best security of a free state, the right of the people to keep and bear arms shall not be infringed; but no person religiously scrupulous shall be compelled to bear arms.[8]

Addressing the First Congress, Mr. Benson moved to strike the CO provision on the grounds that it should be left "to the benevolence of the Legislature." [9] "No man," he said, "can claim this indulgence of right. It may be a religious persuasion, but it is no natural right, and therefore ought to be left to the discretion of the government." [10] Benson's motion was defeated 22-24. This does not mean that a majority of the House rejected Benson's *reasons* for striking the provision. Elbridge Gerry, for example, opposed the exemption because he thought it would enable the government to declare certain people "religiously scrupulous and prevent them from bearing arms." [11] In its final action Congress decided to omit the CO provision, but this, of course, does not mean that Congress did so for the reasons advanced by Benson.

It is possible that Congress deleted the CO provision because it thought that the free exercise clause of the first amendment included the exemption. This does not seem likely, however, in view of the CO provision attached

---

[6] See p. 38, note 2 above. *Welsh* goes beyond *Seeger* in identifying "religion" and "conscience," but in the absence of an "opinion of the Court" its value as precedent is somewhat limited.

[7] Clyde E. Jacobs and John F. Gallagher, *The Selective Service Act* (New York: Dodd, Mead and Co., 1967), p. 57.

[8] *Annals of Congress,* I, 778.

[9] *Ibid.,* pp. 779-80. [10] *Ibid.,* p. 780.

[11] *Ibid.*

to the House version of the Draft Bill of 1814. The bill never became law, but the fact that the House, just twenty-four years after the adoption of the first amendment, saw a need for an explicit affirmation of CO would seem to suggest that such a provision was not considered part of the free exercise clause.[12] Thus, it seems fair to conclude that the legislative history of CO puts an extremely heavy burden of proof on those who hold it is a constitutional right.

A similar conclusion emerges from the judicial disposition of CO cases. These cases abound in dicta which either assert or imply that the exemption is a privilege and not a right.[13] Several authors have pointed out that none of these cases speaks directly to the issue of the constitutional status of CO.[14] To be sure, the Supreme Court's statements on CO as a privilege are mere dicta, but they are dicta that have developed a life of their own. State and federal courts never tire of repeating as sound constitutional doctrine the position that CO is a privilege and not a right.[15]

An interesting argument for CO as a constitutional right is Harry F. Peck's attempt to discount the impressive dicta for CO as privilege by tracing all such statements to *Arver* v. *U.S.*, one of the Selective Service cases of 1918.[16] This is sound strategy, since *Arver* touched on CO only in passing,[17] and therefore provides a very shaky foundation for the abundant dicta against a constitutional right to CO. But before he can rest these data on the bruised reed of *Arver* he must neutralize the adverse effect of *Macintosh* on his argument. *Macintosh* stated the privilege character of CO in no uncertain terms.[18] Since *Girouard* overruled *Macintosh*, Peck

[12] *Ibid.*, XXVIII, 774. For further discussion of other possible motives, cf. Francis J. Conklin, "Conscientious Objector Provisions," *Georgetown Law Journal*, LI, No. 2 (Winter, 1963), 252. For an argument maintaining CO was included in the free exercise clause, cf. Brief for Respondent in *U.S.* v. *Macintosh*, 283 U.S. 611.

[13] *Jacobson* v. *U.S.*, 197 U.S. 11; *Arver* v. *U.S.*, 245 U.S. 366; *U.S.* v. *Schwimmer*, 279 U.S. 644; *U.S.* v. *Macintosh*, 283 U.S. 605; *Hamilton* v. *University of California*, 293 U.S. 245; *In re Summers*, 325, U.S. 561; and *U.S.* v. *Welsh*, 399 U.S. 333.

[14] Theodore Hochstadt, "The Right to Exemption from Military Service of Conscientious Objector to a Particular War," *Harvard Civil Rights-Civil Liberties Law Review*, III, No. 1 (Fall, 1967), 1-66, and Harry F. Peck, Jr., "Selective Service—Right to Counsel, Due Process and the First Amendment," *Marquette Law Review*, LI, No. 4 (Spring, 1968), 409-25.

[15] *Gilham* v. *Reeves*, 263 F. Supp. 378; *Brown* v. *Macnamara*, 263 F. Supp. 686; *Loewing* v. *U.S.* 392 F 2d 218; *U.S.* v. *Annett*, 108 F. Supp. 400; *Uffelman* v. *U.S.*, 230 F 2d 298; *In re Jennison*, 120 NW 2d 515; *Imboden* v. *U.S.*, 194 F 2d 508; and *Rodenko* v. *U.S.*, 147 F 2d 752.

[16] 245 U.S. 366. Cf. note 14, above. See also H. C. Macgill, "Selective Conscientious Objection: Divine Will and Legislative Grace," *Virginia Law Review*, LIV (November, 1968), 1355.

[17] See Chapter I, p. 25.

[18] The following statement of Justice Sutherland is the basis for the Court's interpretations of CO as privilege:

maintains the soundness of the principles behind *Macintosh* demand re-evaluation. For Peck the basic premise in *Macintosh* is the duty of every citizen to bear arms in defense of his country. He maintains this principle was successfully challenged in *Girouard*. As we have seen,[19] Girouard presented a question of statutory construction, i.e., whether the oath mentioned in the Naturalization Act required the prospective citizen to swear to defend his new country by force of arms. Peck's argument really maintains that the dicta in *Girouard* cancel out the dicta in *Macintosh*. To be more precise, he says, the premise underlying *Girouard* has implications which, if made explicit, would lead to dicta contrary to the *already explicit* dicta of *Macintosh!* The boldest conclusion Peck draws from his argument is "that the question still remains open." [20]

The question may still remain open, but there is little evidence to indicate the Court is about to alter what has become a long-standing principle in constitutional law. Peck's argument shows, however, that the Court *could* change this principle without any great embarrassment. Dicta from a 5-4 overruled decision are rather precarious cornerstones for any constitutional doctrine. Nevertheless, at least one court has explicitly rejected the precise argument Peck has advanced.[21] Since it is not likely that other courts will do otherwise, the pages that follow must proceed on the assumption that poor *Macintosh,* despite its many constitutional infirmities, is still alive and vigorous on the issue of CO as a privilege and not a right.

CO as Privilege

The absence of a constitutional right to CO is by no means fatal to the argument for SCO. If the Court and Congress agree that CO is a privilege, their agreement does not license the government to confer the privilege arbitrarily upon some citizens and to withhold it from others.[22] Neither Con-

---

"The conscientious objector is relieved from the obligation to bear arms in obedience to no constitutional provision, express or implied; but because, and only because it has accorded with the policy of Congress thus to relieve him. The alien, when he becomes a naturalized citizen, acquires, with one exception, every right possessed under the Constitution by those citizens who are native born (*Luria* v. *U.S.*, 231 U.S. 9); but he acquires no more. The privilege of the native-born conscientious objector to avoid bearing arms comes not from the Constitution, but from the acts of Congress. That body may grant or withhold the exemption as in its wisdom it sees fit; and if it be withheld, the native-born conscientious objector cannot successfully assert the privilege. No other conclusion is compatible with the well-nigh limitless extent of the war powers as above illustrated, which include, by necessary implication, the power, in the last extremity, to compel the armed service of any citizen in the land without regard to his objections or his views in respect of the justice or morality of the particular war or of war in general."

[19] See Chapter I, pp. 28-30.
[20] Peck, p. 423.
[21] *In re Weitzman*, 284 F. Supp. at 518; also *Imboden* v. *U.S.*, 194 F 2d 508.
[22] *Asbury Hospital* v. *Cass County*, 326 U.S. 207.

gress nor state legislatures can attach unconstitutional conditions to the privileges they confer.[23] The restriction of the CO privilege to total objectors may be vulnerable to constitutional challenges on the grounds that it arbitrarily discriminates against selective objectors. This is the "indirect" argument for SCO.

In essence such a challenge would amount to an equal protection argument at the national level. Strictly speaking, there is no equal protection limitation on Congressional action; the clause pertains only to state governments.[24] In *Bolling* v. *Sharpe*,[25] however, the Court found the principle of equal protection implied in the due process clause of the fifth amendment. The case involved racial segregation in the public schools of the District of Columbia and was decided the same day as the famous *Brown* v. *Board of Education*.[26] Racial segregation in the public schools of the states was struck down as a violation of the equal protection clause. The Court went on to say in *Bolling* v. *Sharpe*:

The legal problem in the District of Columbia is somewhat different, however. The fifth amendment, which is applicable in the District of Columbia, does not contain an equal protection clause as does the Fourteenth Amendment which applies only to the states. But the concepts of equal protection and due process, both stemming from our American ideal of fairness, are not mutually exclusive. The "equal protection of the laws" is a more explicit safeguard of prohibited unfairness than "due process of law," and, therefore, we do not imply that the two are always interchangeable phrases. But, as this Court has recognized, discrimination may be so unjustifiable as to be violative of due process.[27]

Chief Justice Warren added further that if Congress is to restrict "liberty" in accord with due process, there must be some reasonable relation to a proper governmental objective. Since public school segregation is not "reasonably related to any proper governmental objective," it thereby "imposes on Negro children of the District of Columbia a burden that constitutes an arbitrary deprivation of their liberty in violation of the Due Process Clause." [28]

Bolling v. *Sharpe* dealt with the *burden* of racial segregation, whereas SCO treats the *privilege* of conscientious exemption. Nevertheless, *Bolling* is relevant to our purposes because it establishes the principle that any classification of citizens must be based on a reasonable relation to a proper

[23] *Schlochower* v. *Board of Education*, 350 U.S. 551.
[24] "No state shall . . . deny to any person within its jurisdiction the equal protection of the laws." (*U.S. Constitution*, Amendment XIV)
[25] 347 U.S. 497.
[26] 347 U.S. 483.
[27] 347 U.S., at 498-99.
[28] *Ibid.*, at 400.

governmental objective. I shall now consider several cases in which the Courts addressed the classification problem.[29] A brief sample will generate a feeling for how the Court reacts to different types of classification. This should be instructive in determining what lines of argument may be most fruitful for those who see in the present CO exemption an unreasonable discrimination against selective objectors. Three of these cases deal with state legislatures rather than Congress, but since *Bolling* v. *Sharpe* has included equal protection within the due process clause of the fifth amendment, the cases are relevant to our inquiry.

Thomas v. *Collins*[30] involved a Texas statute requiring labor organizers to register with and procure an organizer's card from a designated state official before soliciting membership in labor unions. The conviction of an organizer found guilty of violating this statute was overturned by the Supreme Court. Justice Rutledge conceded Texas had an interest in regulating labor relations within its borders. But when labor leaders are singled out in such a way that the state infringes the preferred freedoms of the first amendment, "the rational connection between the remedy provided and the evil to be curbed, which in other contexts might support legislation against attack on due process grounds, will not suffice." [31] Rutledge went on to give the following test:

These rights rest on firmer foundations. Accordingly, whatever occasion would restrain orderly discussion and persuasion, at an appropriate time and place, must have clear support in public danger, actual or impending. Only the gravest abuses, endangering paramount interests, give occasion for permissible limitation.[32]

The "paramount interest" test won the support of Black, Douglas, and Murphy. Justice Jackson wrote a concurring opinion and the other four justices dissented. Thus, while a majority of the Court decided to overturn the conviction, only four justices accepted the "paramount interest" test as the norm for judging when the state can single out a particular class of citizens in a way that limits their "preferred freedoms."

In *United Public Workers* v. *Mitchell* [33] the Court upheld the dismissal of a government employee who had engaged in political activity prohibited by the Hatch Act. The Court recognized that the Act imposed restrictions on the freedom of government employees which it did not impose on other citizens. This discrimination was justified because the Court saw in the ban

[29] For a comprehensive study of constitutional standards for classifying citizens, see *U.S. Supreme Court Digest*, "Constitutional Law," Key No. 211.
[30] 323 U.S. 516.
[31] *Ibid.*, at 530.
[32] *Ibid.*
[33] 330 U.S. 100.

on political activity a reasonable relation to the efficiency of the public service which Congress wished to protect. The reasonable relation rule of *Mitchell* gives Congress broader regulatory powers than the "paramount interests" tests of *Thomas* v. *Collins;* both cases, however, present first amendment issues.

In *Schware* v. *Board of Bar Examiners* [34] the Court applied the "rational connection" test to overrule the New Mexico Bar Examiners in their denial of admission to Schware. The denial was based on Schware's failure to meet the state's standards of good moral character. In the past Schware had used several aliases, had been arrested but not convicted, and had once belonged to the Communist Party. The Court admitted a state could require "high standards of qualification, such as good moral character or proficiency in its law before it admits an applicant to the bar." [35] These qualifications, however, must have a "rational connection" with the applicant's fitness or capacity to practice law." [36] The Court could find no such connection between Schware's behavior and the conclusion that he was not a man of good moral character.

American Communications Association, CIO v. *Douds*[37] is famous for its tortuous argument that Section 9 (h) of the 1947 National Labor Relations Act raised issues only incidentally related to first amendment freedoms. The section in question denied NLRB services to unions whose officers would not sign "non-Communist" affidavits.

Chief Justice Vinson insisted that the purposes in singling out Communist labor leaders was not to restrict their freedom of speech or belief, but was rather to safeguard the free flow of commerce which Communist labor leaders were wont to disrupt by calling "political strikes." Thus the norm for upholding this special classification of Communist labor leaders is not the "clear and present danger" test associated with first amendment freedoms. The true test for the classification is whether "the remedy provided by 9 (h) bears reasonable relation to the evil which the statute was designed to reach." The evil is the disruption of the free flow of commerce and Vinson has his "reasonable relation." This case represents the zenith (or nadir) of the Court's willingness to permit limitations on first amendment freedoms under the rubric of reasonable relations to a legitimate governmental interest.

Speiser v. *Randall,*[38] like *Schware,* is an example of the reasonable relation test working to the advantage of the individual. The California Constitution granted property tax exemptions to veterans, provided they would subscribe to oaths that they do not advocate the overthrow of the federal or state government by force. The Court could find no reasonable

[34] 353 U.S. 232.
[35] *Ibid.,* at 239.
[36] *Ibid.*
[37] 339 U.S. 382.
[38] 357 U.S. 513.

relation between the oath required and the purpose of the exemption.[39]

This brief sample of cases dealing with classifications gives us some idea of the various ways the Court has handled this question. In reference to SCO it is clear that the government must show at least[40] a reasonable connection between the favored position of CO's and the purposes of the Selective Service Act. It is important to determine just what are the purposes we are discussing. Chief Justice Vinson could uphold Section 9 (h) of Taft-Hartley only because he had previously determined the purpose of the act was to protect commerce and not to harass Communists. In the case of SCO it is important to ask whether we should look at the purpose of the CO provision alone or at the purpose of the entire Selective Service Act. The purpose of the CO provision would seem to be, at least in part, the protection of conscience. It would be difficult for the government to defend its favoritism toward total objectors in this narrow context of protecting conscience. Why *should* it favor total objectors? After all, a conscience is a conscience. The government's position is more plausible, however, if the favoritism to total CO's is seen in the larger context of the purposes of the Selective Service Act. Its purpose, of course, is to raise an army to defend the nation. Under the present system the government knows how many CO's it has before a war begins; under SCO it would not know how many objectors there would be until the guns had sounded. This ignorance could inhibit certain foreign policy decisions. If the Court chose to follow the broad understanding of reasonable relation that it offered in *Mitchell* and *Douds,* the case for SCO would almost surely be defeated.[41]

Compelling State Interest

The case for SCO would be considerably strengthened if the Court went beyond the "reasonable connection" test and demanded that the government show a "compelling state interest" to justify the restriction of the CO exemption to total objectors. This was the test the Court demanded in *Sherbert* v. *Verner.*[42] This case is extremely important for our purposes; it is cited frequently in the briefs for SCO. Here I shall summarize the opinion of the Court and indicate the possibilities its compelling state interest test may have for SCO.

[39] *Ibid.,* at 525-26.

[40] The government may have to show a "compelling interest" to justify the nature of the present CO exemption. Cf. the following section in this chapter.

[41] In *Mitchell* the Court acknowledged that the Hatch Act's provisions limiting the political activities of government employees raised serious questions pertaining to the first, fifth, ninth, and tenth amendments. Nevertheless, it went on to uphold broad congressional regulatory powers as long as they were "within reasonable limits."

[42] 374 U.S. 398.

In *Sherbert* the Court struck down a South Carolina statute which, as applied, denied unemployment compensation to a Seventh-Day Adventist because she refused "without good cause" to accept suitable work when it was offered to her. The reason for her refusal was her conscientious scruple against working on Saturday. Justice Brennan declared this infringement of her free exercise of religion could be justified only by a compelling state interest in the eligibility provisions of South Carolina. It would not suffice to show merely "a rational relationship to some colorable state interest." He then repeated the "paramount interests" test of *Thomas* v. *Collins*. South Carolina failed to show that any compelling or paramount interests were at stake in its denial of unemployment benefits to Sabbatarians.

The significant point in *Sherbert* for our purposes is that it deals with a privilege rather than a right. Sherbert clearly had no right to unemployment compensation. In advancing the compelling interest test Brennan cited *Thomas* v. *Collins* and *NAACP* v. *Button*.[43] These cases applied the paramount or compelling interest test to first amendment *rights,* not privileges. In applying this strict test to privileges, Brennan has clearly gone beyond the cases he cited. He also goes beyond *Speiser* v. *Randall* [44] wherein a reasonable relation test was applied to a condition attached to a privilege. Had California been able to show such a relationship, its non-Communist proviso would have survived. Congress successfully passed this test when *United Public Works* v. *Mitchell* upheld the limitations on political activity placed upon those who enjoyed the privilege of government employment. Sherbert broke new ground in applying to conditions attached to privileges a test which had previously been applied only to situations where government action curtailed first amendment rights.

To interpret *Sherbert* in a way most favorable to SCO, one might argue as follows:

1. The Court has held that Sherbert has no right to compensation, but if anyone gets it she cannot have it denied in a way that would curtail her religious freedom *unless* there is a compelling state interest.

2. An SCO has no right to an exemption from military service on grounds of conscience, but if anyone gets such an exemption, he cannot have it denied in a way that would curtail his religious freedom *unless* there is a compelling state interest.

If the Court applied the compelling interest test, the SCO case would be considerably strengthened. One need only recall Vinson's mighty efforts in *Douds* to establish "reasonable relation" rather than "clear and present

---

[43] Cf. discussion of *Thomas* above, p. 44, and of Button, below, p. 48.
[44] Cf. p. 45, above.

danger" as the relevant question. Once he had established this, the government's triumph was assured. "Compelling interest" could prove to be a difficult test for the government to meet. A brief look is in order at some of the cases where the Court has tried to determine what state interests are compelling.

In *NAACP* v. *Button*[45] the Court overturned the application to the NAACP of a Virginia statute forbidding "the improper solicitation of any legal or professional business." Its attorneys were accused of stirring up litigation and violating the common law prohibitions against barratry, champerty, and maintenance. This was found to be "improper solicitation" within the meaning of the statute. The Court saw in this finding a "serious encroachment . . . upon protected freedoms of expression" which could be justified only by a compelling state interest." Virginia had no such interest.

In re Jennison[46] found the Supreme Court of Minnesota upholding a contempt citation against a person who refused jury duty on the basis of the biblical injunction—"Judge not and you shall not be judged." Upon appeal the judgment was vacated and the case was remanded to the Supreme Court of Minnesota "for further consideration in the light of *Sherbert* v. *Verner.*"[47] The Supreme Court of Minnesota reversed the conviction.[48]

In *Leary* v. *U.S.*[49] the Fifth Circuit found a compelling state interest "in the enforcement of the laws relative to marihuana."[50] The precise interest at stake was nothing less than "the protection of society." On this basis the Court distinguished *Sherbert*.

Finally, in *Sherbert* itself Brennan mentioned *Braunfeld* v. *Brown*,[51] a Sunday closing case, as an example of a state interest which was sufficient to justify infringing the religious freedom of merchants. The interest of the state here was in providing a uniform day of rest.

Thus, the courts have found the uniform administration of welfare laws, the regulation of improper legal solicitation, and the need for jurors as less than compelling state interests, while protecting citizens from the dangers of marihuana and providing a uniform day of rest have passed the test.

[45] 371 U.S. 415.
[46] 120 NW 2d 515.
[47] 375 U.S. 14.
[48] 267 *Minn. Reports,* 136.
[49] 383 F 2d 851. See also *People* v. *Woody*. The fact that drug laws would be relaxed for a sect (in Woody) but not for an individual (in Leary) is not helpful for SCO. The argument for SCO is always based on the rights of an individual, not a sect. This is true as well of the just war doctrine which is not as "central" to the churches that hold it as peyote is to the Native American Church.
[50] 383 F 2d, at 860.
[51] 366 U.S. 599. For a discussion of the relation between *Braunfeld* and *Sherbert,* cf. Galanter, pp. 238-43. Brennan dissented in *Braunfeld* on the grounds that the state had no compelling interest at stake. The majority relied on an alternative means test.

It is difficult, if not impossible, to identify any norm which has guided the courts in putting content into the formula "compelling state interest." The state interest seems to increase in a manner inversely proportional to the burden placed upon the religious freedom of the citizen. This would seem to explain how the Supreme Court could find a greater *state* interest in providing a uniform day of rest than in demanding that a certain citizen act as a juror.

Summary

The purpose of this chapter has been to provide a structure for analyzing the constitutional arguments for SCO. The following schema presents the main outlines of that structure:

1. Since the Court has already come a long way toward equating conscience and religion, an opinion upholding the present CO exemption as a constitutional right would be a mighty stride toward establishing a constitutional right to SCO.

2. Since, however, it is not likely that the Court will find CO is a matter of constitutional right, it is more realistic to base the argument on "indirect" grounds.

3. The effectiveness of an indirect argument for SCO depends on the test the Court puts to the government to justify its present favoritism toward total objectors. Among the many tests the Court *could* put we have considered three. Listed in the order of desirability for the proponents of SCO the tests are:

   a. compelling state interest.
   b. reasonable relation between the "war in any form" condition and purpose of the CO exemption.
   c. reasonable relation between the "war in any form" condition and the purpose of the Selective Service Act.

III
Establishment and Free Exercise

The preceding chapters have set the stage for the consideration of actual cases raising the issue of SCO. The impressive volume of such cases presents a problem of selection.[1] Although the factual details vary from case to case, the constitutional arguments tend to follow the predictable paths of establishment and the free exercise of religion. In this chapter we shall consider three representative cases based on these considerations. The cases in question —U.S. v. Kuebrich, McFadden et al. v. Selective Service Board No. 40, and U.S. v. Kurki—are representative in the sense that they present the main lines of argumentation in SCO cases resting on first amendment grounds.[2] Our purpose in this chapter is to investigate the manner in which the strongest possible case can be made for SCO. Two questions will guide our consideration: (1) Is the best constitutional case for SCO based on the establishment

---

[1] Prominent among the SCO cases omitted from this study are U.S. v. Stewart (Selective Service Law Reporter, II, 7) and Noyd v. Bond (Service Law Reporter, II, 3074). The quarterly index of SSLR gives the most recent information on SCO.

[2] U.S. v. Kuebrich is not reported. The McFadden case can be found in 2 Selective Service Law Reporter (SSLR) 3529. Kurki appears in 255 F. Supp. 161 and 384 F 2d 905. For an interesting departure from the establishment-free exercise approach, see Norman Redlich and Kenneth R. Feinberg, "Individual Conscience and the Selective Conscientious Objector: The Right Not to Kill," New York University Law Review, XLIV (November, 1969), 875. The authors base their argument for SCO on a constitutional right "not to kill." This right is derived from the first, fifth, ninth, and thirteenth amendments. The authors' right not to kill, however, would not free the SCO from noncombat service.

clause, the free exercise clause, or a combination of the two? (2) Within the context of a free exercise argument, how can the selective objector best exploit the favorable possibilities of *Sherbert* v. *Verner?*

Chapter four will treat certain "marginal issues," i.e., constitutional arguments other than the "mainline" considerations of this chapter, while chapter five, the final chapter of Part I, will review the cases currently before the Supreme Court.

U.S. v. Kuebrich

BACKGROUND. On October 20, 1967 Local Board No. 142 in Jerseyville, Illinois classified David Lawrence Kuebrich 1-A. Prior to that time he had enjoyed a 2-S deferment. On December 14 he was ordered to report for induction at Jerseyville on January 9, 1968. At his own request he was "administratively transferred" for induction on January 26, 1968 at Chicago.[3] He reported, as ordered, to the Armed Forces Entrance and Examining Station in Chicago, but "he did then and there knowingly refuse to submit to induction in the armed forces." [4]

On October 31 he appeared before Judge Julius Hoffman in the Federal District Court of the Northern District of Illinois. He was represented by George Pontikes, who, according to Judge Hoffman, is the most experienced Selective Service attorney in the District.[5] Samuel K. Skinner, an Assistant U.S. Attorney, represented the government. On the following day Kuebrich was found guilty of refusing to submit to induction and was sentenced to three years. Bail was denied. On November 12 his attorney filed a notice of appeal.[6]

At Kuebrich's trial the first order of business was the defendant's waiver of his right to be tried by a jury.[7] The Court accepted a stipulation agreed to by both the government and the defendant. The stipulation stated that Kuebrich refused to submit to induction as ordered. With this the government rested its case.

[3] *Trial Record,* pp. 8-9. Hereafter referred to as *T.R.* with appropriate page numbers.
[4] *Ibid.,* p. 9.   [5] *Ibid.,* p. 120.
[6] From file of D. L. Kuebrich, No. 68, CR 218.
[7] This is common in draft resistance cases when the crucial fact—that the accused failed to submit to induction—is uncontested. In such cases a verdict of guilty is a foregone conclusion unless the defense can successfully raise points of law against the charge. One advantage to waiving jury trials is that the judge may be willing to admit testimony he would not have admitted had a jury been present. This can help the defense build a fuller record for appeal—a point stated explicitly by Judge Hoffman (*T.R.,* p. 84).

Defense counsel then moved for acquittal for three reasons. The first two were technical points alleging the Jerseyville Draft Board had failed to follow procedures required by the Code of Federal Regulations.[8] Neither argument impressed the Court.[9] The third reason raised the constitutional argument that the present exemption for total objectors only is an establishment of religion. Defense Counsel had trouble stating his argument because of constant interruptions by the Court. His opening statement went as follows:

Section 6-j of the Selective Service Act provides that any person who, by reason of religious training and belief is opposed to participation in war in any form shall be given exemption as a conscientious objector.

Now, the defendant who has by these two exhibits indicated to the Board that he could not make such a request because he was not, in fact, opposed to participation in war in any form, but, rather, that because of his Roman Catholic training, he was opposed to only wars that his religion or his religious training taught him were unjust, I would suggest to the Court very strongly and urge the Court [10] [at this point Judge Hoffman began a series of questions and musings that covered such topics as the meaning of "dogma" in Roman Catholic theology, the casualties the U.S. has suffered in Vietnam, birth control, Jacqueline Kennedy Onassis, Cardinal Cushing, St. Augustine, and the role of the District Judge in the Federal Court system[11]].

Pontikes resumed his argument:

I think I would be prepared by authorities to substantiate our position that this, in effect, is an establishment of religion, that allowing those persons whose religious training and belief persuades them to be opposed to participation in war in any form, allowing them an exemption, while not allowing those [once again a series of questions and comments by the Court interrupts presentation of the defense attorney's argument].[12]

Then Pontikes made his concluding remarks:

The position we take, your Honor, as I say we are willing to substantiate it by

[8] The regulation in question is 32 CFR 1631.7. Pontikes argued that the wording of the regulation requires that the board itself, and not its secretary, issue the order to report for induction. He also argued that the board failed to produce evidence that it followed the order of call spelled out in the same regulation—delinquents, volunteers, nonvolunteers.

[9] T.R., pp. 27-30.

[10] Ibid., p. 19.

[11] Ibid., pp. 19-23. On the last point Hoffman said he did not think a District Judge should declare a statute unconstitutional "when so many men have served and are serving under that same statute." This question was of such importance for Hoffman that he felt only "our highest court should pass on it." He felt he should "put the burden on the defendant to appeal to the highest Court in the event of a conviction."

[12] Ibid., p. 23.

authorities, and that is that denying those persons who by reason of religious training and belief are opposed to unjust wars, not granting them an exemption is unconstitutional. [sic] [13]

The government replied to the constitutional argument by citing *Seeger*[14]
as upholding the constitutionality of section 6 (j). While *Seeger* did just this,
it did so in the face of a constitutional attack on the Supreme Being clause—
not the "war in any form" provision. This point was indicative of a rather
undistinguished argument in behalf of the government. In justice to Mr.
Skinner, however, one cannot ignore the fact that everyone at the trial
knew Kuebrich's conviction was almost certain. Such an atmosphere cannot
be conducive to challenging an attorney's legal skills.

ESTABLISHMENT AND FREE EXERCISE. Among the SCO cases
we shall study, only *Kuebrich* bases the constitutional argument exclusively
on the establishment clause. Marc Galanter, writing in the *Wisconsin Law
Review*,[15] argues persuasively that "religion" in terms of the establishment
clause must be taken in a more restrictive sense than "religion" in the free
exercise clause. A summary of Galanter's position is in order here to help us
evaluate the two lines of argument.

Galanter maintains there has been a steady erosion during the past twenty-
five years of the objective constitutional standards that once characterized
the Supreme Court's understanding of religion. In 1890 the Court could
say, "the term 'religion' has reference to one's views of his relation to his
Creator, and to the obligations they impose of reverence for his being and
character, and of obedience to his will." [16] In the same year it condemned
polygamy as "a blot on our civilization" and as "contrary to the spirit of
Christianity and of the civilizations which Christianity has produced in the
western world." [17] The contention that polygamy should be protected as
a religious belief was summarily dismissed with the reminder that the Thugs
of India "imagined that their belief in the right of assassination was a religious
belief; but their thinking so did not make it so." [18]

Galanter sees *Murdock* v. *Pennsylvania*[19] as the first significant departure
from the "objective" view of religion. This case overruled *Jones* v. *Opelika*,[20]
decided just a year before *Murdock*. In *Jones* Justice Reed upheld the
application of licensing ordinances to persons selling religious literature. He

---

[13] *Ibid.*, p. 25.   [14] 380 U.S. 163.

[15] Galanter, pp. 217-96.

[16] *Davis* v. *Beason*, 133 U.S. at 342, cited by Galanter, p. 256.

[17] *Late Corp. of the Church of Jesus Christ of Latter Day Saints* v. *U.S.*, 136 U.S.,
at 49; Galanter, p. 256.

[18] *Ibid.*   [19] 319 U.S. 105.

[20] 316 U.S. 584.

distinguished sharply religious rites from religious activities with a commercial character, whereas the majority in *Murdock* granted the sale of religious books "the same high estate under the First Amendment as . . . worship in the churches and preaching from the pulpits." [21]

The *Murdock* majority rejected the view that *any* conduct could be considered religious just because a zealous practitioner said it was, but *Fowler* v. *R.I.*[22] limited even this qualification. In *Fowler* the Court disqualified itself from deciding what sort of activity is religious. "[A]part from narrow exceptions not relevant here . . . it is no business of Courts to say that what is a religious practice or activity for one group is not religion under the protection of the First Amendment." [23]

On the issue of what beliefs (as opposed to actions) are religious, the Court in *U.S.* v. *Ballard*[24] accepted a totally subjective standard. Courts cannot enter into a judgment on the truth of religious beliefs, but only on whether they are sincerely held.

The theistic nature of religion, as we have already seen, was successfully challenged in *Torcaso* v. *Watkins*[25] and *Seeger*.[26]

If the Court has come close to saying that religion, like beauty, is in the eye of the beholder, this must, according to Galanter, be understood in terms of the free exercise of religion—not establishment. While there is considerable conceptual clarity in giving "religion" the same meaning in both clauses, this clarity must be sacrificed in view of the Court's broad understanding of religion.[27] Galanter aptly points out the problems that may ensue if religion is taken as meaning the same thing in both clauses:

[If] we begin with the broad definition which is emerging in the free exercise area and work back to establishment, this equivalence leads to somewhat paradoxical results. Is the government forbidden to adopt and enforce policies which express paramount convictions or ultimate concerns? Is it forbidden to support teachings which embody or proceed from such convictions or concerns? Are such teachings and policies "religious" merely because they occupy a parallel position in the

---

[21] 319 U.S., at 109; Galanter, p. 259.   [22] 345 U.S. 67.

[23] *Ibid.*, at 69-70; Galanter, p. 260. The irrelevant "narrow exceptions" include the well-established condemnation of polygamy.

[24] 322 U.S. 78.   [25] 367 U.S. 488.

[26] 380 U.S. 163.

[27] See Rutledge's dissent in *Everson*, 330 U.S. 1, for a position advocating that religion means the same in both clauses. Whether the Court's understanding of "religion" is desirable is, of course, a distinct question from the massive fact of its presence. Since it is "there," a double standard for religion is the only way to make any sense out of it. One hesitates to imagine the reaction of W. W. Crosskey had he been asked if the same word could have two different meanings within the same amendment! See his monumental work, *Politics and the Constitution* (Chicago: University of Chicago Press, 1952), I, 3-14.

thoughts of their advocates or proponents? Even when they are not claimed to be religious? If religion embraces a whole class of beliefs when they are claimed to be such by their adherents, does it include all the beliefs of that class when no such claim is made for them? Or when the religious characterization is attached by someone other than the adherent himself? Is the teaching of secular subjects in religious schools a secular matter because the school authorities deem it such? Or is it a religious matter because opponents of aid to schools deem it religious? If government is constitutionally disabled from saying that it is religious, is it similarly disabled from saying that something is religious when its practitioners say it is not? [28]

If the Court allows each person to determine what is religious for him, it must restrict this right to the free exercise clause. Otherwise a citizen could maintain the "Americanism" taught in the public schools is a religion and conclude that tax support for public schools is unconstitutional.[29]

The Supreme Court has shown a willingness to decide what is religion and what is not religion in establishment cases. Thus in *Gallagher* v. *Crown Kosher Super Market*[30] it held that Sunday closing laws, though religious in origin, can no longer be considered religious in the sense of involving an establishment. In *Eagle* v. *Vitale*[31] the Court held certain prayers in public schools were an establishment of religion, but the recitation of historical documents or the singing of anthems with references to a Supreme Being were not. Finally, in *Schempp* v. *Pa.* the Court found that the objective study of the Bible was permissible while public recitation at the beginning of class was not.[32]

This digression on establishment will help us evaluate the arguments we shall encounter in *Kuebrich* and the other cases as well. If a free exercise argument is raised, we can expect the Court to be generous in considering the claim "religious" if the SCO so labels it. We can then look for such tests as "reasonable relation," "compelling state interest," and "no alternative means."[33] When an establishment argument is raised, as in *Kuebrich,* the crucial question is whether the defendant can establish the religious character of his objection to the satisfaction of the Court.

KUEBRICH'S POSITION. The need to establish the religious character

---

[28] Galanter, p. 265.

[29] For the problem of standing, see *Flast* v. *Cohen,* 392 U.S. 83.

[30] 366 U.S. 617.　　　　　　　　　　　[31] 370 U.S. 421.

[32] 374 U.S. 244. For further discussion of the double standard of religion, see Van Alstyne, "Constitutional Separation of Church and State: The Quest for a Coherent Position," *American Political Science Review,* LVII (1963), 865. See also *Sheldon* v. *Fannin,* 221 F. Supp., at 775. "The former (establishment clause) looks to the majority's concept of the term, religion, the latter (free exercise clause) the minority's."

[33] For a discussion of reasonable relation and compelling interest, cf. Chapter II, above. For a discussion of no alternative means, cf. *Braunfeld* v. *Brown,* 366 U.S. 599.

of Kuebrich's SCO claim dictated the strategy Pontikes followed. He had Kuebrich tell his own story, highlighting the religious influences on his decision. This was followed by "expert testimony" offered by three Catholic priests to underscore the religious nature of Kuebrich's decision.[34]

The first priest to testify was the Rev. Gerald Grant, S.J., associate professor of Sociology at Loyola University, Chicago. He stated that the just war theory, which guided Kuebrich's thinking, is part of the general moral teaching of the Church. He recounted the history of the doctrine and showed how the salient criteria of the doctrine corresponded with Kuebrich's account of how he decided the Vietnam war was unjust. Next came the Rev. Robert J. Braunreuther, S.J., a psychologist with impressive credentials in pastoral counseling. He maintained that a Catholic could reasonably feel bound in conscience to follow the just war doctrine. Finally, the Rev. Victor Balke, a longtime friend of Kuebrich, testified to the defendant's sincerity in making his decision.

The "expert testimony," of course, could only supplement Kuebrich's own story of how he reached the decision that brought him before a federal court. Perhaps it is best to let Kuebrich speak for himself: [35]

Pontikes: Would you explain to the Court what steps you took to come to the conclusion that as a Roman Catholic you were compelled to find that the war in Vietnam was unjust?

Kuebrich: I think I would like to address myself to two things. Well, to begin with, I guess I didn't really think a lot about the war until—I believe it was the spring of 1965. At that time I was a student at Washington University in St. Louis. At that time we started bombing North Vietnam. Various professors, groups of ministers, and so forth, would sign petitions, take out ads in the *New York Times,* something like this, and there was a flurry kind of across the country about campus teach-ins, things like this.

At the university I attended, a part of the faculty did sign the petition, sending it to the President, thinking that this was a kind of a very inhumane thing to do, and also took issue on the level of religious politics.

At that time, one of my professors, my philosophy professor who had left Germany in the second World War and lived in France when France was involved in Vietnam, a couple of times I heard him talk about the war in Vietnam, and I suppose that that was when I first began to think about it seriously. But I felt very much at that time that if the United States was involved in a war, it was probably a just war.

[34] The prosecution objected to most of this testimony as immaterial. The Court sustained the objection, but allowed the questioning of the witnesses to go on as "offer of proof."

[35] I have given Kuebrich's testimony at some length to give the reader an example of how a selective objector works out his decision. We will have occasion to return to Kuebrich's testimony in several of the following chapters.

Probably the next thing that made me think about the war was in January of '66. I was reclassified 1-A. Then I had thought, well, it was the kind of war that was unpopular, and I kind of felt that the war was probably foolish and immoral, but really not too much, and I hadn't really studied the war on my own and I didn't —I was willing at that time, but I had a broken leg and so I got a deferment. Then I was almost inducted and my Draft Board gave me a graduate school deferment which I accepted.

But during all this time I kind of became more and more concerned because, at that time, I thought I should refuse induction, but I wasn't going to.

In graduate school I began to read very much about the war on my own and it was becoming more and more unpopular.

Pontikes: When did you reach the conclusion finally in your mind that it was firmly fixed that the war was an unjust war?

Kuebrich: I think around September of '66.

Pontikes: Did you talk with any of your co-religionists or priests in the Church at that time about this matter?

Kuebrich: No, I hadn't. At that time, I wasn't going to church and so I was really only speaking to a few clergymen, you know, as friends. But I don't really know how to say when I decided the war was unjust, because if I would have really thought it was at that time, when I almost received an induction order, I wouldn't have gone to Vietnam, but I was willing to go at that time or go and possibly end up there.

I think it was during the winter of '67 that I decided that the proper thing for me to do—excuse me, the winter of '66, or '66-'67, with the beliefs I had that I could not and, in fact, never would participate in this war, and that, in fact, I couldn't even continue to participate with the Selective Service System, but I was not willing to sever my relationship at that time and I had a privileged deferment and it seemed like to me a rather bizarre thing to do in a way.

And then things just intensified in my own mind until I finally decided that I no longer wanted a student deferment, because I thought that it was participation in an unjust law and so during the summer of '67, I decided that I would no longer participate with the Selective Service.[36]

Defense counsel then asked his client what criteria he had used in arriving at his decision. Kuebrich replied:

In my high school religion courses and in various theology texts I have read since then, there are laid down certain criteria which each individual should apply to a conflict which his nation is involved in. Through correspondence with a former professor of mine at the seminary and through reading on my own various Catholic periodicals and various books in which these criteria were applied, the four criteria are basically that the war be declared by legitimate authority; that it be a just cause; that there be observed the principle of proportionality whereby the good that will be gained by the conflict will outweigh the damage

[36] *T.R.,* pp. 41-44.

and destruction and carnage that is involved in the process; and there be civilian immunity.

Many of the people that I read—in fact, the ones I have seen that have addressed themselves to this question find that our present engagement in Vietnam is unjust and I have been led to believe that I agree also with that analysis.

Pontikes: Which of the four criteria, you have derived from your reading in various Catholic sources, do you feel are violated by the war?

Kuebrich: There has been quite a bit said and I have seen a couple of people—for instance, Gordonson[37] points out that this war is not declared by legitimate authority because there has not been a state of war declared by Congress. I really don't know too much about that. It seems to me it is more like a political or constitutional issue than a moral issue, although there is always, I guess, some overlap there.

But the idea of civilian immunity—and this was said in Vatican II by the Cardinals of the Roman Catholic Church, that this criteria was relevant and that there couldn't be indiscriminate destruction of civilians. In 1966 when the Roman Catholic Bishops made their statement concerning the Vietnam war, they quoted that paragraph also.

It seems like to me that it is undeniable a lot of people that are reporting upon Vietnam have pointed out that the United States does have what they call free fall zones, which areas are just set off and everything is destroyed in those areas.

I remember also in the spring offensive a general pointed out that we had to destroy the city in order to save it. The city was utterly destroyed, and it seems like to me, and these various people have pointed it out, that it is a clear-cut violation of the civilian immunity.

Pontikes: Any other of the criteria?

Kuebrich: On the question of proportionality, it is very hard to come to certain figures about this because you suspect that everyone has bias and still I have paid a lot of attention to this, and to quote even from what our Government sources present—and I suppose that they would not make the carnage worse than what it actually is—they have pointed out that we have killed over 400,000 Vietnamese soldiers. They also point out that as a conservative estimate, to consider there are four casualties for every person killed, this would mean approximately 2,000,000 people as of September of this year have been injured in this war.

The United States has had 25,000 killed and it has had 178,000, I believe, wounded during this same period. This also only includes the casualties that are in South Vietnam, so that you have there over 2,000,000 in a population of 60,000,000 which means that 1 out of 68 people in Vietnam has been wounded or killed during this war.[38]

Also we have as of August of '67—and I haven't seen more recent figures on this—over 2,000,000 refugees in Vietnam. They said that they were flowing in at

[37] Kuebrich said "Gordon Zahn," an articulate pacifist. The court reporter did not understand what he had said.

[38] Kuebrich's arithmetic is a bit confusing, but his point is clear.

the rate of over 750,000 a year. During the spring offensive, they said there were 500,000 refugees. So I think at a minimum rate, there would be over 3,000,000 now.

It has been pointed out by everyone, Senator Kennedy's investigating committee, AID officials, that it is a tragedy and really a scandal the way these refugee camps are conducted. Of normal Vietnamese children, 60 to 70 percent attend school in these camps—10 to 15 percent attend school [*sic*]. I saw an interview with a doctor who had worked in these camps and it was shown on TV and in this case very much was made of the napalming of the children. This doctor said that in these camps he never has examined one child not suffering from acute malnutrition.

Pontikes: You have come to the conclusion and all this evidence led you to believe the proportionality proposition has been violated, is that correct?

Kuebrich: Yes, that and other evidence. . . .

Pontikes: And on the basis of this evidence, you reached what you say—from what you derived from your reading and consultation, you reached the conclusion as to justness or unjustness of the war in Vietnam, is that correct?

Kuebrich: Yes. Well, also based upon another criteria which is a just cause, and I believe that that is even more crucial than either of the other two. I don't believe that we have a just reason for our presence in Vietnam. I realize that I was giving a lot of empirical information which is necessarily involved in some way of applying the just war criteria, but I think that you are saying that perhaps it is not really relevant right now, and so I won't continue.[39]

There can be no doubt that Kuebrich followed procedures approved by his church in attempting to decide whether a given war is just. He had reasonably accurate knowledge of the principles involved. He investigated the facts as best he could and he consulted with people well versed in the area in question.[40] To the extent that he conformed his judgment to the norms approved by his church, his decision was certainly "religious." The problem for government is whether the conclusions such a decision-making process leads to can be considered religious for establishment purposes. Is Kuebrich's view of the war sufficiently similar to the admittedly religious view of the total objector to justify his contention that the preference given to the latter is an establishment of religion? A free exercise argument would have enabled Kuebrich to clear the religious hurdle, but for establishment purposes it would seem the Courts could reasonably find that only total objection was "really" religious. As Galanter has shown, the Courts are much more willing to decide what is or is not religion in cases concerning establishment than in free exercise cases. Since this is an establishment case, a judicial decision that only total objection is "religious" would be in order. There would be no establishment of religion in 6 (j) because the

[39] *T.R.,* pp. 47-52.
[40] Cf. Heribert Jone, *Moral Theology,* trans. Urban Adelman (Westminster, Md.: Newman Press, 1961), p. 92.

path of total objection lies open to all who choose to tread it—Roman Catholics included.[41]

If the Courts cannot define religion in this way, how would they answer the Catholic taxpayer who sees an establishment of religion in the financial support given to the "religion" of Americanism (all men created equal, endowed with certain inalienable rights, religious pluralism, etc.) taught in the public schools, while similar support is denied the parochial schools. The best way to handle this complaint would seem to be a judicial finding that the American values taught in the public schools, though not without religious implications, are not sufficiently "religious" to support the taxpayer's objection. In view of the broad understanding of religion in *Torcaso* and *Seeger* the Court could hardly deny that there was some support of "religion" in the public schools. To defeat the Catholic taxpayer's objection, the Court need only reserve to itself the right to determine how much religion is "really" religion for establishment purposes. If the Court surrenders this right, it would enter the chamber of horrors Galanter described above.[42] To apply this reasoning to Kuebrich, the Courts need only note the strong political overtones of the defendant's beliefs—his interpretation of the President's war powers, his negative judgment on the advisability of free fall zones, his willingness to second guess the military officer in the field on the necessity of destroying a city to "save" it, his views on the unsatisfactory administration of refugee camps, and his willingness to prefer his judgment to that of the government in determining how much human suffering is too much.

These political convictions could permit the Courts to find that Kuebrich's decision was not sufficiently religious to qualify as "religion" for establishment purposes.

It is, of course, no solution to the fundamental question Kuebrich raises to dismiss his decision as not religious within the meaning of the establishment clause.[43] His decision was obviously both political and religious. But within the limited context of the establishment argument, it seems fair to say the government can effectively defeat Kuebrich's contention as long as the Courts retain the right to decide what is or is not religion for establishment purposes.

Judge Hoffman's reaction to Kuebrich's statement that he was not attending

[41] "Pastoral Constitution on the Church in the Modern World" (*Gaudium et Spes*), No. 79, *The Documents of Vatican II*, ed. Walter M. Abbott (New York: Guild Press, 1966), p. 294. Hereafter cited as *Vatican II.*

[42] Cf. p. 54, above.

[43] In Chapter VI the question of politics and religion is discussed in some detail. Kuebrich is correct in insisting upon the connection between these two areas of human experience. The problem for government is to decide to what extent it can do the same without inviting anarchy in the name of religion.

church regularly is instructive. He questioned Kuebrich at some length [44] on his failure to attend Sunday Mass regularly. Addressing the same question, Father Balke saw little significance in Kuebrich's departure from certain formal practices of his religion. He still has the "Roman Catholic mentality which he acquired over 22 years, and I think this is to be kept in mind in this case, that the mentality that he has is a Roman Catholic one." [45]

Most theologians would probably agree with Balke, but Judge Hoffman, approaching the question from a different angle, was anxious to keep the religious genie within the bottle of readily identifiable religious practices. Kuebrich's failure to conform to these practices tended to discredit the religious nature of his claims in the eyes of the judge.

In conclusion, it would seem that in the light of Galanter's analysis of the double standard of "religion" in the first amendment, an SCO argument based on establishment alone is futile. SCO's cannot avoid bringing some political consideration into their religious decisions. This necessity makes the SCO vulnerable to the Court's willingness to decide what is religious in establishment cases.

McFadden et al. v. Selective Service System Local Board No. 40

BACKGROUND. *McFadden* presents an SCO case that is different from *Kuebrich* both in form and substance; in form, because it is a civil action and, in substance, because it rests on the free exercise clause as well as the establishment clause.

In September, 1968 James F. McFadden and thirteen co-plaintiffs sought judicial review of a Selective Service classification in the District Court for the Northern District of California. They also petitioned that a three judge court be convened to issue an injunction on constitutional grounds against the enforcement of Section 6 (j) of the Uniform Military Service and Training Act.[46]

The plaintiffs were eleven Catholic priests, a seminarian, and two Catholic laymen. They all maintained that Section 6 (j) "unconstitutionally discriminates against Catholics and in favor of members of traditional peace sects, such as the Quakers, by denying conscientious objection status to Catholics solely by reason of difference in the doctrinal and theological statement of grounds for conscientious objection." [47]

[44] *TR,* pp. 55-59.   [45] *Ibid.,* p. 96.

[46] "Plaintiffs' Brief," pp. 5-6. This typescript brief was sent to me through the courtesy of Richard Harrington, attorney for the Plaintiffs. A three-judge court must be convened before a permanent injunction can be issued against the enforcement of a federal statute on constitutional grounds. 28 U.S.C. 2282.

[47] "Plaintiffs' Brief," pp. 3-4.

McFadden, one of the laymen, had received a 1-A classification from Local Board No. 40. The clergymen either held ministerial exemptions[48] or were over age.[49] Their immediate interest in the case was their contention that the Military Training and Service Act made it impossible for them to exercise their ministry. Section 12 (a) makes it a felony to counsel others to resist the draft.[50] The priests contended that the absence of an SCO provision in 6 (j) put them in the position of committing a felony if they counsel selective objectors to follow the just war teaching of the Catholic Church.

The U.S. Attorney for the Northern District of California served as counsel for Draft Board No. 40. At the end of September he filed a motion to dismiss the complaint. His brief rejected the constitutional arguments of both clergy and laymen with a flat assertion that neither Section 6 (j) nor the Selective Service Regulations[51] allows any discrimination against Catholics.[52]

The government brief focused its attention on the question of the Court's jurisdiction. There could be no review of McFadden's classification, the government contended, because Congress had precluded such a review "except as a defense to a criminal prosecution." [53] The brief maintained Congress had the constitutional power to restrict the jurisdiction of the federal courts in this way.[54]

The government supplemented its attack on the jurisdiction of the Court by pointing out that McFadden had not exhausted his administrative remedies and therefore there was no "case or controversy." [55] Nor was there a case or controversy as far as the co-plaintiffs were concerned, since none of them could be put in the 1-A category because of his age and/or his ministerial exemption.

On September 30 Judge Lloyd Burke upheld the position defended by the U.S. Attorney:

The Court, having considered all documents on file and the arguments of counsel, and being fully advised, made the following determinations:

[48] Category IV-D; see 32 *CFR* 1622.43.   [49] Category V-A; see 32 *CFR* 1622.50.
[50] 50 *USC* App. 462 (a).   [51] 32 *CFR* 1622.44.
[52] "Defendant's Brief," pp. 7-8. This typescript brief was also sent through the courtesy of Richard Harrington.
[53] 50 *USC* App. 460 (b) (3). The government's interpretation of this statute may be considerably modified by the Supreme Court's decision in *Oesterreich* v. *Selective Service Board No. 11*, 393 U.S. 96. See also *Petersen* v. *Clark*, 289 F. Supp. 949, and *Gabriel* v. *Clark*, 287 F. Supp. 369.
[54] *U.S. Constitution*, Article III, Section 2, Clause 2.
[55] "Defendant's Brief," p. 6. See *Witmer* v. *U.S.*, 327 U.S. 114, and *Falbo* v. *U.S.*, 320 U.S. 549.

1. There is no substantial constitutional question concerning the validity of 50 USC App. 456 (j);[56]

2. To the extent that plaintiffs seek review of questions of classification or processing, or the threat thereof, by selective service, the Court lacks jurisdiction pursuant to 50 USC App. 460 (b) (3);

3. To the extent that plaintiffs do not seek such review of questions of classification or processing by selective service, there is no case or controversy between plaintiffs and defendants;

4. The complaint fails to state a claim upon which relief can be granted.

Accordingly, it is hereby ordered that plaintiffs' motions to convene a three judge court and for summary judgment be and hereby are denied; it is further ordered that defendants' motion to dismiss be and hereby is granted.[57]

On October 9, Richard Harrington, Attorney for the Plaintiffs, made a motion for a new trial which was denied by Judge Burke. On October 30, Harrington filed a "Notice of Appeal" to the U.S. Court of Appeals for the Ninth Circuit requesting that a three judge court be convened to review McFadden's constitutional argument. The appeal was denied as far as McFadden himself was concerned. The Court of Appeals did agree, however, to convene a three judge court to hear the complaint of the clergymen "if they show after a hearing that there is an immanent threat of their being prosecuted for their counselling." [58]

THE CONSTITUTIONAL ISSUES. McFadden's brief raised three constitutional issues maintaining that sections 6 (j) and 12 (a) of the Uniform Military Training and Service Act violate "freedom of speech and religion and deny Catholics equal protection of the law." The free speech issue pertained to the clergymen alone. The other two issues concerned both McFadden and the clergymen. The precise nature of the "freedom of religion" issue never became entirely clear, but it seems most likely that the argument is based on *both* the establishment and free exercise clauses.

The equal protection position is clearly subordinate to the freedom of religion argument, although, again, its precise place in McFadden's strategy is not clear. It would seem to be relevant only as a second-line argument for an establishment case. Thus, if the Court should find, as it did in *Kuebrich,* that Section 6 (j) did not involve an establishment of religion, McFadden

---

[56] 50 *USC* App. 456 (j) is Section 6 (j) of the Uniform Military Training and Service Act.

[57] From the "Order of Dismissal" released by the Clerk of the U.S. District Court, San Francisco; courtesy of Mr. Harrington.

[58] 2 *Selective Service Law Reporter* (SSLR) 3529.

could still raise the equal protection question of whether the favoritism toward total CO's was a reasonable classification.[59]

To the extent that McFadden relies on the free exercise clause, his equal protection argument would seem to be useless. As pointed out above the Court is extremely generous in declaring beliefs and practices "religious" for free exercise purposes.[60] Presumably, McFadden would have little trouble crossing this hurdle. The crucial question would then be whether the *government* could pass a "compelling state interest" test, i.e., could the government show a compelling interest in restricting CO status to those who object to war in any form? If it could, it could obviously pass a reasonable relation test as well. If it could not, McFadden would have won his case and there would be no need to consider the equal protection position.

McFadden's attorney, however, chose a scatter-shot approach for his constitutional attack—apparently hoping that one of the arguments would appeal to Judge Burke. For our purpose it is necessary to look for more precision than the Courtroom situation demanded.

EVERSON AS PRECEDENT. The first constitutional argument against Section 6 (j) is based on the Court's holding in *Everson* v. *Board of Education*.[61] When McFadden cites *Everson* his freedom of religion argument is clearly in establishment territory. Here he must face the same problem Kuebrich faced—is his claim religious? His account of the reasons why he objects to the Vietnam war has the same political overtones that burdened Kuebrich's case.[62] If Galanter's analysis has any merit, it would seem McFadden would have serious difficulty maintaining the religious character of his decision for establishment purposes.

McFadden offers two arguments to support his contention that Section

[59] As noted above, Chapter II, p. 46, he would do well to raise the "reasonable relation" question in reference to the purposes of the CO exemption rather than in reference to the purposes of the Selective Service Act.

[60] Cf. pp. 53-55, above.

[61] 330 U.S. 1.

[62] Plaintiffs submitted as "Exhibit A" a letter from McFadden to his draft board in which he tried to explain the reason for his seeking an exemption on grounds of conscience. The letter read in part:

"Let me begin by saying that I regard the acts being performed by our government and its forces as a direct violation to the spirit of Christianity. I reject the State Department's dictum that we are involved in Viet Nam because of a sincere concern for the integrity of another country; rather, I judge that we are attempting to coercively superimpose an American Anglo-Saxon reality image upon an Asian people. Further, I reject the party line that we are trying to thwart a Gengis Khan-type invasion from the hinterlands into the defenseless lowlands; rather, I judge that we have chosen *one* side in a civil war; moreover, we have chosen to support a Saigon faction which cannot be said to reflect all of Viet Nam."

6 (j) establishes the religion of the Quakers. The first of these arguments
is stated as follows:

The Everson case held that the state might consistently with the First Amendment provide transportation to all children in the state attending schools—parochial
or otherwise—accredited by the state. Attendance at school was required by the
state.

An improper discrimination between religions would be apparent if a state or
the federal government enacted a law that the government would pay for transportation to schools operated by the Society of Friends, but deny payment for
transportation to Catholic schools, upon the standard stated that transportation was
permissible to schools teaching religious opposition to all war, but transportation
should not be allowed to Catholic schools teaching the doctrine set out in the
complaint—the 'just war' doctrine as it is often abbreviated.[63]

The government brief did not reply directly to this argument. Had the
government chosen to do so, it would not have had much trouble distinguishing the SCO question from the hypothetical situation McFadden suggests.
The "Sunday Closing cases" [64] held that the state had to have some
legitimate secular goal as its primary objective to justify "incidental" burdens
on religious practices. A "uniform day of rest" was found to meet this
requirement. In McFadden's example it is difficult, if not impossible, to
imagine what secular goal—legitimate or otherwise—the state would have
in refusing to pay the transportation costs of "just war" children. In the
case of Section 6 (j), however, there is a legitimate secular goal behind
the favoritism shown to total objectors. That goal is to fill the manpower
needs for national defense.[65]

The second argument, that 6 (j) establishes the Quaker religion, was
put in these words:

If the plaintiffs in McFadden v. Selective Service Board No. 40 would simply
convert to religious belief and membership in the Society of Friends, they would

[63] "Plaintiffs' Brief," pp. 11-12.
[64] Two Guys from Harrison-Allentown, Inc. v. McGinley, 366 U.S. 582; McGowan
v. Maryland, 366 U.S. 420; Gallagher v. Crown Kosher Super Market, 366 U.S. 617,
and Braunfeld v. Brown, 366 U.S. 599.
[65] Whether the "discrimination" against just warriors would pass the "no alternative
means" test of Braunfeld v. Brown is, of course, another question. In a telephone
conversation on February 21, 1969, Mr. Harrington told me he would rely heavily
on Braunfeld in his appellate brief. Presumably, he will argue that even though the
burden placed on SCO's may be justified by a legitimate secular goal, this goal could
be attained by "means which do not impose such a burden" Braunfeld at 607. See
Donald A. Giannella, "Religious Liberty, Nonestablishment, and Doctrinal Development,
Part I: The Religious Liberty Guaranteed," Harvard Law Review, LXXX (May, 1967),
1381-1431, for a discussion of such tests as no alternative means and secular purpose.

enjoy the preference accorded to Friends of not facing prosecution for felony attended by a jail term of five years and fine up to $10,000 for refusing military service or counselling such refusal.

To attach a criminal penalty to conduct otherwise lawful after inquisition into religious doctrine and because the statement of doctrine by one religion is different from the statement of doctrine by another religion is precisely the government conduct prohibited by the First Amendment.[66]

The obvious flaw in this argument is, as the government brief points out, that the norm for the CO privilege is not membership in a church, but "subjective belief." [67] There is no discrimination against Catholics as such. Indeed, any Catholic who chooses to object to all wars can qualify for the exemption. Such a choice would meet with the approval of the highest teaching authority in the Roman Catholic Church.[68]

SHERBERT AS PRECEDENT. McFadden shifts the grounds of his argument when he enlists *Sherbert* v. *Verner* [69] in his attack on 6 (j). As has been noted, *Sherbert* was a free exercise case. McFadden interprets *Sherbert* as meaning that once "a privilege has been extended to some on grounds of religious belief, it may not be withheld from others merely because their religion is different." [70] He offers the example of a statute exempting from military service "persons who by religious training believe that there is no life after death, while compelling service of persons who by religious training subscribe to belief in life after death." [71] He suggests that such a statute would be unconstitutional because of the holding in *Sherbert* that, "It is too late in the day to doubt that liberties of religion and expression may be infringed by the denial of or placing of conditions upon a benefit or privilege." [72]

McFadden's use of *Sherbert* overlooks an important element in the reasoning behind that case. Mrs. Sherbert did not win her case simply because she showed her religious beliefs were impaired by the unemployment laws of South Carolina. She won because South Carolina failed to show that a "compelling interest" required the state to impose this burden upon her. In *Sherbert* there is no absolute imperative against placing burdens on religious beliefs. Such burdens must always be balanced against state interests with the scales weighted heavily, but not decisively, in favor of the claims of religion. McFadden's example of the preference given to those who do not believe in eternal life is, of course, riddled with constitutional infirmities—*Sherbert*

[66] "Plaintiffs' Brief," pp. 12-13.
[68] *Documents of Vatican II*, p. 292.
[70] "Plaintiffs' Brief," p. 14.
[72] *Ibid.*, citing 374 U.S. at 404.

[67] "Defendant's Brief," pp. 7-8.
[69] 374 U.S. 398.
[71] *Ibid.*

or no *Sherbert. But on the basis of Sherbert,* it would be unconstitutional not because the burden was placed on those who believe in an afterlife, but because the state would surely fail to show a compelling interest to justify the burden.

U.S. v. Kurki

BACKGROUND. *U.S.* v. *Kurki*[73] presents a stronger case for SCO than *Kuebrich* and *McFadden.* Like *McFadden,* it improves on *Kuebrich* by concentrating on the free exercise clause.[74] *Kurki* goes beyond *McFadden,* however, in attempting to show that the United States has no "compelling state interest" in favoring CO's over SCO's.

On August 10, 1965 Irving Kurki, a selective objector, appeared at his Local Draft Board Office in Racine, Wisconsin in accordance with an order for induction issued on July 20, 1965. After receiving the notice of induction, Kurki informed his local board that he would not serve in the Army. Nevertheless, he complied with the induction notice to the extent that on the day appointed he reported to the Local Board Office. Upon his arrival, however, he began distributing leaflets critical of the United States' effort in Vietnam and urged his fellow registrants to follow his example by refusing to serve. An employee of the Local Board asked Kurki if he intended to board the bus for the induction center at Milwaukee. When he replied in the negative, he was asked to leave the office at once and he did so. Three months later he was indicted for failing to report for induction and on August 9, 1966 was found guilty and sentenced to two years in prison.[75]

His attorneys[76] based his defense on two lines of reasoning. The first dealt with the proper meaning of the statutes and Selective Service Regulations Kurki had allegedly violated. Was the fact that he *intended* not to serve sufficient to convict him of failing to report for induction when, in fact, he had reported and had left the Racine office only when asked to do so? The second argument was a constitutional case based on the free exercise clause.

Judge Reynolds of the United States District Court for the Eastern District of Wisconsin rejected both of Kurki's arguments. His main objection to the constitutional argument was that Kurki's beliefs were *political,* not religious. Consequently, Kurki's appeal to the Seventh Circuit developed at great length the religious character of his beliefs. Kurki lost his appeal in a 2-1

[73] 255 F. Supp. 161, 384 F 2d 905.

[74] Kurki also raises an establishment argument, but it is subordinate to his principal argument which is based on the free exercise clause.

[75] "Plaintiffs' Brief" in petition for *certiorari,* pp. 3-6.

[76] Harold P. Sutherland and David Loeffler of Milwaukee. I am grateful to Mr. Sutherland for making available certain documents relevant to Kurki's case.

decision with Judges Knoch and Cummings affirming the lower Court and Judge Kiley dissenting.[77] Judge Kiley's dissent was based on the first question, whether Kurki had actually failed to report for induction. He did not touch the constitutional issue. The two-judge majority held that since Kurki did not appeal his 1-A classification within the Selective Service System itself, he had not "exhausted his administrative remedies,"[78] and, therefore, "the District Court should not have received evidence as to whether he was actually a CO within the meaning of Section 6 (j)."[79]

Kurki's appeal to the Supreme Court for a writ of *certiorari* was denied. His appeal, however, was based exclusively on the question of whether he had failed to report for induction, since this was the only issue the Judges of the Seventh Circuit found relevant. Hence, the proponents of SCO can take comfort in the fact that by the time the Supreme Court denied *certiorari*, *Kurki* was no longer an SCO case.

In this section I will focus attention on the brief Kurki submitted to the Seventh Circuit. In this brief Kurki's lawyers developed most fully the constitutional case in reply to Judge Reynolds' finding in the District Court that Kurki's beliefs were not religious.

RELIGION AND POLITICS. Irving Kurki's objections to the Vietnam war are more overtly political than those of Kuebrich and McFadden. In the "Declaration of Conscience" which he distributed at the Local Board in Racine he gave his views as follows:

President Johnson has blatantly violated last November's "Mandate for Peace." Instead of stopping the war against the people of Vietnam he has escalated it. Today nearly one hundred thousand U.S. troops occupy this war-torn country; before the year is over this figure will double.

THE U.S. HAS NO LEGAL RIGHT TO BE IN VIETNAM. Our actions there constitute a clear violation of both the United Nations Charter and the 1954 Geneva Accords.

THE U.S. HAS NO MORAL RIGHT TO BE IN VIETNAM. In the name of "freedom" we are suppressing freedom. We are burning villages and killing women and children. U.S. intervention means nothing but continued suffering for the people of Vietnam, and a continued risk of nuclear holocaust for the rest of the world.

The rape of Vietnam must be stopped. For my part, I cannot conscientiously become a cog in the U.S. war machine; I am refusing to submit to induction. I ask you to do the same. I urge you to join me in striving for a fundamental change in

[77] 384 F 2d 905.
[78] *Ibid.*, at 907.
[79] *Ibid.*

U.S. foreign policy. Don't let Johnson's crimes become your crimes. REFUSE TO
FIGHT IN VIETNAM.

IRV KURKI[80]

His letter to the Draft Board giving his reasons for refusing to serve
and his testimony at his trial were laden with similar "this-worldly" considerations. Nevertheless Kurki attempted to parlay *Seeger* and a convenient
interpretation of 6 (j) into an argument that his beliefs were religious and
not political.[81]

Section 6 (j) defines religious training and belief as follows:

Religious training and belief in this connection means an individual's belief in a
relation to a Supreme Being involving duties superior to those arising from any
human relation, but does not include essentially political, sociological, or philosophical views or a merely personal moral code.[82]

Kurki's brief maintained the word "essentially," as used in the statement,
meant that religious and political beliefs were mutually exclusive. Whatever
is religious cannot be political. He then appealed to *Seeger's* highly subjective test of what constitutes "religion" to underscore the religious character
of his beliefs.[83] Kurki was not a religious man in any orthodox sense,
but his political beliefs were for him areas of "ultimate concern" occupying
in his life "a place parallel to that filled by the God of those admittedly
qualifying for the exemption." [84] Therefore, under *Seeger,* Kurki's beliefs
are religious and, further, under the "mutually exclusive" interpretation
of 6 (j) their religious character purges them of any political content.[85]

Thus Kurki's attorneys expanded the area of religion by applying *Seeger*
to their client's belief and, at the same time, they contracted the meaning
of politics by their "mutually exclusive" interpretation of 6 (j). In this way
they attempted to get around Judge Reynolds' finding Kurki's beliefs
political. In effect, their argument defines out of existence the political
character of any belief tinged with ultimate concern. The most interesting
point in Kurki's argument is that he says in the practical context of the
courtroom what Galanter [86] had said in academe—that under *Seeger,* in
the question of whether a given belief is "religious," "saying makes it so."

---

[80] *Plaintiff's Brief in the U. S. Court of Appeals for the Seventh Circuit,* Appendix,
p. 114. Hereafter referred to as *Plaintiff's Brief—7th Circuit.*

[81] *Ibid.,* Appendix, pp. 121-28.   [82] *Ibid.,* p. 37, citing 50 *USC App.* 456 (j).

[83] Cf. Chapter I, pp. 33-37.   [84] *U.S.* v. *Seeger,* 380 U.S. at 176.

[85] Kurki exploits an ambiguity in *Seeger* to his own advantage. Clark's opinion
at times seemed to call for more "content" than his "parallel place" test would
suggest. Cf. 380 U.S. at 173.

[86] See pp. 53-55, above.

COMPELLING STATE INTERESTS. *Kurki* and *McFadden* pursue similar strategies by first claiming their beliefs are religious and then arguing that the burdens placed on their beliefs violate *Sherbert* v. *Verner*.[87] As we have seen,[88] McFadden rests after demonstrating the mere fact that discriminatory burdens have been placed on certain religious beliefs. Here, *Kurki* goes beyond *McFadden* and correctly interprets *Sherbert* to require not only that discrimination be shown, but also that the discrimination cannot be justified by a "compelling state interest."

Kurki raises three points in his contention that the government has no compelling interest in discriminating against SCO:

1. A change in the law would not impose an administrative burden on the state because the number of CO's has always been "infinitesimal." [89]
2. During World War II Britain's CO provision was "broad enough to encompass the defendant and others like him," [90] but very few objectors took advantage of this liberal provision.
3. The problem of testing for sincerity would be no worse under SCO than at present for "if an individual is willing to lie or dissimulate in order to obtain exemption he will certainly do it as readily where a particular war is concerned as where all [wars are concerned]." [91]

Unfortunately, these arguments do not seem to be as "compelling" as the state interests Kurki would discredit.[92] His first point, the infinitesimal number of CO's, is weak because one of the reasons for the negligible number of CO's is the fact that the exemption has always been restricted to total pacifists. SCO would broaden the grounds on which the exemption would be granted. During wartime it would increase the number of men qualifying for the exemption. Whether this increase would be substantial or negligible would vary from war to war and from time to time within the same war. In general, the number of total objectors can be known in advance of a decision to go to war. Hitherto this number has, as Kurki contends, always been quite small. There is no reason to think this number will increase substantially in the near future. But, even if it should, the Selective Service System would have a reasonably accurate estimate of how many CO's there are at a given time. If this number increased considerably over the years, the government would have to take this into consideration

[87] 374 U.S. 398.
[88] See pp. 61-63, above.
[89] *Plaintiffs' Brief—7th Circuit*, p. 73.
[90] *Ibid.*, pp. 73-74.
[91] *Ibid.*, p. 75.
[92] For examples of what the Courts have considered "compelling interests," see Chapter II, pp. 46-49, above. In *U.S.* v. *O'Brien*, 391 U.S. 367, Chief Justice Warren suggests that the Supreme Court is willing to go a long way to meet what the government considers necessary for the efficient administration of the Selective Service System.

in conducting its foreign policy. Under SCO this number would never be known before a war and could fluctuate wildly during a war depending on the mood of popular opinion.

Neither is the British experience in World War II particularly instructive, since one would hardly expect many Englishmen to be *selective* objectors to *that* war. Unfortunately, not evey nation fights for a cause as clearly justifiable as England's resistance to Hitler. If this were the case, Kurki's second point would be well taken. But a brief review of modern history suggests that the British experience in World War II was the exception rather than the rule. It is much more difficult to imagine a British selective objector, than it is to imagine an American objecting to the Korean War or an Italian to World War I.

Finally, the sincerity problem would be greater under an SCO provision than at present, not because CO's are less likely to be liars, but because, if they lie, they are more likely to be caught. It is easier to investigate a claim of total objection because this usually involves membership in a peace church or some comparable secular organization. Such membership would not, of course, by itself suffice to establish a citizen's pacifist credentials. But when an objective fact—like membership in a religious or secular peace group—is supplemented by affidavits from friends who testify to the long-standing pacifist beliefs of a registrant, a local board has solid grounds for granting a CO exemption. Under the present system it is the "road to Damascus" CO who presents the difficult case. His claim has no roots, and though he may be quite sincere in his pacifism, he often has trouble convincing his draft board. Under an SCO provision, all roads would lead to Damascus. In the early years of a war, sudden conversion would be the rule rather than the exception, since the objector's opposition to a particular war ordinarily would not antedate the beginning of that war.[93]

Although *Kurki* surpasses *McFadden* in its grasp of the relevance of *Sherbert* for SCO, the argument could have been stronger. In *Sherbert* the Court said that *even if* South Carolina could show that intolerable administrative burdens would accompany an unemployment system that took Mrs. Sherbert's religious scruples into consideration, "it would still

---

[93] In the case of a long war, however, objective criteria for evaluating a claim of SCO would be more readily available—e.g., active involvement in "peace movements." An SCO provision before a war or during its early stages might encourage registrants to join peace movements to impress their draft boards with their "sincerity." If, however, an SCO provision were enacted after several years of warfare had elapsed, participation in peace movements could provide a meaningful criterion for judging sincerity. On the other hand, a widespread peace movement enjoying massive support might be a contra-indication for an SCO enactment precisely because so many registrants could justly support a sincere claim to selective objection. In such circumstances, the more prudent course might be to end the war rather than pass SCO.

plainly be incumbent upon the appellees [S.C.] to demonstrate that no alternative forms of regulation would combat such abuses without infringing First Amendment rights." [94] Kurki overlooked the fact that should his effort to challenge the government's compelling interest in favoring total objectors fail, he could still demand that the government show there is no alternative method of protecting such interests without discriminating against selective objectors.[95]

EVALUATION OF KURKI. We have already seen how Kurki's argument surpasses that of Kuebrich and McFadden. He also makes a strong argument that the government has failed to show any reasonable relation between the burden placed on SCO's and the purpose of the exemption.[96] As has been shown, if one makes a "reasonable relation" argument,[97] it is better to consider the terms of the relation as the favoritism toward total objectors and the purposes of the *exemption* rather than the same favoritism and the purpose of the Selective Service Act as a whole. Also, in challenging the reasonableness of discrimination against SCO's, he develops a "national interest" argument which has always enjoyed an honorable place in the American approach to conscientious objection.[98]

These arguments were not rejected by the Seventh Circuit, but were dismissed because the issue was not "ripe" for adjudication.[99] Future proponents of SCO would do well to study Kurki's argument. If they could improve on its one glaring weakness—the failure to present a serious challenge to the government's compelling interest in the discrimination against SCO's—they might be able to establish a constitutional argument for selective objection.

[94] 374 U.S. at 407.

[95] Perhaps a volunteer army would be such an alternative means. Under *Sherbert* it would seem that the government would have to show why this is *not* an alternative means. Cf. *The Draft: a Handbook of Facts and Alternatives*, ed. Sol Tax (Chicago: University of Chicago Press, 1967), pp. 191-286.

[96] *Plaintiff's Brief—7th Circuit*, pp. 75-78.

[97] Chapter II, p. 46

[98] Chapter I, pp. 23-24. His argument is twofold: (1) It is not in the best interest of the military establishment to have unwilling soldiers in its ranks, and (2) no nation can survive for long unless it respects the rights of conscience. The second argument relies heavily on a famous article written by Harlan F. Stone, "The Conscientious Objector," *Columbia University Quarterly*, XXI (1919), 253.

[99] 384 F 2d at 907.

IV
The Marginal Issues

In the previous chapter the three cases reviewed revealed different methods of approaching SCO within the framework of the establishment and free exercise clauses. Since these considerations dominate the literature on SCO, it seems only right to consider other approaches as marginal. In this chapter the "marginal issues" raised in three further SCO cases will be considered: *U.S.* v. *Spiro*, *U.S.* v. *Sisson*, and *U.S.* v. *Mitchell*.[1] Although these cases are outside the "mainstream" of SCO argumentation, they present questions that cannot be lightly dismissed. In the first case, *U.S.* v. *Spiro*, the defendant argued that the Supreme Court had already recognized the right to selective objection in granting CO status to Jehovah's Witnesses who would fight in theocratic wars.[2] In the second case, *U.S.* v. *Sisson*, Judge Wyzanski reached first amendment grounds in upholding a qualified form of SCO, even though Sisson's defense rested on other grounds. In the third case, *U.S.* v. *Mitchell*, we shall consider the question of whether the Nuremberg Trials set a precedent that would permit Americans to refuse to serve in the Army because of the allegedly "aggressive war" the U.S. is waging in Vietnam.

U.S. v. Spiro

BACKGROUND. Stephen Spiro first registered with the Selective Service System in December, 1957. For the next four years he enjoyed a student

[1] *U.S.* v. *Spiro*, 384 F 2d 159; 390 U.S. 956. *U.S.* v. *Sisson*, 297 F. Supp. 907; 399 U.S. 267. *U.S.* v. *Mitchell*, 369 F 2d 323; 386 U.S. 972.

[2] Cf. Chapter I, pp. 30-32, above.

deferment while attending the University of Chicago on an "on and off basis."[3] During a drop-out period early in 1962 he was reclassified by his local board in New Jersey. In April of the same year he took an Air Force qualifying examination and a few months later submitted an application for the Naval Reserve. In the fall of 1962 he took a job with the National Office of the Student Peace Union. It was at this time that he first notified his local board that he was a CO. He was classified 1-A-O. This classification meant that Spiro would be required to serve in the Army but in a non-combatant capacity.[4] He appealed this decision in the hope of getting a 1-0 classification, the category for those who object to any form of participation in military affairs.[5] This appeal was denied.[6] Spiro was ordered to report for induction on January 6, 1965. He reported to the induction center, but failed to take the "one step forward." Subsequently, he was indicted for refusing to submit to induction and found guilty by Judge Wortendyke of the United States District Court for the District of New Jersey. The Court of Appeals for the Third Circuit upheld Judge Wortendyke[7] and on March 4, 1968 the Supreme Court denied *certiorari*.[8]

Spiro's argument in support of his claim for the exemption was based on the just war doctrine as expounded by reputable Catholic authors.[9] He placed great stress on what he understood to be a willingness, under certain circumstances, on the part of the U.S. government to deploy nuclear weapons against civilian population centers of hostile nations.[10] He said he would fight in a conventional or even a nuclear war as long as the principle of civilian immunity was preserved.[11] However, he did not feel that this principle would be observed and, consequently, felt obliged to oppose on grounds of conscience *any* war the U.S. might enter upon.[12]

More significant, however, is the position Spiro took in a letter to the

---

[8] *U.S. Supreme Court Briefs and Records,* 390 U.S. 956. *U.S.* v. *Spiro,* "Petition for Writ of Certiorari to the U.S. Court of Appeals for the Third Circuit," p. 7. Hereafter referred to as *Spiro's Brief.*

[4] *Ibid.,* p. 4; cf. 32 *CFR* 1622.11.

[5] *Spiro's Brief,* p. 4; cf. 32 *CFR* 1622.14.

[6] *Spiro's Brief,* p. 4.

[7] 384 F 2d 916.

[8] 390 U.S. 956. See *New York Times,* Tuesday, March, 5, 1968, p. 26.

[9] *Spiro's Brief* mentions *Breakthrough to Peace,* edited by Thomas Merton; *Modern War and Basic Ethics* by John Ryan; and *Morality and Modern Warfare,* edited by John Nagle.

[10] *Spiro's Brief,* Appendix, p. 5a.

[11] Spiro's position must be pieced together from various letters he wrote and summaries of his position offered by his counsel and the courts. Here I rely on a letter from the Chief of the Conscientious Objector Section of the Department Justice to the Chairman of the Appeal Board of the New Jersey Selective Service System. The letter is reproduced in *ibid.,* pp. 26a-30a.

[12] *Ibid.,* p. 5a.

New Jersey Selective Service Board of Appeals. Here he developed more fully his understanding of the just war theory. Not only did he consider unjust any war the U.S. might wage at present, but he went on to state that in his opinion, no war has ever met the criterion required for a just war. In his own words:

> Although I said that I could participate in a just war, even in a combatant status, this was surely a theoretical statement. If I had wings I could fly. I maintained that this "just war" is, in the real world, not capable of occurring; that as a result of the Sin of Adam and the consequent corruption of Human Will, it is inconceivable that a just war will ever happen—since there never has been one, as far as I can tell, and I hardly expect that Men will suddenly change. Consequently, I must refuse military service.[13]

CONSTITUTIONAL ISSUES. It was Spiro's rigid understanding of the just war doctrine that provided the basis of his constitutional argument. Although he would fight in a just war, the fact that he felt there never has been and never will be such a war placed him, he argued, in the same constitutional position as Jehovah's Witnesses who will fight only in theocratic wars. In *Sicurella* v. *U.S.*,[14] Spiro contended, the Supreme Court granted the CO exemption to theocratic warriors and should do the same for just warriors who believe that *de facto* no war is ever just. In his appeal for *certiorari* Spiro maintained that a failure to do so is a discrimination which violates the establishment and free exercise clauses of the first amendment and the due process clause of the fifth amendment.

The government brief attempted to distinguish *Spiro* from *Sicurella* on the grounds that Sicurella opposed all use of carnal weapons. Thus, the wars in which Sicurella would fight would be spiritual battles, not "shooting wars." If Spiro's rigid norms of a just war were ever met, he would then be fighting in the kind of war that "Congress had in mind . . . when it referred to participation in war in any form—actual military conflicts between nations of the earth in our time—wars with bombs and bullets, tanks, planes and rockets." [15]

---

[13] *Ibid.*, p. 33a.

[14] 348 U.S. 385. *Spiro's Brief* goes over what is now familiar territory to the reader. For his establishment argument, he cites *Schempp*. The free exercise argument relies on *Fowler, Ballard,* and *Sherbert* and the due process argument (with equal protection overtones) is based on *Bolling* v. *Sharpe*. See Chapter I, pp. 30-32, for a discussion of the problem of whether "in any form" modifies "participation" or "war." In cases involving Jehovah's Witnesses the courts connect the phrase with "participation." The best defense of this interpretation appears in "Memorandum from Counsel for Captain Dale E. Noyd to the Secretary of the Air Force Personnel Board Headquarters," prepared by Marvin Karpatkin of the American Civil Liberties Union.

[15] *U.S. Supreme Court Briefs and Records,* 390 U.S. 956, *U.S.* v. *Spiro,* "Brief for the U.S. in Opposition," p. 8, citing *Sicurella* v. *U.S.*

The Courts simply ignored the constitutional issue. Judge Wortendyke found it sufficient to hold that the "evidence disclosed beyond a reasonable doubt that the defendant Stephen Spiro was properly classified by the appropriate Selective Service authorities as 1-A for Military Service in the Armed Forces of the U.S." [16]

Judge Staley, speaking for a unanimous Court of Appeals, found there was a "basis in fact" for the Draft Board's denial of the CO claim. He added, "Once this conclusion is reached, we are without jurisdiction to delve into the legal and theological implications of appellant's belief." [17]

In this way the Court of Appeals avoided any explanation of how Spiro's position differed from that of theocratic warriors who have qualified for the exemption. The government's rejoinder—that Sicurella would not use carnal weapons—was inadequate, because, as we have seen, Sicurella indicated he would use force in defending "Kingdom interests." [18] Other Jehovah's Witnesses had been even more explicit in stating their willingness to use "carnal weapons" in warfare should God so order them. In U.S. v. Taffs[19] and U.S. v. Hartmann[20] registrants who affirmed their readiness to fight in theocratic wars without any repudiation of carnal weapons had their CO claims upheld. The repudiation of carnal weapons by Sicurella served only to obscure what the Appellate Courts have held consistently—that theocratic warriors are considered bona fide CO's.[21]

If we pierce the veil of judicial restraint that enabled the Third Circuit to dispose of Spiro on administrative grounds, it may at first seem strange that Spiro should have lost his case. After all, Spiro maintained there never has been and never will be a just war, whereas the Witnesses acknowledge that there have been theocratic wars and that there may be another one at Armageddon.[22]

Thus, Spiro lost his case even though his position is closer total objection to war than that of the Jehovah's Witnesses whose claims have been upheld. Perhaps the reason the Courts are more lenient toward theocratic warriors than toward a just warrior like Spiro is found in the government's sense

---

[16] Cited in Spiro's Brief, Appendix, p. 9a.

[17] 384 F 2d 956. This statement is hard to understand in view of Spiro's constitutional defense. The "basis in fact" rule (Estep v. U.S., 327 U.S. 114) would not keep the Courts from striking down a Selective Service Regulation that said Jehovah's Witnesses could be classified as CO's but Roman Catholics could not. The "basis in fact" that a registrant really was Roman Catholic would not keep the Courts from delving further into the constitutionality of the regulations.

[18] Chapter I, pp. 30-32.

[19] 208 F 2d 239. [20] 209 F 2d 366.

[21] For references to CO cases, see p. 32, n. 74, above.

[22] Sicurella v. U.S., 348 U.S. at 390. See also Hartmann v. U.S., 209 F 2d at 370 citing the article, "Why Jehovah's Witnesses Are Not Pacifists," in The Watchtower, February 1, 1951.

of incompetence in matters of religion. In our regime there would be something unseemly about the government entering into a dispute with a citizen on the question of whether God had or had not commanded a particular war. As long as the theocratic warrior confines the wars in which he would fight to the distant past of the Old Testament or to the distant future of Armageddon, the government, for all practical purposes, can treat him the same way it would treat a total objector.[23]

In basing his argument on *justice,* Spiro moved into an area in which, unlike religion, government should have the highest competence. The man who refuses to fight in a war because it is unjust presents a threat to his government. He says it has failed precisely in the area in which it should excel—the pursuit of justice. To be sure, Spiro softened the blow by saying no nation has ever waged a just war. He did not *single out* the United States for his moral disapproval as did Kuebrich, McFadden, and Kurki. Nevertheless, in basing his attack on "justice," he challenged the government in a very sensitive area.

On a constitutional level the government might have a difficult time showing precisely what compelling state interest permitted it to classify the Jehovah's Witnesses as CO's while denying this same classification to a man with Sprio's extremely rigid interpretation of the just war doctrine. Perhaps it was to avoid this constitutional issue that the Third Circuit refused to go beyond the "basis in fact" rule of *U.S.* v. *Estep.*[24] Regardless of the constitutional merits of Spiro's case, at the more fundamental level of the nature of government, Spiro's case is quite different from that of Sicurella and the other Witnesses. As a selective objector with justice as the basis of his selection, Spiro presents a more political challenge than the Witnesses who would fight only at the command of God.

U.S. v. Sisson

BACKGROUND. John H. Sisson's troubles with Local Board No. 114 began shortly after his graduation from Harvard in June, 1967. He registered at the Boston Architectural Center for a few weeks in the fall of 1967, but dropped this endeavor when he decided he could not in good conscience apply for a student (2-S) deferment. He then worked as a reporter for *The Southern Courier,* a newspaper published in Montgomery, Alabama.

---

[23] If, however, the theocratic warrior maintained that God told him to fight in Korea but not in Vietnam his claims would probably be no more successful than those of Kuebrich, McFadden, and Kurki. As long as his "selection" of wars is restricted to the distant past or distant future, the problem he presents is minimal. For all practical purposes he will not fight in any war at all.

[24] 327 U.S. 114. See also Alexander M. Bickel, *The Least Dangerous Branch* (Indianapolis: Bobbs-Merrill, 1962), chap. iv: "The Passive Virtues."

In February, 1968 he wrote to his Massachusetts draft board to request Selective Service System Form No. 150, the form that must be completed by conscientious objectors. He failed to execute this form for two reasons. The first was that he "could not honestly make a claim to conscientious objection to war in any form as it is put on the Form 150." The second reason, which concerned his unwillingness to accept a student deferment as well as a CO exemption, was his belief that the exemption and deferment systems discriminate against the poor and the uneducated.

On March 18, 1968, Local Board No. 114 notified Sisson that he was to report for induction on April 17. Sisson reported on the scheduled day and went from the local board to the induction center at Boston where he refused to take the symbolic "step forward." [25] Shortly thereafter he was indicted for violating the Military Selective Service Act of 1967 and found guilty on March 21, 1969.[26] The government had no trouble proving what no one denied—that Sisson had failed to submit to induction as ordered. Sisson's attorney, John G. S. Flyn, abandoned the familiar first amendment question in favor of an attempt to persuade the jury that Sisson's refusal to accept induction had not been "wilful." The argument seemed to confuse motive and intent. The latter refers to whether one acts deliberately, i.e., wants to do what one does, whereas the former usually refers to *why* one performs a certain action. Defense counsel summoned two academic critics of the Vietnam war, Richard Falk of Princeton and Howard Zinn of Boston University. The purpose of their testimony was to show that reasonable men could believe what Sisson believed about the wisdom, justice, and legality of the Vietnam war. Prodded by constant objections from the U.S. attorney to the admissibility of such evidence, Flyn insisted he was not debating the merits of the Vietnam war, but was merely showing that reasonable men could share Sisson's beliefs.[27] In his closing argument Flyn took the jury back to Germany of thirty years ago when young men like Sisson were told to march into Poland and all too few raised the question Sisson had raised. All this was rather loosely connected with the only relevant question, viz., whether Sisson's refusal to step forward had been "wilful." [28]

In his charge to the jury Judge Wyzanski destroyed whatever Flyn had hoped to accomplish. He instructed the jurors that

the words "unlawfully, knowingly and wilfully" as used in this indictment, in these regulations and in this statute mean deliberately, intentionally, knowingly. And it makes no difference whatsoever if the defendant has the finest motive in the

[25] 294 F. Supp. 511 and Trial Record of *U.S* v. *Sisson,* pp. 14-67. Hereafter cited as *T.R.*

[26] 294 F. Supp. 511.

[27] *T.R.,* pp. 93-94 and p. 112.

[28] *T.R.,* pp. 126-33.

world, it makes no difference whatsoever whether as a matter of reasonable belief he thought a particular war was or was not contrary to an international obligation, contrary to the Constitution of the United States, contrary to good order, morals, justice or any ethical or other consideration.

The only question that as a matter of law a Jury has a right to consider is whether the defendant if he failed to perform an act required under the statute and regulations was acting knowingly in the sense of with mental awareness, wilfully in the sense of intentionally and with free choice.[29]

With this instruction in mind, it was no wonder that the jury needed only twenty minutes to return a verdict of guilty. Sisson was released on his own recognizance and told to appear later for sentencing, but on April 1, 1969 Judge Wyzanski declared Section 6 (j) unconstitutional as applied to Sisson and granted the defense's motion in arrest of judgment. In granting an arrest of judgment rather than simply acquitting Sisson, Wyzanski offered the government an opportunity to appeal his ruling and thereby enable the Supreme Court to address his constitutional argument for SCO.[30] On June 29, 1970 the Supreme Court found that Wyzanski had erred in granting the motion for an arrest of judgment and dismissed the government's appeal "for lack of jurisdiction."[31] This meant an acquittal for Sisson without a Supreme Court decision on the merits of Wyzanski's opinion. The Court promised to consider the question of SCO in *Gillette* v. *U.S.* and *Negre* v. *Larsen*.[32]

JUDGE WYZANKI'S OPINION. Although *Sisson* began as a "marginal issue" case, Judge Wyzanski's opinion brought it into the first amendment line of reasoning. He began with a recognition of broad Congressional powers of conscription. However, this power is not simply unlimited:

This court's assumption that Congress has the general power to conscript in time of peace is not dispositive of the specific question whether that general power is subject to some exception or immunity available to a draftee because of a constitutional restriction in favor of individual liberty.[33]

Having introduced a limiting principle on Congress' power to conscript, Wyzanski then suggested a balancing test between the needs of national security and Sisson's freedom of conscience:

This is not an area of constitutional absolutism. It is an area in which competing

[29] *T.R.,* pp. 147-48.

[30] For a thorough and extremely interesting treatment of the significance of Sisson's motion in arrest of judgment, see Isidore Silver, "Sisson's Complaint, Wyzanski's Ploy," *Commonweal,* XC (June 20, 1969), 385-89.

[31] 399 U.S. 270.   [32] See Chapter V.   [33] 297 F. Supp. 907.

claims must be explored, examined, and marshalled with reference to the Constitution as a whole.

There are two main categories of conflicting claims. First there are both public and private interests in the common defense. Second there are both public and private interests in individual liberty.

Every man, not least the conscientious objector, has an interest in the security of the nation. Dissent is possible only in a society strong enough to repel attack. The conscientious will to resist springs from moral principles. It is likely to seek a new order in the same society, not anarchy or submission to a hostile power. Thus conscience rarely wholly disassociates itself from the defense of the ordered society within which it functions and which it seeks to reform not to reduce to rubble.

In parallel fashion, every man shares and society as a whole shares an interest in the liberty of the conscientious objector, religious or not. The freedom of all depends on the freedom of each. Free men exist only in free societies. Society's own stability and growth, its physical and spiritual prosperity are responsive to the liberties of its citizens, to their deepest insights, to their free choices,—"That which opposes, also fits."

Those rival categories of claims cannot be mathematically graded. There is no table of weights and measures. Yet there is no insuperable difficulty in distinguishing orders of magnitude.

The sincerely conscientious man, whose principles flow from reflection, education, practice, sensitivity to competing claims, and a search for a meaningful life, always brings impressive credentials. When he honestly believes that he will act wrongly if he kills, his claim obviously has great magnitude. That magnitude is not appreciably lessened if his belief relates not to war in general, but to a particular war or to a particular type of war. Indeed a selective conscientious objector might reflect a more discriminating study of the problem, a more sensitive conscience, and a deeper spiritual understanding.

It is equally plain that when a nation is fighting for its very existence there are public and private interests of great magnitude in conscripting for the common defense all available resources, including manpower for combat.

But a campaign fought with limited forces for limited objects with no likelihood of a battlefront within this country and without a declaration of war is not a claim of comparable magnitude.

Nor is there any suggestion that in the present circumstances there is a national need for combat service from Sisson as distinguished from other forms of service by him. The want of magnitude in the national demand for combat service is reflected in the nation's lack of calls for sacrifice in any serious way by civilians.[34]

He then concluded:

Sisson's case being limited to a claim of conscientious objection to combat service in a foreign campaign, this court holds that the free exercise of religion clause in the First Amendment and the due process clause of the Fifth Amendment prohibit

[34] *Ibid.*, at 908-9.

the application of the 1967 draft act to Sisson to require him to render combat service in Vietnam.

The chief reason for reaching this conclusion after examining the competing interests is the magnitude of Sisson's interest in not killing in the Vietnamese conflict as against the want of magnitude in the country's present need for him to be so employed.[35]

The precise meaning of Wyzanski's statement—that the Constitution "prohibits the application of the 1967 draft act to Sisson to require him to render combat service in Vietnam"—was not altogether clear. He said only that the "in any form" clause cannot be *applied* to Sisson for *combat* service in *Vietnam*. Lest there be any doubt on this point, he concluded his decision with the following bold-face declaration:

To Guard Against Misunderstanding, This Court Has Not Ruled That:

(1) The Government Has No Right to Conduct Vietnam Operations; or

(2) The Government Is Using Unlawful Methods in Vietnam; or

(3) The Government Has No Power to Conscript the Generality of Men for Combat Service; or

(4) The Government in a Defense of the Homeland Has No Power to Conscript for Combat Service Anyone It Sees Fit; or

(5) The Government Has No Power to Conscript Conscientious Objectors for Non-combat Service.

Indeed the Court Assumes Without Deciding that Each One of These Propositions States the Exact Reverse of the Law.

All That This Court Decides Is that as a Sincere Conscientious Objector Sisson Cannot Constitutionally Be Subjected to Military Orders (Not Reviewable in a United States Constitutional Court) Which May Require Him to Kill in the Vietnam Conflict.[36]

It is clear from this statement that Wyzanski did not uphold a general constitutional right to SCO in the sense in which the term is ordinarily used. The proponents of SCO do not restrict their argument to Vietnam alone. Their argument moves at the level of principle. As will be pointed out in Part II, the proponents of SCO would not be happy with a situation in which a man's conscientious scruples against fighting in Vietnam were respected while those of a man opposed to fighting in the Dominican Republic were ignored. Sisson made it clear that he would not be satisfied with an arrangement that would do no more than keep him out of Vietnam:

I refused induction because I believe the war in Vietnam, that is the United

[35] *Ibid.*, at 910.

[36] *Ibid.*, at 912. The bold face type appears in the opinion released to the press, not in the *Federal Supplement*.

States war making in Vietnam, to be wrong on every ground by which I could judge it and to be immoral, and to be illegal and to be unjust and unjustifiable in any way, and because it went against my principles and my best sense of what was right. Therefore, I felt that by accepting induction that *even though I might not be sent to Vietnam*, I would be consenting to the Government's waging of war in Vietnam, and I believed it my duty not to consent with that action because I did not consent in my own mind.[37]

Even more significant was Wyzanski's distinction between combat and noncombat service. Under Wyzanski's ruling Sisson could have been required to serve in the military in a noncombatant capacity. Sisson would surely find this unsatisfactory since noncombatant military personnel are as important to the war effort as combatants. Their purpose is to serve the objectives of the command to which they are attached. Wyzanski's concern to deliver Sisson from a situation in which he would have to *kill* another man did not meet Sisson's problem. Sisson's difficulty was not that *he* would have to kill in Vietnam, but rather that anyone at all was being killed in a situation he considered morally intolerable.

It is fortunate that the Supreme Court did not attempt to decide the SCO issue within the framework presented by Wyzanski. Had the Supreme Court sustained Wyzanski's argument, Sisson's draft board could still order him to report for induction with the understanding that he would be placed either in a combat unit not destined for Vietnam or in a noncombat unit destined for Vietnam. For Sisson neither of these alternatives would be acceptable.[38]

In trying to accommodate Sisson's conscience, Wyzanski failed to grasp the nature of selective objective. Noncombatant military service is suitable for men with moral scruples against killing in any circumstances, but who have no moral difficulties in supporting the objectives of the government. Sisson's case was quite different. He could not in good conscience cooperate with the objectives of his country. Thus, his moral scruples have a political dimension unknown to noncombatant military personnel. Had Wyzanski's views prevailed, we would have had the worst of both worlds; we would have been burdened with the theoretical and administrative problems of SCO without having satisfied the conscientious demands of the selective objector. In a word, Wyzanski's opinion either went too far or it did not go far enough. For if the state has no compelling interest in sending Sisson into combat in Vietnam, what compelling interest does it have in inducting him in a noncombat status? Fortunately, the Supreme Court will have the opportunity to take up SCO in cases which present the issue more clearly.[39]

[37] *T.R.*, p. 74 (italics added).
[38] *T.R.*, pp. 75-80; 82-84.
[39] Wyzanski's understanding of SCO is quite similar to that of Kingman Brewster,

U.S. v. Mitchell

BACKGROUND. The case for SCO often founders on the shoals of sincerity. Unlike the traditional CO, the selective objector cannot present objective evidence, like membership in a peace church, to support his claim. In the final analysis his case rests on the subjective norm of how he looks at the morality of a particular war. This subjective appeal discredits his case in the eyes of the government because if the government respects one man's view of the war, it cannot ignore the view of another. The traditional requirements for CO status—objection to *all* wars by reason of *religious* training and belief—offers the government some basis for explaining why Jones goes to war while Smith stays at home.

U.S. v. *Mitchell* [40] presents a version of the SCO argument that would skirt the difficulties of basing one's case on "that's how I look at it." Mitchell's appeal to positive law and legal precedent was a "tougher" argument than that of the other SCO's because he relied on law as it is rather than as it ought to be. He defended his refusal to report for induction by arguing that the United States was waging an aggressive war in South Vietnam and that he as a participant in such a war would be liable to criminal prosecution under the Nuremberg precedent.

His argument was rejected in the Federal District Court; Mitchell was convicted of failing to report for induction. The Second Circuit affirmed the conviction with Judge Medina speaking for a unanimous Court. The Court held that the Selective Service System was based on Congress' power to raise and support armies, whereas the manner (legal or illegal) in which these armies are used is a question concerning the President's power as Commander-in-Chief. Thus, the alleged illegality of the American presence in South Vietnam (aggressive war, war crimes, etc.) was not a Selective Service question. Mitchell's failure to report for induction was simply a violation of the Selective Service Act and, as such, had nothing to do with the nature of the war in Vietnam. Medina's argument would seem to suggest that Mitchell could not raise his Nuremberg defense until he had orders for Vietnam. Perhaps at that point he could petition for a writ of *habeas corpus*.[41]

---

president of Yale University. See his remarks before the Senate Subcommittee on Administrative Practice and Procedure of the Senate Committee on the Judiciary; 91st Congress, First Session, Persuant to S. Res. 39 (G.P.O. Washington, 1969), pp. 239-41. The Subcommittee reacted favorably to Brewster's remarks on SCO; see its Report: "A Study of the Selective Service System: Its Operation, Practices, and Procedures," pp. 2-3. For a criticism of Wyzanski's line of reasoning, see my article, "Judge Wyzanski and Selective Conscientious Objection," *America*, CXXII (Feb. 21, 1970), 182-85.

[40] 386 U.S. 972.
[41] 369 F 2d 323.

When Mitchell appealed to the Supreme Court, the government made three arguments for affirming the conviction. The first was that the Court could not decide the question Mitchell raised without violating the political questions doctrine. Mitchell's brief invited this response by stating that this was the most important case to come before the Court since *Dred Scott*. The reference to *Scot* seemed to betray a gross insensitivity to the Court's role in the political process. It could not have been very helpful to Mitchell's cause, since not even the most "activist" Court would be attracted by the prospect of reliving the Dred Scot experience.[42]

The government's second point challenged Mitchell's standing to sue on the grounds that there was no evidence that Mitchell would go to the scene of the allegedly aggressive war. This argument responded to the challenge in Mitchell's brief to Judge Medina's distinction between the respective powers of President and Congress. Mitchell insisted that the Selective Service System was a necessary adjunct to the "agressive war." [43]

The third point in the government's brief was a curt dismissal of the relevance of Nuremberg. There was nothing in the Nuremberg trials, the government contended, to support the position that a soldier could refuse to serve in a war he failed to approve.[44]

The Supreme Court denied *certiorari* with Justice Douglas dissenting. There is no way of knowing which, if any, of the government's arguments the Court found impressive, but we can reasonably conjecture that the political question argument did not go unnoticed. Mitchell's defense rested on the expectation that the Federal Courts would declare the Vietnam enterprise a war of aggression. Not even Douglas' dissent went this far. He confined his remarks to the narrow issue of whether the aggressive war question could be raised as a defense. Had Douglas' view prevailed, Mitchell would have had the consolation of seeing the American Court system become the forum for a "great debate" on the Vietnam war. This would have been a political achievement of no small proportion. But there was no guarantee that any jury or judge, including Douglas, would agree with the substance of Mitchell's argument, viz., that the United States was waging a war of aggression and that Mitchell could be prosecuted by an international tribunal for allowing himself to be inducted into the United States Army.

It is unfortunate for us (as well as for Mitchell) that the Supreme Court denied *certiorari*. Had Mitchell had his way our study of SCO would have been blessed with reams of briefs, opinions, and editorials defending and attacking Mitchell's contention that the Nuremberg trails committed every

[42] *U.S Supreme Court Briefs and Records*, 386 U.S. 972-975. *Mitchell* v. *U.S.*, "Brief for U.S. in Opposition," pp. 2-3. Hereafter referred to as *Government Brief*.
[43] *Ibid.*, p. 3.   [44] *Ibid.*, p. 4.

civilized nation to refrain from drafting those who contended their government had initiated a war of aggression until a domestic court had judged the merits of the government's action. It is not surprising that the Court chose to avoid this controversy by simply denying *certiorari*.

NUREMBERG AS TREATY. Fortunately, the groves of academe provide a happier home than the marble temples of justice for those who would think the unthinkable. In our discussion of SCO we can shuffle off the coils that restrained the Supreme Court and consider Mitchell's argument more directly. The clearest statement of his Nuremberg defense appears in the brief petitioning the Supreme Court for *certiorari*. After rehearsing the American adherence to the London Charter, the horrors of the Vietnam war, and the obligation to abide by treaties, the brief asks, "May not a citizen refuse to obey a national law rendered invalid by a treaty in order to avoid possible punishment under existing treaty obligations?" [45]

Justice Douglas' dissent provides a basis for enumerating the monumental tasks that Mitchell's defense would require. For Douglas the case presents five questions:

(1) whether the Treaty of London is a treaty within the meaning of Article VI, Cl. 2;

(2) whether the question as to the waging of an aggressive "war" is in the context of this criminal prosecution a justiciable issue;

(3) whether the Vietnam episode is a "war" in the sense of the Treaty;

(4) whether petitioner has standing to raise the question;

(5) whether, if he has, the Treaty may be tendered as a defense in this criminal case or in amelioration of the punishment. [46]

To reach the question raised in Mitchell's brief it would seem an affirmative answer would be required to each of Douglas' questions. This would be no simple task, especially in the case of questions one and three. The Treaty of London is a "treaty" in the sense that several nations are parties to it, but it would not qualify as a "treaty" in the constitutional sense because it was not submitted to the Senate for ratification. Technically, it was an executive agreement; but this technical point is not fatal for Mitchell's case, since there is little, if any, difference in legal effects between treaties and executive agreements. Thus, executive agreements do not terminate at the close of the administration of the President who entered into them nor do they necessarily fail to qualify, along with treaties and congressional

---

[45] *U.S. Supreme Court Briefs and Records*, 386 U.S. 972-975. *Mitchell* v. *U.S.*, "Petition for a Writ of Certiorari to the U.S. Court of Appeals for the Second Circuit," p. 12. Hereafter referred to as *Mitchell's Brief*.

[46] 386 U.S. 972.

statutes, as the supreme law of the land.[47] To reach the substance of Mitchell's argument, we shall consider the Treaty of London as a treaty in the sense of Article VI, clause 2.

Douglas' third question—"whether the Vietnam episode is a war in the sense of the Treaty"—raises a more serious difficulty for Mitchell. The treaty in question, the London Agreement of August 8, 1945, is concerned only with "the Prosecution and Punishment of the Major War Criminals of the *European Axis.*"[48] Since the Treaty that established the courts of Nuremberg was concerned only with prosecution of Axis war criminals, there would seem to be no way in which Mitchell could give an affirmative reply to Douglas' third question. The failure to answer this question in the affirmative means that the Nuremberg Trails, *as part of a treaty,* have no relevance for the Vietnam "episode."

Even if there were a way of avoiding the difficulties presented by Douglas' five questions, Mitchell's appeal to Nuremberg *as treaty* would still be quite dubious. As we have seen, the crucial question in his brief is, "May not a citizen refuse to obey a national law rendered invalid by a treaty in order to avoid possible punishment under existing treaty obligation?" In order to answer this question in the affirmative, one must presume that the treaty in question is *subsequent* to the national law it would render invalid. Article VI of the Constitution states that laws of the United States made in pursuance of the Constitution and treaties made under the authority of the United States are the Supreme Law of the land. When a federal law conflicts with a treaty, the established practice of the Courts is to accept the more recent enactment as supreme.[49] Mitchell was convicted of violating the Selective Service Act which was passed many years after the London Agreement of 1945. His brief, therefore, reversed the order of constitutional priorities in its presumption that the treaty under which the Nuremberg Trails took place would "render invalid" the "national law" he had violated.

In the light of this consideration, then, it seems fair to conclude that even if the Courts were not limited by the political questions doctrine, they would have little trouble disposing of Mitchell's contention that the Treaty of London prevented the United States government from inducting him into the Army to fight in Vietnam. The reasons for this conclusion are: (1) Mitchell's failure to take into consideration the temporal sequence of the Treaty and the Selective Service Act he violated, and (2) his failure to

[47] C. Herman Pritchett, *The American Constitution* (2d ed.; New York: McGraw-Hill Book Co., 1968), p. 359.

[48] *Trials of War Criminals Before the Nuremberg Military Tribunals Under Control Council Law No. 10* (Washington, D.C.: Government Printing Office, n.d.), p. ix (emphasis added.)

[49] Pritchett, p. 362.

answer satisfactorily the questions considered indispensable by the only Justice impressed by his argument.

NUREMBERG AS PRECEDENT. Although Mitchell's brief relies primarily on the Nuremberg Trials as the result of a treaty, there is a second line of argumentation that is not vulnerable to the criticisms leveled against the treaty approach. This might be described as a "Nuremberg as precedent" argument. Its basic thrust is that the Nuremberg Trials created a body of international law that serves as a binding precedent today. Since the Nuremberg Trials acknowledged the principles of individual responsibility for crimes committed in the name of the state, the argument runs, the United States cannot draft a citizen and force him to commit such crimes because he might have to answer for his deeds to an international tribunal. Thus, compulsory military service, in the absence of a judicial determination denying the aggressive character of the American involvement in Vietnam, deprives a citizen of his liberty without due process of law.

This argument has one clear advantage over the "Nuremberg as treaty" approach. Its scope is not limited to soldiers fighting in the armies of the European Axis Powers. If Nuremberg is a precedent at international law, it can transcend the narrow limits of its origin. There are, however, several serious difficulties with the "Nuremberg as precedent" argument.

The first difficulty is the long-standing practice of national courts favoring national law over international law. When there is a conflict between an Act of Congress and a provision of international law, American courts will follow the Act of Congress. While this may cause considerable embarrassment on the international scene, it would seem to be but a corollary of the nation-state system. Thus, even if the Nuremberg principle of personal responsibility were a precedent at international law, an Act of Congress drafting men regardless of their opinions of the justice of a particular war would take precedence over that principle.

The second difficulty with the "Nuremberg as precedent" argument is the dubious nature of precedent in international law. The standard textbooks warn students trained in the common law that they "must be constantly on guard against assuming that precedents are regarded as binding authorities in International Law."[50] *The Statute of the International Court of Justice* says judicial decisions are only "subsidiary means" (along with the writings of highly qualified publicists) for the determination of rules of law.[51]

[50] William W. Bishop, Jr., *International Law: Cases and Materials* (2d ed.; Boston: Little, Brown & Co., 1962), p. 37. See also J. J. Brierly, *The Law of Nations* (5th ed.; Oxford: University Press, 1956), p. 64; Oppenheim-Lauterpacht, *International Law* (8th ed.; London: Longman, Green & Co., 1957), p. 31; Charles G. Fenwick, *International Law* (4th ed.; New York: Appleton-Century-Crofts, 1965), p. 91.

[51] *Statute of the International Court of Justice*, Article 38.

This "subsidiary" use of prior decisions can take place only "subject to the provisions of Article 59." [52] That article states: 'The decision of the Court has no binding force except between parties and in respect of that particular case." [53] William W. Bishop suggests the role of nonbinding precedents is to contribute to the development of "customary law" by showing what principles have been commonly accepted as international law.[54] The Nuremberg principle of "absolute liability," i.e., the principle that superior orders are no defense for war crimes and crimes against the peace, was certainly not "commonly accepted" in the years before and during World War II. The military manuals of the United States, the United Kingdom, France, and Germany granted military personnel immunity from prosecution for nearly all crimes committed under orders. The American and British manuals introduced the principle of absolute liability in late 1944, but this was done to bring the Allies' rules of liability into line with the liability the victors would soon demand of the vanquished.[55]

These considerations indicate the difficulty Mitchell would have in establishing the precedential character of Nuremberg. Nevertheless, his cause is not entirely hopeless. The General Assembly of the United Nations has adopted a resolution upholding the principles of the Nuremberg Trials as international law. While this resolution has no binding force, it might be considered what Hans Kelsen has called "a worthy example for the decision of subsequent similar cases." [56] This is a rather weak estimate of the value of Nuremberg as precedent in the light of the weight it must bear in Mitchell's argument. But, for the sake of that argument, let us consider it as the wedge that opens the door of precedent. This will enable us to consider just what the substantive value of Nuremberg really is. In other

[52] *Ibid.*
[53] *Ibid.*, Article 59.
[54] Bishop, p. 37.
[55] See Martin Redish, "Nuremberg Rule of Superior Orders," *Harvard International Law Jornal,* IX (Winter, 1968), 175-78.
[56] H. Kelsen, "Will the Judgment in the Nuremberg Trial Constitute a Precedent in International Law?" *International Law Quarterly,* I (Summer, 1947), 164. Kelsen responds with an emphatic "no" to the question he raises in the title of his article. His point of departure is the statement of Justice Jackson in his "Report to the President" of October 15, 1946 to the effect that the rules of law applied by the I.M.T. to the German war criminals have been incorporated into a "judicial precedent." Kelsen maintains a precedent must establish a new rule of law; it cannot simply apply an existing rule. It was the Treaty of London, not the International Military Tribunal, that created a new rule of law, i.e., personal responsibility for criminal acts of the state. The Tribunal simply applied what the Treaty had legislated. The Treaty itself cannot be considered a precedent becaues it deals only with an *ad hoc* situation, viz., the prosecution of war criminals of the European Axis Powers. As indicated in the text, Kelsen concedes that a decision which is not a precedent may still be followed in the future if it is recognized as a "worthy example" for the decision of subsequent similar cases. He does not think the Nuremberg decision is a "worthy example," but the General Assembly of the U.N. apparently does not agree with him on this point.

words, let us prescind from the procedural difficulties involved (1) in establishing the Nuremberg Trials as precedent and (2) in getting American Courts to apply the precedent in the face of conflicting domestic statutes. Let us do this to see just what relevance Nuremberg has for Americans ordered to fight in Vietnam.

Before we begin our investigation we must define with greater precision the meaning of "the Nuremberg Trials." There were two sets of trials at Nuremberg. The first was the trial of major war criminals before the International Military Tribunal. This Tribunal was established by the London Agreement of August 8, 1945; the Charter of the International Military Tribunal was issued to the contracting parties in pursuance of the Agreement. The Tribunal consisted of four members and four alternates. Each of the Signatory Powers (the United States, the United Kingdom, France, and the Soviet Union) appointed one member and one alternate. The second set of Nuremberg Trails was established under Allied Control Council Law No. 10. The London Agreement "concerning prosecution and punishment of Major War Criminals of the European Axis" was made an integral part of this law. Under Control Council Law No. 10 each occupying power could try within its zone those suspected of being war criminals. The Trials held in the American zone took place at Nuremberg.

In addition to the meaning of "Nuremberg," we should also distinguish the various counts on which the war criminals were indicted. This will help us determine what charges might possibly be brought against Mitchell before an International Tribunal for accepting induction into the United States Army.

There were five counts on which a war criminal could be indicted:

1. Crimes against the peace.
2. Conspiring to commit a crime against the peace.
3. War crimes.
4. Crimes against humanity.
5. Membership in a group or organization declared to be illegal by the International Military Tribunal.

Among the crimes against the peace we find "waging a war of aggression." Under this formula it was at least theoretically possible for every German soldier to be tried as a war criminal.[57] This could be a strong point in Mitchell's favor.

[57] Article 6 of the Charter of the International Military Tribunal reads as follows: "The tribunal established by the Agreement referred to in Article 1 hereof [the London Agreement of August 8, 1945] for the trial and punishment of the major war criminals of the European Axis countries shall have the power to try and punish persons who, acting in the interests of the European Axis countries, whether as individuals or as *members of organizations,* committed any of the following crimes [italics added].

"The following acts, or any of them, are crimes coming within the jurisdiction of the Tribunal for which there shall be *individual responsibility:*

"(a) CRIMES AGAINST THE PEACE: namely, planning, preparation, initiation, or

The crime of conspiring to commit a crime against the peace would not affect Mitchell; conscripted privates were not considered conspirators. In describing the crime of conspiracy, the International Military Tribunal stated: "Hitler could not make war by himself. He had to have the co-operation of statesmen, military leaders, diplomats, and business men." [58]

War crimes and crimes against humanity usually collapse into the single category of war crimes. Crimes against humanity had to be added to cover Nazi atrocities committed before the war and those perpetrated against German Jewish citizens during the war. These offenses were not "war crimes," i.e., violations of the rules of war. The crimes against humanity would, therefore, be irrelevant to the Vietnam situation. War crimes, however, would be a relevant category for Mitchell. As the My Lai tragedy has taught us, the ordinary soldier might well be the perpetrator of such crimes either under orders or on his own initiative, e.g., by torturing prisoners of war, murdering civilians, plundering public or private property, etc.

Membership in an illegal group would not affect Mitchell if Nuremberg were used as a "precedent." The German Army was never considered an illegal group. Even the notorious S.A. escaped this charge. Further, the International Military Tribunal declared that members of illegal groups who had been "drafted by the state" should not themselves be considered criminals.[59]

Of the five possible charges on which Mitchell could be indicted by a future Tribunal following Nuremberg, only two—crimes against the peace (waging aggressive war) and war crimes—would seem to apply to him.

Mitchell's vulnerability to the charges of waging aggressive war and committing war crimes rests only on the *wording* of the Charter establishing the International Military Tribunal.[60] If Nuremberg is to be used as a "precedent," we must look more closely at how these words were actually

---

waging of a war of aggression, or a war in violation of international treaties, agreements or assurances, or participation in a Common Plan or Conspiracy for the accomplishment of any of the foregoing; . . . [italics added]."

The relevant questions are: (1) does the ordinary soldier "wage" war and (2) if so, does he wage war in such a way as to be a major war criminal. Mitchell's argument needs an affirmative reply to both questions. See "Symposium: War Crimes Trials," *University of Pittsburgh Law Review*, XXIV (October, 1962), 73 ff.

[58] *Trial of the Major War Criminals Before the International Military Tribunal* (Nuremberg, 1947), II, 225-26. Hereafter cited as *IMT*.

[59] *Ibid.*, XXII, 500.

[60] See note 57, p. 89, above, for wording of the crime of waging war. Article 6 of the *IMT* Charter gives the following actions as war crimes "for which there shall be individual responsibility.

"WAR CRIMES: namely, violations of the laws or customs of war. Such violations shall include, but not be limited to, murder, ill-treatment or deportation to slave labor or for any other purpose of civilian population of or in occupied territory, murder

applied. "Precedent" can never be derived from the mere wording of a charter or statute. The underlying assumption of an argument from precedent —whether that precedent be binding or merely persuasive—is that one looks at how the words of a law were interpreted in a concrete case. Is there anything in the manner in which the courts at Nuremberg interpreted "war crimes" and "waging aggressive war" that would support Mitchell's contention that a man in his position would be in real danger of prosecution by a future Tribunal which took Nuremberg as a precedent?

This question can be answered in three steps: (1) How strictly did the courts at Nuremberg interpret such principles as the "duty to resist" and "absolute liability"? (2) What sort of men did the prosecution wish to bring to justice? (3) What sort of men were actually convicted for waging wars of aggression and committing war crimes?

The wording of the Nuremberg charter is quite strict in holding subordinates responsible for criminal actions performed under orders.[61] The International Military Tribunal, however, interpreted this responsibility in a manner more lenient than the wording of the Charter might suggest:

That a soldier was ordered to kill or torture in violation of the international law of war has never been recognized as a defense to such acts of brutality, though, as the charter here provides, the order may be urged in mitigation of the punishment. The true test, which is found in the criminal law of most nations, is not the existence of the order, but whether moral choice was in fact possible.[62]

The Court did not give any detailed example of what circumstances would render moral choice impossible. Hence, there is no way of determining with certainty whether the threat of a prison sentence for failing to report for induction would be enough to remove moral choice. At any rate, the "moral choice" rule is surely more lenient than the unadorned words—superior orders are no defense—would suggest.

The American courts of Control Council Law No. 10 suggested a slightly different interpretation from that of the International Military Tribunal. The defense of superior orders cannot be sustained if a soldier "accepts a

---

or ill-treatment of prisoners of war or persons on the seas, killing of hostages, plunder of public or private property, wanton destruction of cities, towns or villages, or devastation not justified by military necessity."

One cannot exclude the possibility that Mitchell—or any soldier in any army—might find himself in a situation where he is ordered to commit one of the above crimes.

[61] Article 8 of the Charter of the *IMT* states: "The fact that the Defendant acted pursuant to an order of his government or of a superior shall not free him from responsibility, but may be considered in mitigation of punishment if the Tribunal determines that justice so requires."

[62] *IMT, I,* 224.

criminal order and executes it *with a malice of his own.*" [63] This norm seems to burden the prosecution with a need to prove *mens rea* in addition to proving the possibility of moral choice.

H. F. Donnedieu de Vabres, one of the French judges at the International Military Tribunal, has written extensively on the question of personal responsibility and the Nuremberg Trials. His basic principle is that legitimate authority can be used as a defense only if the commanded action was indeed "legitimate"—i.e., within the competence of the one commanding. Then, following the International Military Tribunal, he qualifies this rigorous stance by arguing that if freedom of choice (*liberté morale*) was not available to the subordinate, his action could be defended by the principle of *force majeure.*

In determining when a man can honestly maintain his freedom of choice has been taken away, de Vabres offers the following norms: (1) Civilians can make this plea less readily than military personnel, since the latter are under more stringent discipline. But a civilian in a dictatorship where the will of the leader is the law can raise this defense with greater plausibility than a civilian in a free society. (2) Among military personnel only senior officers can be held responsible for actions committed in a war of aggression which are violations of public law, but not of the laws of war. (3) Lower ranking military personnel who violated the laws of war can defend their action by citing such circumstances as the presence of the Commanding Officer at the scene of the crime, the detail in which the order was given, etc.[64]

These norms give little support to Mitchell's case for refusing induction. Mitchell's status as a conscripted private would go a long way toward absolving him of legal responsibility even if he should be sent to Vietnam and ordered to perform some act contrary to the laws of war.

What sort of men did the Nuremberg Trials intend to bring to justice? The opening statement of Justice Jackson, the American prosecutor before the International Military Tribunal, indicates that men like Mitchell would have nothing to fear from a tribunal that followed Nuremberg as precedent:

The case presented by the U.S. will be concerned with the brains and authority of all the crimes. These defendants were men of a station and rank which does not soil its own hands with blood. They were the men who knew how to use lesser folk as tools. We want to reach the planners and designers, the writers and the leaders without whose evil architecture the world would not have been so long

---

[63] *Trials of War Criminals Before the Nuremberg Military Tribunals Under Control Council Law No. 10,* IV, 471 (italics added). Hereafter referred to as *CCL No. 10.*

[64] Henri Felix Donnedieu de Vabres, *Le Procés de Nuremberg* (Paris, n.d.), pp. 278-83.

scourged with the violence and lawlessness, and wracked with the agonies and convulsions, of this terrible war.[65]

After citing the Charter's refusal to allow "superior orders" as a defense, Jackson continued:

Of course, we do not argue that the circumstances under which one commits an act should be disregarded in judging its legal effect. *A conscripted private* in a firing squad cannot expect to hold an inquest on the validity of the execution. The Charter implies common sense limits to liability just as it places common sense limits upon immunity. But none of these men before you acted in minor parts. Each of them was entrusted with broad discretion and exercised great power.[66]

The prosecution of war criminals under Control Council Law No. 10 followed the International Tribunal in its concentration upon military leaders. The Executive Order establishing the American Courts envisioned by the Control Council stated quite clearly that the prosecution would deal only with "Leaders of the European Axis Powers and their Principal Agents and Accessories." [67]

The word "accessories" invites our third question. Is there any evidence from Nuremberg that men like Mitchell could be convicted of being accessories to the commission of war crimes?

In all the cases heard at Nuremberg both before the International Military Tribunal and under Control Council Law No. 10, there was only one non-commissioned officer indicted for committing war crimes. This was Mattias Graf, a member of the S.S. *Einsatzgruppen* that handled the murder of thousands of Jews. He was a second lieutenant (*Untersturmführer*) at the end of the war, but while he was associated with the S.S. activity under the Court's scrutiny he had held the rank of corporal (*Unterscharführer*), sergeant (*Scharführer*), and master sergeant (*Oberscharführer*). He was acquitted on the charge of committing war crimes. In acquitting him the Court relied heavily on the fact of "Graf's non-commissioned officer's status in an organization where rank was of vital importance." [68]

Graf was found guilty on the charge of being a member of an illegal group. His sentence was limited to the time he had already spent in prison awaiting trial. This conviction is no precedent for Mitchell since one of the reasons the S.S. was declared an illegal group was because membership in it was voluntary.[69] Graf was in the S.S. because he wanted to be there.

The records give no support to the possibility that Nuremberg could be

[65] *IMT*, II, 104-5.
[67] Executive Order No. 9679.
[69] *Ibid.*, p. 587.
[66] *Ibid.*, pp. 149-50 (emphasis added).
[68] *CCL No. 10*, IV, 585.

used as a precedent for prosecuting Mitchell on the charge of waging an aggressive war, though, admittedly, the sweeping language of the Charter could have been interpreted that way. As a matter of fact, however, there were only two members of the German military convicted on this charge. These men were at the highest echelon of the military establishment—Generals Keitel and Jodl.

In summary, then, the "Nuremberg as precedent" argument is vulnerable to the following questions: (1) What binding force does precedent in general and Nuremberg in particular have at international law? (2) Even if Nuremberg is a binding precedent at international law, how can a domestic court apply it in the face of a conflicting Act of Congress? (3) Even if the Courts could find a way to do this, what relevance would Nuremberg have for conscripted privates?

In our consideration of *U.S.* v. *Mitchell* there has been a certain element of political fantasy. The idea of General Giap or Mao Tse Tung establishing a tribunal on the basis of Nuremberg to try American "war criminals" is difficult to imagine. The legalistic arguments in *Mitchell* may be examples of mere shadowboxing. Most likely, Mitchell's real intent was to get the Courts to provide a forum for debating the war, while the government's goal was to whisk him off to jail without having to face the embarrassment this debate might present.

Nevertheless, the legal arguments are important for our purposes. Mitchell departed from the SCO cases discussed earlier in this study. He relied on positive law rather than on the dictates of conscience alone to support his position. If Mitchell's case had any real merit, it would mean that a limited form of SCO was already part of our domestic law. This would shift the entire grounds of this discussion which has centered on the *conflict* between the conscience of the individual and the positive law. Thus it was imperative to answer Mitchell's argument somewhat more fully than the Courts had. At present SCO is a question of private choice, not of international law.[70]

---

[70] The most thorough study of the relevance of Nuremberg for Vietnam is a very recent book by Telford Taylor, *Nuremberg and Vietnam: An American Tragedy* (Chicago: Quadrangle Books, 1970). Taylor was the U.S. Chief Counsel to the prosecution at Nuremberg. For an interpretation of "Nuremberg" somewhat at odds with my own, see Anthony A. D'Amato, "War Crimes and Vietnam: The 'Nuremberg Defense' and the Military Service Resister," *California Law Review*, LVII (November, 1969), 1055-1110. Professor D'Amato's article focuses on the degree to which a "Nuremberg Defense" would assist a soldier (i.e., a man already in service) in refusing to carry out certain orders. He addresses the question of the draft resister only in passing.

V
SCO and the Supreme Court

In the closing chapter of the first section of this book, three cases will be considered briefly which are to be presented for oral argument before the Supreme Court during the 1970-71 term. The present study would be incomplete without mention of these cases, since, if the Supreme Court ever does address the issue of SCO, it will probably do so in one of the cases considered in this chapter.

On June 29, 1970 the Supreme Court granted a writ of *certiorari* petitioned by Louis A. Negre in the case of *Negre* v. *Larsen*.[1] Negre is a private in the United States Army who requested a discharge because he had become a conscientious objector. The method of processing "in service" CO's was outlined in a Defense Department Directive of May 10, 1968 and incorporated into Army Regulations three months later.[2] In accordance with this procedure, Negre filed his petition and conferred with the base chaplain and psychiatrist at Fort Ord who commented favorably upon his sincerity. He then had an interview with a "hearing officer" whose task it is to recommend to the commanding officer the sort of action to be taken on the petition. The findings of the hearing officer, if approved by the commanding officer, are then forwarded to Departmental Headquarters for a decision. The hearing officer found that Negre's conscience would not allow him to perform any violent actions in warfare. He therefore recommended that Negre be transferred to a noncombatant unit rather than

[1] *New York Times*, June 30, 1970, p. 1. 418 F 2d 908 (1969).
[2] DOD Directive, 1300.6; Army Regulation 635-20, 17 August 1968.

discharged as a CO. The Department of the Army rejected this recommendation on the grounds that Negre did not object to all wars but only to wars he considered unjust and that he therefore did not qualify for noncombatant status.[3] After an unsuccessful appeal to the Army Board for Correction of Military Records, Negre filed a petition for *habeas corpus* in Federal District Court for the Northern District of California. This petition was denied and the denial was upheld by the United States Court of Appeals for the Ninth Circuit. The Supreme Court issued its writ of *certiorari* to the Ninth Circuit.

The essence of Negre's argument is the familiar complaint that the present provision for CO's discriminates against adherents of the just war doctrine and that this discrimination is unconstitutional. While the argument is not new, the Court's favorable action on the petition for the writ of *certiorari* means the Supreme Court will finally have an opportunity to address directly the problem of SCO.

There is a possibility, however, that if the Court so chooses, it could uphold Negre's petition for discharge as a CO without reaching the question of selective conscientious objection. There is some indication in Negre's statement of his beliefs that he is really a pacifist rather than a just warrior. Although he explicitly embraces the just war theory, he quotes with approval Cardinal Ottaviani's argument that the nature of modern warfare demands that "in practice it will never again be lawful to declare war." [4] His brief cites many statements from scripture and Roman Catholic authorities to buttress his position, but *without exception* these statements would support traditional pacifism as readily as SCO.[5] What is most remarkable is that in citing the American Catholic Bishops' Letter of November, 1968, *Human Life in Our Day,* he omits the passage in which the bishops explicitly call for SCO!

It may be that the Supreme Court will reject Negre's petition for discharge from the Army. If, however, the Court wishes to uphold Negre without getting into the embarrassing corollaries of SCO (which will be considered at some length in the second part of this book), the wisest

[3] From Appendix D of the brief submitted by Negre in his petition for *certiorari.* Hereafter referred to as "Negre's Brief."

[4] Negre's Brief, Appendix F, p. 12.

[5] *Ibid.* Among the passages from scripture one finds the following: "Then Jesus said to Peter: Put again thy sword into its place, for all that take the sword shall perish with the sword." (Matt. 26:52). "But I say to you, Love your enemies; do good to them that persecute and calumniate you." (Matt. 5:44). "You shall not kill." (Exod. 20:13). Among the Roman Catholic authorities Negre cites, we find Pope John's statement that "it is irrational to believe that war is still an apt means of vindicating violated rights" and Pope Paul's admonition to the United Nations: "If you wish to be brothers, let the weapons fall from your hands. . . . No more war. War never again."

course may be to emphasize the pacifist character of Negre's belief. This would be in accord with the findings of Lieutenant Colonel Charles Richard, the chaplain who interviewed Negre at Fort Ord. Chaplain Richard found that Negre "feels war, especially this war, is immoral." [6] If the Court is uneasy about the ramifications of SCO, it would have reasonable grounds for sidestepping the issue by declaring Negre a pacifist. A Court that does not blush at declaring Welsh a "religious" man should have no trouble making a pacifist out of Negre.

On the same day that the Supreme Court granted Negre's petition for *certiorari* it issued a similar writ to the Second Circuit for the SCO case, *U.S.* v. *Gillette*.[7] The issues raised by *Gillette* are similar to those in *Negre* with the one important exception that Gillette is a civilian. The *selective* character of Gillette's conscientious objection is clearer than that of Negre. Gillette is certainly no pacifist; he would be willing to fight if the United States were attacked as well as to enforce a United Nations decision against a country accused of breaking the peace.[8] Thus, his case presents the issue of selective objection a bit more clearly than Negre's.

If the Court should choose to avoid confronting the issue of SCO in *Gillette,* it would seem that the only course it could follow would be to find that Gillette's beliefs were not sufficiently "religious" to merit the CO exemption. In this way the Court could prescind from the SCO question by finding Gillette's principles "essentially political" and that he was therefore disqualified from *any* type of exemption for conscientious objectors. There seemed to be some doubt about the religious character of Gillette's beliefs, but the lower courts gave him the benefit of the doubt because of the Supreme Court's broad understanding of "religion" in *Seeger.* Since *Welsh* has extended the meaning of "religion" even further, it does not seem likely that the Court will deny Gillette's claim for the CO privilege on religious grounds. Indeed, if the Court wished to avoid the SCO question, it could have followed the easier path of simply denying *certiorari* in both *Negre* and *Gillette.* Its failure to do this suggests that the Court is willing to resolve the difficult issues involved in SCO. If this is the case, the Court might do well to focus on *Gillette* rather than *Negre,* since the possibility that the latter is really a pacifist might obfuscate the issue.

The third case scheduled to appear before the Supreme Court is *U.S.* v. *McFadden*.[9] In chapter three we investigated at some length *McFadden* v. *Selective Service Board No. 40,* a civil action brought by James McFadden to enjoin his draft board from ordering him to report for induction. His petition was denied by the Federal District Court and this decision was

---

[6] *Ibid.* p. 19. [7] 420 F 2d 298 (1970).
[8] *Ibid.* at 299.
[9] *Selective Service Law Reporter* (SSLR) 3529; 309 F. Supp. 502.

upheld by the Court of Appeals for the Ninth Circuit. His draft board thereupon issued an induction notice which McFadden refused to obey. He was arrested and indicted for violating the Selective Service Act. This was the origin of the second McFadden case—the criminal action, *U.S. v. McFadden.*

Late in February of 1970 McFadden filed a motion to dismiss the indictment on the familiar grounds that Section 6 (j) of the Selective Service Act was unconstitutional. But this time McFadden had a new argument. In *U.S. v. Bowen*[10] (decided on December 24, 1969) Judge Weigel of the Federal District Court for the Northern District of California declared section 6 (j) unconstitutional for its failure to recognize the rights of selective conscientious objectors. McFadden relied heavily on *Bowen* in presenting his argument. Judge Zirpoli acceded to McFadden's petition and issued an order granting the motion to dismiss the indictment. Although *U.S. v. Bowen* preceded *U.S. v. McFadden,* the latter is the more important case for our purposes because *Bowen* cannot be appealed and therefore will never reach the Supreme Court. In *Bowen* section 6 (j) was struck down *after* Bowen had been tried. The government cannot appeal an acquittal under such circumstances without running into problems of double jeopardy. In *McFadden,* however, it was an *indictment* that was dismissed; the defendant was never brought to trial. Hence, the government can appeal Judge Zirpoli's finding that 6 (j) is unconstitutional and, if the appeal is successful, can bring McFadden to trial. The government immediately went before the Court of Appeals for the Ninth Circuit, but because a Federal Judge had declared part of an Act of Congress unconstitutional, the Appellate Court referred the appeal to the Supreme Court.[11]

In light of the analysis presented in chapter three, *U.S. v. McFadden* presents a stronger case for SCO than *Negre* or *Gillette.* In *McFadden* it is the United States, not the defendant, who appears as appellant. To deny a constitutional right to SCO in *McFadden,* the Supreme Court will have to reject not only the lawyers' arguments in the briefs, but the opinion of a Federal Judge as well. What is even more important for our purposes, Judge Zirpoli's argument follows the approach we outlined in chapter three. After several false starts,[12] he relies on *Sherbert* v. *Verner*[13] to demand that the United States show a "compelling state interest" in drafting a selective conscientious objector. He holds that the government has failed to meet

[10] *Selective Service Law Reporter* (SSLR) 3421.

[11] 18 *U.S.C.A.* 3731.

[12] For example, the Judge seemed unduly concerned with establishing the religious character of McFadden's beliefs. He cited *U.S* v. *Ballard,* 322 U.S. 78 (1944), to support his contention that the courts are not free to say a certain belief is not "religious." He then went on for several pages trying to prove what he is not permitted to deny—that McFadden's beliefs are religious.

[13] 374 U.S. 398.

this test and that the statute is therefore unconstitutional.[14] Thus, in terms of the argument in chapter three, *McFadden* presents the strongest possible argument for SCO. The second section of this book—and especially chapter seven—will investigate in some detail just what interests, compelling or otherwise, the state might have in denying a right to selective conscientious objection.

[14] In addition to the "compelling state interest" test he also uses the "no alternative means" test of *McGowan* v. *Maryland* 366 U.S. 420 (1961) and *Braunfeld* v. *Brown* 366 U.S. at 608-9 (1961). Further, he cites with approval Judge Weigel's attack on 6 (j) in *Bowen* as a violation of the establishment clause.

PART II
THE POLICY QUESTION

In those days there was no king in
Israel, every man did that which was right
in his own eyes.

Judges 21:25, AV

VI

The Catholic Case for SCO:
Just Wars and Vatican II

The first section of this book considered the constitutional case for SCO. The specific focus was whether our fundamental law commits our society to uphold the right of selective conscientious objection. Constitutional discussions are necessarily technical in nature because the judicial process requires that judges rely—or at least say they rely—on such considerations as precedent, rules of procedure, and legislative intent. Judicial realism has not yet reached the point where the people will support a constitutional ruling based on nothing more than the Court's candid statement that a particular course is sound public policy. This second section will be free of the restraints imposed by the nature of the judicial process and consider directly the wisdom of SCO as public policy. Here focus will shift from the Courts to Congress where it is quite appropriate for a senator or representative, unlike a judge, to say he supports a particular program because he thinks it is a good idea. Indeed, if the argument of the first section of this book is correct—*i.e.,* if there is no constitutional right to SCO—it will be *only* through favorable Congressional action that SCO could become public policy.[1] The present chapter will consider the practical question of how the strongest

---

[1] Even if the Supreme Court should uphold a right to SCO, this would not mean SCO is necessarily sound public policy. The fact that a question is settled at a constitutional level does not insure the wisdom and justice of the decision. One need only recall how the Supreme Court "settled" the issue of slavery in the territories or "settled" the meaning of the due process clause of the fourteenth amendment during the *lassez-faire* era. If the Court should uphold a constitutional right to SCO one might read the following three chapters from the point of view of whether or not the Court has acted wisely.

pressure group for SCO is likely to react if its lobbying proves fruitless. The following two chapters will take up the theoretical arguments for and against SCO.

In studying the constitutional case for SCO the objectors' word had to be taken as true. For constitutional purposes we acknowledged they were in a religious dilemma simply because they said they were. In this section, where the wisdom of SCO as public policy will be considered, a closer look can be taken at the religious argument behind the alleged dilemma.

This "closer look" is especially important in the case of Roman Catholic selective objectors. In their appeals to the just war doctrine and the teachings of *Vatican II*, they try to assimilate their position to that of the Quakers. Just as the Quaker must object to all wars, so Catholics *must* object to all unjust wars. The courts can defeat this argument by discerning a compelling state interest in drafting selective objectors, but Congress must face a different problem. Even if there is no constitutional right to SCO, Congress must decide whether SCO is sound policy. In reaching that decision Congressmen would have to see whether the failure to enact SCO would alienate the Catholic population in the U.S. In investigating this problem it is important to determine if the just war doctrine and *Vatican II*—the major sources of the Catholic selective objector's argument—put Catholics in such a predicament that in some present or future war they, as a group, would be forced to choose between God and Caesar. To answer this question a legislator would have to know if Catholic selective objectors are in a religious dilemma because of the demands of their church,[2] or because they have gone beyond these demands and conscientiously, but voluntarily, chosen to place this moral burden upon themselves. If the latter is the case, Congress would

[2] This is the position taken by the National Council of Churches in its *amicus curiae* brief in *McFadden et al.* v. *Selective Service System Local Board No. 40*, pp. 9-10.

"According to paragraph 3 of the amended complaint, the plaintiff McFadden is a Roman Catholic by religious training and belief, and has had his education in several Roman Catholic institutions of learning. 'He is unable to participate in war at this time by reason of his religious training and belief and applied for the status of conscientious objector.' (Trial Record, p. 54.)

"According to paragraph 4 of the amended complaint, the plaintiff Bowen is likewise a Catholic by religious training and belief. He claimed exemption as a conscientious objector because 'by reason of his religious training and belief, he was prohibited from participating in any form in any wars which after examination of his conscience did not meet standards fixed by the Catholic religious training and belief for participation in war.' (Trial Record, p. 55.)

"Paragraph 5 of the amended complaint's prayer for judgment requests a judgment (Trial Record, p. 59): '5. Enjoining defendants and each of them from refusing to exempt Catholics who claim and establish that they conscientiously must refuse service by reason of their religious training and belief, and from refusing to accord such Catholics alternative service.' "

be invulnerable to the charge of discriminating against *Catholics* by its failure to enact SCO.

This is the sort of question a court cannot handle because the judicial system deals with individuals. It would be out of place for a court to decide the orthodoxy of a citizen's belief.[3] Public policy, on the other hand, is general in character and deals with the citizenry as a whole. Here questions of orthodoxy are quite appropriate for they bear directly on the impact of proposed legislation upon large segments of society. A legislator should have some idea of the meaning of the just war doctrine and the teachings of *Vatican II* if he is to determine realistically whether the present CO provisions are likely to present serious conscience problems for Catholics in general.[4]

There is no doubt that selective conscientious objection enjoys wide support in the Catholic community. The American Catholic Bishops strongly endorsed SCO in their pastoral letter of November 15, 1968.[5] The ten American Jesuit Provincials sent a joint letter to every member of the Senate in which they urged the Senators "to modify Selective Service regulations (the draft) to allow selective conscientious objection, as recently espoused by the United States Catholic Conference." [6] The next chapter will point out that the Catholic press never tires of discussing the issue and, as has already been noted, many SCO's are themselves Catholics. Despite this widespread support for SCO, the prudent legislator may want to know just how intensely the Catholic community is committed to selective objection. Is the absence of SCO as offensive to Catholics as the absence of a CO provision would be to Quakers?

This chapter will critically discuss the argument that a Catholic selective objector "cannot do other" simply because he is a Catholic. While selective objection is consistent with Roman Catholic teaching, that same teaching is so qualified that it would be almost impossible for a Catholic to maintain that his church, either in its teaching or governing authority, would ever *demand* of an ordinary citizen conscientious objection to a particular war. Thus the burden of this chapter will be to develop the theme that the proponents of SCO interpret Catholic doctrine on war and peace far more rigorously than the church itself has ever understood it. If this attempt is successful it will provide at the level of public policy an answer to the

[3] *Kedroff* v. *St. Nicholas Cathedral*, 344 U.S. 94, and *Presbyterian Church etc.* v. *Mary Elizabeth Blue Hall Memorial Presbyterian Church*, 393 U.S. 440.

[4] For what is, perhaps, the most trenchant statement affirming the alleged discriminatory character of the absence of SCO, see Peter J. Riga, "Selective Conscientious Objection: Progress Report," *The Catholic World*, CCXI (July, 1970), 161-65.

[5] The title of the letter is "Human Life in Our Day." It is published by U.S. Catholic Conference, 1312 Massachusetts Avenue, N.W., Washington, D.C.

[6] Letter from the Conference of Major Superiors of Jesuits (May 20, 1970).

complaint that the absence of SCO discriminates against Roman Catholics. The detailed discussion of the traditional Roman Catholic teachings on the just war, then, is not intended to criticize or uphold that teaching. It is simply to investigate the Catholic tradition to see how seriously we should take the complaint of discrimination against members of just war churches.[7]

The Just War

It is beyond the scope of this essay to provide a systematic treatment of the just war doctrine.[8] Its main thrust has been the insistence that warfare, like any other form of human activity, must be justified in terms of a higher law. No group of men may attack another group without some principles to support and guide their destructive behavior. Thus, the principle of the just war attempts to offer political societies the same sort of guidelines the doctrine of legitimate self-defense offers the individual. The overall purpose of such principles is to curtail, control, and perhaps even civilize the recourse to violence. There is nothing distinctively Roman Catholic about the doctrine, although it has long been associated with the teachings of that church.[9] Theologians debate whether the doctrine is distinctively Christian or part of the secular Western tradition of higher law.[10]

[7] For examples of the discrimination argument, see National Council of Churches' brief for McFadden in *McFadden et al.* v. *Selective Service System Local Board No. 40, passim.* (Future references to McFadden's appeal to the 9th Circuit will be given as *McFadden, 9th Circuit.* References to McFadden's action in the District Court for the Northern District of California will be given simply as *McFadden.*) See also the flyer released by CADRE after the sentencing of David Kuebrich. In bold print at the top of the page there appeared the following: "Chicago Catholic Imprisoned. Protests Religious Discrimination. Sentenced to 3 Years." The opening paragraph read as follows:
"On November 1, the Feast of All Saints, Mr. David Kuebrich, 25, was convicted and sentenced to three years' imprisonment for refusing induction. Dave, who devoted one and a half years of his life to preparing for the Catholic priesthood before choosing to serve God and men in a different vocation, and who until recently was working toward a Ph.D. in English from the University of Chicago, refused to be inducted into the army and is now in prison because *he is a true Catholic,* a young man who takes his Catholicism seriously . . ." (italics in the original). Finally, see "The Draft and Conscience," *Commonweal,* LXXXVI (April 21, 1967), 140.

[8] For a detailed discussion of the development of the just war doctrine, see Alfred Vanderpol, *La doctrine scolastique du droit de guerre* (Paris: Desclée & Cie, 1919). For a contemporary Protestant position see Paul Ramsey, *The Just War* (New York: Charles Scribner's Sons, 1968). See also Paul Ramsey's *War and the Christian Conscience* (Durham: Duke University Press, 1916). For an interpretation of the American understanding of the just war doctrine see Robert W. Tucker, *The Just War: A Study in Contemporary American Doctrine* (Baltimore: Johns Hopkins University Press, 1960).

[9] Ramsey, *The Just War,* pp. xii-xiv.

[10] Ramsey explains the just war doctrine as an outgrowth of the New Testament ethic of love of neighbor. This love may at times require a Christian to take up the sword to defend the innocent. (*The Just War,* p. 143). John Courtney Murray maintains the doctrine is not necessarily Christian: "It emerges in the minds of all men of reason

Such questions need not delay us here. For our purpose it is sufficient to state the general conditions which must be met if a war is to be considered just. An adequate statement of contemporary Catholic understanding of the conditions for a just war appears in Austin Fagothey's *Right and Reason,* a standard textbook, credited by James McFadden with influencing his thinking. At the end of a lengthy chapter on the just war, Fagothey gives the following summary:

There are *four conditions for a just war:*

1. *Lawful authority.* War is an act of the state as such and must be properly authorized. This authorization gives the soldier his right to kill and use force. So long as there is hope, guerilla fighting and underground resistance movements are lawful, even when the government that authorized them has fallen.

2. *Just cause.* This can be only the attempted or accomplished violation of a nation's strict rights. There must be *sufficient* proportion between the good intended and the evil permitted. War must be the *last resort* after the breakdown of all feasible forms of negotiation. There must be *fair hope* of success or there can be no proportion. The cause must be *known to be just;* if it is doubtful, subordinates can form their consciences and trust to the wisdom of their leaders.

3. *Right intention.* Objective grounds for war may exist, yet the nation may fight it for the wrong motives. *Punitive war* is accepted by the older writers and, despite objection, seems still applicable; on this basis the punishment of war criminals can be defended.

4. *Right use of means.* A war otherwise justifiable can become wrong by the way it is fought. The natural law allows almost anything in a just war except the direct killing of the innocent. The killing of the guilty (combatants), even direct killing, is allowed on the principles of national self-defense and of retributive justice. The treatment of prisoners, spies, noncombatants, and hostages; the use of bombing, siege, blockade, submarine warfare, and poison gas; the handling of enemy property and respect for the rights of neutrals; these and similar matters are but vaguely indicated by the natural law and are determined by custom and international agreement. Such contracts must be kept unless they are substantially broken by the other side. But no nation may do something intrinsically wrong because the other side does so.[11]

---

and good will when they face two inevitable questions. First, what are the norms that govern recourse to the violence of war? Second, what are the norms that govern the measure of violence to be used in war? In other words, when is war rightful and what is rightful in war? One may indeed refuse the questions, but this is a form of moral abdication, which would likewise be fatal to civilization. If one does face the questions, one must arrive at the just war doctrine in its classical form, or at some analogue or surrogate, conceived in other terms." Excerpted from "War and Conscience," an address delivered by Murray at Western Maryland College shortly before his death in 1967. It is reproduced in James Finn (ed.), *A Conflict of Loyalties: The Case for Selective Conscientious Objection* (New York: Pegasus, 1969), p. 21. See also Everett E. Gendler's "War and the Jewish Tradition," in the above-cited volume edited by James Finn.

[11] Austin Fagothey, *Right and Reason* (2d ed.; St. Louis: C. V. Mosby, 1959), pp. 577-78.

Various authors give slightly different formulations of the cardinal points of the just

Fagothey's statement reflects the careful use of words characteristic of the scholar. It is instructive to see how these principles are translated into the idiom of public debate. For example, in his trial David Kuebrich described the just war doctrine as follows:

In my high school religion courses and in various theology texts, I have read since then, there are laid down certain criteria which each individual should apply to a conflict which his nation is involved in.

Through correspondence with a former professor of mine at the seminary and through reading on my own various Catholic periodicals and various books in which these criteria were applied, the four criteria are basically that the war be declared by legitimate authority; that it be a just cause; that there be observed the principle of proportionality whereby the good that will be gained by the conflict will outweigh the damage and destruction and carnage that is involved in the process; and that there be civilian immunity.[12]

There is no need to quarrel with Kuebrich's statement of the just war doctrine. Considering the difficult circumstances in which he found himself, he did well indeed. What is of interest, however, is Kuebrich's tendency to simplify the doctrine along with his emphasis on the role of the individual in applying the just war criteria.

The tendency to simplify is a common characteristic of the proponents of SCO. In reading the literature and listening to speakers supporting selective objection, one detects an "automatic" application of the principles to the Vietnam situation. Every war is either just or unjust. All we must do is investigate the situation and apply the principles and we shall be able to determine whether the Vietnam war passes the justice test. Thus, Peter Riga writes in *Modern Society:*

The answer to our problem is quite clear: since there can be unjust wars, the individual can become truly a person only by taking himself in hand in responsibility and judge the actions of government in the light of the gospel and the traditional teaching of his Church about a just war. He has no other choice if he wishes to be a person and a Christian. After serious investigation, if he

---

war doctrine. I have selected Fagothey's book because it is widely used in Catholic colleges as an ethics textbook and, therefore, is somewhat representative of the way students and professors in Catholic institutions approach the just war question. Although the tone of Fagothey's summary is a bit "hawkish," the fact that James McFadden, himself an SCO, would refer to the book as influencing his thinking suggests Fagothey's treatment is rather well balanced. I felt it was particularly advantageous to cite a volume published *prior* to the Vietnam war. With articles and books of more recent vintage, there is always the danger that the author has written with one eye on Southeast Asia and that his interpretation of the just war doctrine may conveniently support a pre-determined conclusion.

[12] *U.S. v. Kuebrich, T.R.,* p. 47.

considers the actions of his government to be immoral, he must refuse to serve in the armed forces *in any capacity* (this would seem to rule out any participation in the military, even as a non-combatant, since his presence simply frees another to war for him).[13]

In his testimony on behalf of David Kuebrich, Gerald Grant, a priest and a professor of sociology, gave the following answer to the question of how "the average Roman Catholic" would decide the justice of his nation's cause:

The process, Mr. Attorney, is quite similar to the process that you would use in a court of law. As a matter of fact, it is called in our theory a court, the internal court of conscience. He would have to examine the facts in light of the principles. The principles are the ones I sketched out. Do the facts in the case bring the cause of war sufficiently under the law so that it is fulfilling the requirements of the moral law and, therefore, is just? [14]

This approach to the just war tradition is surely too simple. There are two massive questions men like Kuebrich, Riga, and Grant ignore. The questions are (1) to what extent does the just war theory concern ordinary citizens, and (2) to what extent should these citizens concede to their government a "presumption of justice"—or, in Fagothey's words—"trust to the wisdom of their leaders."

THE CITIZEN AND THE JUST WAR. Proponents of SCO eagerly wrap their arguments in hoary tradition. They are careful to point out that the just war doctrine is not the creation of the current "resistance" movement, but is rather the product of centuries of doctrinal development beginning with Augustine and running through Aquinas, Suarez, and Vitoria down to our own times.[15] Since the argument for SCO rests so heavily on tradition, it is only fitting that we look at that tradition to determine with what relevance it can be applied to the current debate on SCO. The

[13] Peter J. Riga, "Selective Conscientious Objection," *Modern Society*, July-August, 1968, p. 113.

[14] *U.S.* v. *Kuebrich, T.R.*, p. 76. Father Grant's approach to the just war doctrine recalls Justice Robert's method of testing the constitutionality of a statute: "When an act of Congress is appropriately challenged in the courts as not conforming to a constitutional mandate, the judicial branch of the government has only one duty—to lay the article of the Constitution which is invoked beside the statute which is challenged and to decide whether the latter squares with the former" (*U.S.* v. *Butler*, 297 U.S. 1).

[15] Calvin Trillin, "U.S. Journal: Clovis—No, Sir, I Can't Go" (*New Yorker*, XLIV [March 30, 69], 107); Defendant's Brief in *U.S.* v. *Spiro*, 390 U.S. 956 (cert. denied), p. 5, Appendix, pp. 7a and 29a; deposition of the Rev. Peter J. Riga in *McFadden*; plaintiff's Brief in *McFadden, 9th Circuit, passim*; statement of The Rev. Gerald Grant in *U.S.* v. *Kuebrich, Trial Record*, p. 68.

specific question to be investigated is the extent to which the traditional just war doctrine was intended to guide the ordinary citizen.

In the *City of God* Augustine does, indeed, uphold a distinction between just and unjust wars, but he has little to say on the relevance of this distinction for the individual soldier. As far as the latter is concerned, Augustine's main point is to insist that he resort to violence only when commanded by those in authority and never on his own initiative. If a soldier were to kill a man without proper authorization, he would be a murderer. If, however, he refused to kill when commanded to do so, "he would be guilty of disobedience and contempt for authority." [16] In the *Contra Faustum,* however, Augustine makes it clear that the justice of a particular war is not the concern of the ruler alone:

A just man may with a good conscience fight on behalf of a king, even a pagan king, if in the efforts to preserve peace it is certain that what has been commanded him is not contrary to the command of God *or it is not certain whether the commands are contrary to the command of God.* In this way the blame for commanding something evil would be on the king's conscience, but the soldier in his subordinate capacity would be innocent.[17]

Augustine's formulation of the principles that allow a citizen to participate in warfare is more complex than the statements of men like Kuebrich, Grant, and Riga. The complexity of Augustine's statement comes from his awareness that the citizen may not be able to make a clear-cut decision on the morality of a particular war. Contemporary proponents of selective objection seem to suggest that after a thorough investigation, a citizen will always be able to decide whether or not a war is just. Augustine acknowledges the very real possibility that a prospective soldier may never resolve his doubts about the justice of a particular war. In such a case he would permit the citizen to fight. If the war really is unjust, the moral fault lies with the king, not the soldier. Thus, for Augustine, there are two situations in which a man can fight: (1) if he is certain that the order given him is not contrary to the law of God; or (2) if he is *not* certain that the order *is* contrary to the law of God. He is forbidden to fight only if he is *certain* that the command is contrary to God's law.

Thomas Aquinas' statement on the just war doctrine seems to be addressed

[16] The words quoted appear in the following context:

"A soldier who kills another man in response to a command issued by legitimate authority is not guilty of the crime of homicide. Indeed, if he fails to obey the command, he would be guilty of disobedience and contempt for authority. But if he acts on his own initiative, he is guilty of murder. Therefore, just as he is punished if he acted on his own, so also, he is punished if he fails to act when commanded" (*De Civitate Dei,* I, 26 [translation mine]).

[17] Contra Faustum, XXII, 75 (emphasis added; translation mine).

to kings and princes rather than to "private persons." He lists three conditions that must be met before a war can be justified: approval by legitimate authority, just cause, and right intention.[18] It is only the first of these that even mentions "private persons." But here the intention is quite clearly to restrict the legitimacy of massive violence to those situations authorized by government. That is, the requirement of the just war doctrine that a war be approved by legitimate authority is not a limitation on the power of government. On the contrary, it is an ethical norm that allows the government to restrain "vigilante" violence on the part of its citizens. This is simply a development of Augustine's position in *The City of God.* The second and third conditions, just cause and right intention, are stated without any reference to the ordinary citizen.

Thus, in his discussion of the just war, it seems that Aquinas is more concerned with helping political leaders make their decision for or against war on sound moral grounds than with providing the citizens with guidelines for judging the morality of their leaders' decisions. His main concern with the private citizen is to caution him against any recourse to violence that is not approved by the proper authorities. This is seen clearly from the way in which he handles an objection to his just war exposition. The objection is based on Matthew 26:52, "All who take up the sword will perish by the sword." The substance of the argument was that God inflicts punishment only for sin. But to perish by the sword is punishment. Therefore taking up the sword must be sinful.[19] In reply Aquinas maintains "taking up the sword" refers only to those who would kill another without the authorization or command of any legitimate superior. He continues:

When a private person uses a sword at the behest of a prince or a judge or when a public official does the same from a desire for justice—acting, as it were, under the authority of God—they themselves do not "take up the sword." Rather they make use of a sword entrusted to them by another. Hence they should not be punished.[20]

The teaching of Aquinas on the just war doctrine, then, would seem to be an attempt to limit and control the use of violence. Of the three Thomistic norms—approval by legitimate authority, just cause, and right intention—only the first concerns the citizen. And here his task is not to judge the wisdom of his rulers' decision, but to abstain from violence initiated on his own without the approval of the public authorities.

[18] *Summa Theologica,* II/2, 40:1. The fourth condition—use of legitimate means—is taken up in article three of the same question.
[19] *Ibid.*
[20] *Ibid., ad primum* (translation mine).

The authors of the late medieval and early modern periods follow Augustine's teaching that one may participate in warfare as long as it is not certain that the war is unjust.[21] The two most prominent political commentators of the sixteenth century, Suarez and Vitoria, follow this Augustinian principle, but go on to ask the more interesting question of whether the subjects are obliged to investigate the justice of the war in which they are to serve. Both authors reply in the negative. Vitoria says:

The subjects of a humble station who are neither admitted into nor heard within the councils of the king or of the state, are not obliged to study the causes of the war. They may go to war trusting in their superiors.[22]

Suarez makes a similar reply:

Ordinary soldiers who are subjects of princes need not weigh the causes of the war. When they are summoned, they may go to war, provided it is not obvious to them that the war is unjust. The reason for this is that as long as the injustice of the war is not clear, it is sufficient for them to follow the opinion of the prince and his advisers.[23]

This brief survey of four leading spokesmen of the just war doctrine, then, shows that one (Aquinas) does not even raise the question of the citizen's duty to investigate the justice of a particular war. Vitoria raises the question only to deny any such obligation for those "who are neither admitted into nor heard within the council of the king or of the state." Augustine and Suarez allow a soldier to participate when the justice of a particiular war is in doubt. Since few areas are more dubious than international relations, a principle that would justify resolving doubts in favor of government would seem to relieve the conscientious burdens of soldiers in most cases.

In summary, then, the just war tradition cannot *oblige* a man to refuse military service as long as he is not certain that a particular war is unjust. Nor is he even obliged to investigate the justice of the war if the issue is in doubt. With a clear conscience he could take part in the war relying on the judgment of those who govern him. It is for this reason that Paul Ramsey, a contemporary Protestant student of the just war theory, maintains that the traditional teaching of the Catholic Church "held this doctrine to be primarily addressed to the leaders of nations." [24]

A proponent of selective objection might complain that an argument from

[21] Vanderpol, p. 104. [22] Cited *ibid.*

[23] Francisco Suarez, *Opera Omnia*, Vol. XII: *Disputatio* xiii, *De Bello* (Paris: Apud Ludovicum Vives, 1858). (Translation mine.)

[24] Ramsey, *War and the Christian Conscience*, p. 132. Ramsey thinks that today the doctrine must be addressed to all citizens.

tradition is more than a textual study of authors of the distant past. A tradition is both ancient and *alive*. If we are to avoid shallow fundamentalism we must constantly reinterpret the words of the past in the light of contemporary circumstances. No tradition can survive if it is governed exclusively by the dead hand of the past. To apply the just war theory to the debate on SCO we cannot ignore the democratic character of American society.[25] It is all right for Vitoria and Suarez to say "subjects of a humble station" need not investigate the decisions of the prince, but such a directive falls on deaf ears in a modern society with a relatively high degree of civic education.

This is a reasonable objection, but if we are to update the just war theory in terms of the responsibilities of democratic citizenship, we must not close our eyes to other aspects of modern life, e.g., the involvement of "civilian" peasants in guerilla warfare and the fact that, unlike the professional armies of the Middle Ages, our armies are comprised of conscripted soldiers. These military changes are as important for the just war theory as the political developments from subject to citizen.

One of the main reasons many objectors find the Vietnam war unjust is the alleged failure of the U.S. to heed the prohibition against killing or injuring noncombatants. The protection of civilian personnel has an honorable history in just war literature.[26] The Second Vatican Council reaffirmed this principle when it vigorously condemned as "a crime against God and man" any act of war "aimed indiscriminately at the destruction of entire cities or of extensive areas along with their population." [27]

Selective objectors to the Vietnam war frequently cite the tradition of civilian immunity and the Council's condemnation of indiscriminate destruction as the basis for finding the war unjust. The difficulty with this argument is that it fails to tell us who the civilians are and what sort of destruction is "indiscriminate" in modern guerilla warfare. If by "combatant" we understand uniformed personnel, we face the relevance problem we had when we discussed just wars in terms of subjects and princes. Paul Ramsey argues persuasively that we must broaden the understanding of "combatant" if we apply the just war theory to guerilla warfare.

In contemporary insurgency, the fact is that a peasant is often a civilian by day and a combatant by night. Others are close cooperators all or some of the time and therefore technically combatants also. In short, the decision of the insurgents to conduct war by selective terror results in a situation in which a whole area is inhabited mainly by "combatants" in the ethically and politically relevant sense that a great number of the people are from consent or from constraint the bearers

[25] Donald Wolf, "Vietnam Morality: Who Judges What, When, How?" *The Catholic World,* CCVII (June, 1968), 108-9.

[26] Vanderpol, pp. 148-50.   [27] *Vatican II,* p. 294.

of the force to be repressed. "There is no profound difference between the farmer and the soldier," wrote Mao-Tse-Tung; and so saying made it so. The *insurgents themselves* have enlarged the target it is legitimate for counter-insurgents to attack, so far as the principle of discrimination is concerned and it is therefore mainly the principle of proportion that limits what should be done to oppose them. Since in the nature of insurgency the line between combatant and non-combatant runs right through a great number of the able-bodied people in a given area, male or female, above, say, ten years of age, and since anyone may cross over this line in either direction by the hour, it is not the business of any moralist to tell the soldiers and military commanders who are attempting to mount an effective counter-insurgency operation that this cannot be done in a morally acceptable way because under these circumstances they have no legitimate military target. In devising a military riposte, it will not be those who are directing the counter-insurgency who illicitly enlarge the target and chose to fight the war indiscriminately. Instead the tragedy is that they *have* an enlarged legitimate target because of the decision of the insurgency to fight the war by means of peasants. Whether because he is idealistically persuaded or terrorized, many a South Vietnamese lad qualified as a combatant without malice. It is a terrible human tragedy when American soldiers discover among the casualties after a Viet Cong attack the body of a twelve-year-old boy, his maps on him, who an hour before had shined their shoes near the compound; but I do not see how it is possible to accuse them and not the Viet Cong of the wickedness.[28]

A second difficulty in updating the just war theory to fit contemporary circumstances is the fact that American soldiers are conscripted into military service. The medieval soldier was usually a professional. If he refused to fight, he would have to find a new livelihood, but, unlike his modern counterpart, he would not be imprisoned. Carletti is the only author who takes up explicitly the question of when a subject can follow his prince in a war he knows is unjust. A subject may do this only if the failure to obey would cause him to lose "his fief or other goods."[29] Thus, for Carletti, the just war doctrine would allow participation in a war one knows to be unjust if the refusal to serve would lead to serious loss. In updating this principle one might argue that the obligation *not* to participate in an unjust war is softened by the fact that the reluctant warrior will be imprisoned for his refusal.

Thirdly, we must consider the principles behind our rejection of the idea that a citizen in a democratic society has no obligation to investigate the justice of a particular war. Such a position contradicts a basic premise of sound democratic theory—the personal responsibility of all citizens to promote

[28] Ramsey, *The Just War*, p. 435.
[29] Cited in Vanderpol, p. 104. Robert Bellarmine develops the point that a man who *must* fight has less responsibility to investigate the justice of the cause than one who volunteers (see Fagothey, p. 565).

the common good or, more simply, civic virtue. A good citizen in a democracy cannot absolve himself from the responsibility of looking into the merits of major policy questions. One of the reasons Vitoria says "subjects" need not bother about whether a war is unjust is that they cannot do anything about it anyway.[30] In a democracy it is precisely because the citizen can do something about a war he finds unjust that he must investigate the whole question.[31]

To update the just war doctrine in the name of civic virtue we must not restrict the responsibilities of citizenship to intelligent investigation. The citizen shares the responsibility for the survival, stability, and well-being of the nation. Is it enough for him to decide that a war is unjust and then refuse to serve? Unlike Vitoria's subject, a citizen can do something. He can use his vote, and his freedom of speech and press to urge an end to the war.[32] In this way he contributes to the common good as a responsible citizen.[33] Under SCO he would be granted a leave of absence from the political arena. He could still vote and speak against the war, but he would do so as one exempted from the ordinary burdens of citizenship.[34]

Such an exemption would present no difficulty for those who consider democracy a form of government whose sole purpose is the protection of individual rights. If, however, democracy is based on the responsibility of sharing the enterprise of promoting the common good, such an exemption is hard to justify. Then it would be necessary for those who update the just war theory to show how selective objection would not only ease the conscience of the individual, but would also enable that same individual to fulfill his obligation to promote the common good. This may not be an insurmountable task, but it would seem to be essential for any argument that would avoid an extremely individualistic understanding of democracy.

Finally, the Catholic objector to the Vietnam war cannot ignore the manner in which the Second Vatican Council "updated" the just war theory. Its statement in *The Pastoral Constitution on The Church in the Modern World* was strongly antiwar. It did acknowledge, however, that "governments cannot

[30] Vanderpol, p. 104.

[31] An exception to this is the limitation put upon the free speech of men in uniform. One could argue persuasively that such "muzzling" of the citizen-soldier often has no relation to national security. This, however, would be an argument for changing military regulations, not for SCO.

[32] See Herbert J. Storing, "The Case Against Civil Disobedience," *Essays on Civil Disobedience,* ed. Robert Goldwyn (Chicago: Rand McNally and Company, 1969).

[33] See Chapter VII, pp. 156-62, below, for "national interest" arguments in support of SCO.

[34] A selective objector might consider his free speech and suffrage as a starting point for his protest against the war. But what should he do if these means are ineffective? Should he submit to majority rule, or does the "moral" character of his position require that he be exempt from the ordinary rules of the political process? For a discussion of this point, see Chapter VII, pp. 135 ff.

be denied the right to legitimate defense once every means of peaceful settlement has been exhausted." [35] Instead of restating the traditional conditions for a just war, the Council stressed the need to restrain the folly that would lead the world into the horrors of *total* war. In laying such heavy emphasis on the danger of *total* war, the conciliar statement invites the interpretation that limited warfare could be justified as a means of preventing total war. The prevention of total war is, of course, one of the reasons why the United States abandoned the policy of massive retaliation and developed a military force capable of pursuing effectively the goals of limited warfare.[36] The prevention of a far greater war in the future is one of the arguments frequently offered in support of American involvement in Vietnam. The value of such arguments is quite dubious, but can anyone honestly say they are *certainly* wrong? If one cannot say this, it is difficult to establish an *obligation* to refuse to serve in Vietnam within the framework of the just war theory.

The purpose of the arguments developed in this section is to "relax" the rigid stance taken by Catholic objectors to the Vietnam war. I have tried to show that the just war doctrine—both in its traditional and updated forms—leaves the selective objector a great deal of room in which to maneuver within the bounds of Catholic orthodoxy before he can claim his religion demands that he refuse to serve in a particular war. No one argument or any combination of them need convince anyone that the war in Vietnam is just. One need only raise *a substantive and legitimate doubt about the injustice* of the war to deliver a Catholic objector from the obligation of refusing to serve. In the complex area of international relations such doubts are not difficult to raise. The Catholic objector who refuses to serve in a war whose injustice is not certain may well be a man of the highest personal integrity, but he cannot claim that he is compelled to do so by the demands of his church.[37] Because of the complex nature of international

---

[35] *Vatican II*, p. 293.

[36] This is a basic theme in Maxwell Taylor, *The Uncertain Trumpet* (New York: Harper, 1960).

[37] The problem of the doubtful conscience is one of the most interesting and complex questions in Roman Catholic casuistry. The basic principle is that one must not act with a doubtful conscience. The doubtful conscience must be rendered certain. There are two ways of doing this—direct and indirect. The direct method is simply to investigate the matter fully to see if one can arrive at certitude. If not, one must resort to the indirect method of appealing to certain principles of moral analysis. In applying the indirect method one must distinguish "doubts of law" (*dubia juris*) and "doubts of fact" (*dubia facti*). In questions of doubts of law the prevailing doctrine is that of "probablism." Its basic principle is that "an uncertain law does not oblige" (*lex incerta non obligat*). If there are two conflicting interpretations of a law and both are "probable," then neither interpretation is "certain." There can be no certitude if an opposite opinion is probable. It makes no difference if one opinion is "more" probable than the other. As long as the less probable opinion is really probable, the more probable opinion cannot be certain and therefore need not be followed. For example, church law requires abstinence from meat on Ash Wednesday and Good Friday. Does the law include whale meat as "meat"?

affairs and the ambiguity of the just war doctrine, it seems reasonable to conclude that the absence of an SCO provision cannot be fairly interpreted as a sign of congressional disregard for the consciences of Catholics.[38]

THE PRESUMPTION OF JUSTICE. At this point in our analysis we have seen the need for *certainty* that a war is unjust before a Catholic can derive from his church's teaching an *obligation* to refuse to serve. As long as the issue is in doubt, he may participate. Thus, in the just war tradition doubts are resolved in favor of the government. Given the bewildering nature of international affairs, this principle goes a long way toward softening the impact of the just war doctrine on the individual citizen. The reason behind this principle is the traditional doctrine that the citizen owes his government a presumption of justice. In the absence of such a presumption the duty to obey legitimate authority would be drastically curtailed since the justice of so many decisions of public policy is often dubious.

As we have seen, the medieval and early modern commentators on the just war doctrine denied that subjects have a duty to investigate the justice of a particular war. This does not mean, of course, that they *must not* do this. What happens, then, if they choose to investigate the justice of a particular war and their investigation leaves them in a state of doubt? The traditional answer is that they must obey the prince. This is the teaching

---

The more probable opinion among canonists is that whale meat is meat. Nevertheless one may follow the "less probable" opinion and eat whale meat on Ash Wednesday because the probability of the more lenient opinion renders the more severe opinion "uncertain."

In doubts of fact one cannot apply probablism because this could lead to serious harm to others. Thus, if a hunter "doubts" whether something moving in the bushes is a deer or a dear friend, he cannot shoot on the assumption that it is "probably" a deer. In cases of doubts of fact, the basic principle is "follow the safer course" (*pars tutior sequenda*). Applying this principle to the case of a citizen who has doubts about the justice of a war, Suarez maintains he must obey those who govern him. His reason is that this is the safer course since the citizen can be certain the ruler has the right to command even though it may be doubtful whether a particular exercise of that right is justified (p. 750). Vitoria takes a similar stand in his *De Jure Belli,* as cited by Vanderpol, p. 133.

This sort of casuistry is less common among Roman Catholics today than it had been before *Vatican II.* It is especially offensive to the progressive wing of the Catholic Church which has little patience with such legalism. Nevertheless, no theologian that I know of has maintained that probablism is no longer within the pale of Roman Catholic orthodoxy. As long as this is the case those who argue for an *obligation* to object to a particular war by reason of Roman Catholic religious training and belief will have great difficulty establishing their point.

[38] The American Catholic bishops have supported SCO in their pastoral letter *Human Life in Our Day* (November 15, 1968). The fact that they support it does not mean the failure to enact SCO would be considered "discrimination" against Roman Catholicism. The bishops often lobby for programs that affect the interests of the Catholic Church and the public interest in general. They seldom claim, however, that they have been discriminated against when their efforts are ineffective.

of Antonin, Carletti, Cajetan, Vitoria, Suarez, Vasquez, and Lupus.[39] The following statement of Suarez is representative of the position of these canonists and theologians:

> When subjects are in a state of doubt (doubt of fact, that is) they must obey their superiors. There is a good reason for this. In such doubts the safer course must be followed. Since the prince has the law on his side, it is safer to obey him. To confirm this position, recall that a judge's servant can execute the sentence without examining it, provided its injustice is not obvious. This is the common doctrine as found in Cajetan . . . , de Soto . . . , and Sylvester. . . .[40]

The proponents of SCO frequently reject this aspect of the just war theory. For example, Gordon Zahn writes:

> The indifference, scorn, or retaliation stirred by such acts of dissent and dis-obedience as burning draft cards are, I am sorry to say, supported by the traditional theological definitions of the citizen-ruler relationship offered by our major religious communities. Since all authority is seen to originate in God, the authority of the secular ruler has been divinized to the point that he can command the obedience of the citizen as a *moral* obligation. This may not hold, of course, when the act commanded is certainly immoral—but here, too, there is a convenient escape hatch which combines recognition of one's "limited access to all the facts" with the proviso that one is to give the "presumption of justice" to the state where doubt is present. Is the citizen perhaps troubled by the form of government or by the obviously irreligious or openly anti-religious behavior of its leaders? Then let him remember that all forms of government are morally indifferent and that the sinfulness of the evil ruler does not free the citizen from his obligation to render him obedience. The dice are always loaded in favor of "legitimate authority," and the faithful are assured that whatever actions they perform out of obedience in good faith will be viewed as meritorious and any evil that may be involved will be charged against those who gave the order.[41]

Zahn's characterization of the presumption of justice as "a convenient escape hatch" is certainly questionable. Nevertheless, he acknowledges that this presumption is part of the traditional just war teaching. He challenges the wisdom of the presumption and, perhaps, for this very reason rejects the just war doctrine in favor of pacifism.[42] Zahn's candid recognition of the presumption of justice, however, is far more helpful for those who accept the just war doctrine than the approach of those who simply ignore

---

[39] Vanderpol, pp. 132-33.

[40] Suarez, p. 750 (translation mine).

[41] Gordon Zahn, *War, Conscience and Dissent* (New York: Hawthorn Books, 1967), p. 133.

[42] Zahn gives an account of his pacifism in *The Military Chaplain* (Dublin: University of Toronto Press, 1969).

this presumption. There is, of course, no need to accept a principle that grants the government a presumption of justice, but this liberty cannot be conceded to adherents of the just war tradition for the simple reason that the presumption is part of the tradition. The participants in public debate must not wrap their argument in venerable tradition unless they are willing to accept that tradition. Selective objection to war does not justify selective perception of tradition.

Selective perception, however, is very common among SCO's. For example, a young man in San Francisco sent a letter to his draft board in which he stated the reasons for his belief that the Vietnam war was unjust. After outlining his position he concluded, "If I am wrong, then it is the obligation of our government to refute all my points in order to prove me wrong." [43] An imprisoned selective objector maintained there was no more reason to give the benefit of the doubt about the justice of a war to his own government than to the enemy.[44] And a young seminarian, indicted for destroying draft records, called for resistance "in some concrete way" from those who are convinced the war in Vietnam is unjust as well as from those who "have serious reservations about it." [45]

This tendency to ignore or reject the presumption of justice was deplored by one of the most distinguished proponents of SCO. In a graduate address at Western Maryland College the late John Courtney Murray cited a statement issued by the Seminarians' Conference on the Draft. The statement maintained that the principles of the just war doctrine demand "that every war be opposed until or unless it can be morally justified in relation to these principles." [46] Murray observed, "The dear seminarians have it backward." He went on to show that the nature of the state as a moral and political agent requires that once a decision has been reached, "at least a preliminary measure of internal authority must be conceded by the citizens to this decision, even by those citizens who dissent from it." [47] If this concession were not forthcoming, the moral character of the state would be meaningless. For this reason, Murray argues, the just war theory has always maintained "that the presumption stands for the decision of the community as officially declared. He who dissents from the decision must accept the burden of proof." [48]

[43] Deposition of James McFadden in *McFadden*.
[44] From notes taken in a personal interview with David L. Kuebrich at the federal penitentiary at Springfield, Missouri, December 22, 1968.
[45] Circulated statement of Joseph Mulligan of Bellarmine School of Theology, Christmas, 1968.
[46] John C. Murray, "War and Conscience," in Finn (ed.), *A Conflict of Loyalties*, p. 26.
[47] *Ibid.*
[48] *Ibid.*, p. 27. After his statement that the seminarians "have it backward," Murray went on to say:
"The root of the error here may be simply described as a failure to understand that

It is not likely that SCO's would challenge Murray's position that the state is the agent of a moral community. To do so would be self-defeating. For if the state is an amoral institution, its officers have no obligation to respond to moral values. They would be perfectly justified in turning a deaf ear to SCO's who ask for military exemption on grounds of conscience precisely because of the moral character of the case for SCO. The very existence of the debate over SCO is a tacit recognition of the moral character of the state. Once the moral character of the state is acknowledged, the presumption of justice would seem to follow inexorably. For what meaning can there be in speaking of the state as the agent of a moral community if we are not willing to grant "at least a preliminary measure of internal authority" to the decisions of that agent?

One possible explanation of the tendency of selective objectors to withhold the presumption of justice may be that they have confused a presumption for authority with a presumption for war. Donald Wolf has developed skillfully the notion of a presumption against war:

[H]uman life is a primary and ultimate human value. Thus in the decision to be made between war and no-war, the presumption in any particular case falls on the side of no-war. The scales from the beginning are weighted against war in any form; the burden of proof is on the advocates of war and not on those who oppose war. This being the case, before a war begins and even after it has begun, the opinion of the dissenter—whether it be on grounds of legally-defined conscientious objection to all war or because of political and/or moral objections to a particular war—must be fully accepted, not just tolerated as an undesirable and difficult problem to war mobilization. Dissent against war is a truly human

provision of the just-war doctrine which requires that a war should be 'declared.' This is not simply a nice piece of legalism, the prescription of a sheer technicality. Behind the provision lies a whole philosophy of the State as a moral and political agent. The provision implies the recognition of the authority of the political community by established political processes to make decisions about the course of its action in history, to muster behind these decisions the united efforts of the community, and to publicize these decisions before the world.

If there is to be a political community, capable of being a moral agent in the international community, there must be some way of publicly identifying the nation's decisions. These decisions must be declared to be the decisions of the community. Therefore, if the decision is for war, the war must be declared. This declaration is a moral and political act. It states a decision conscientiously arrived at in the interest of the international common good. It submits the decision to the judgment of mankind. Moreover, when the decision-making processes of the community have been employed and a decision has been reached, at least a preliminary measure of internal authority must be conceded by the citizens to this decision, even by those citizens who dissent from it. This, at least in part, is what Socrates meant by respect for the 'conscience of the laws.' This is why in the just-war theory it has always been maintained that the presumption stands for the decision of the community as officially declared. He who dissents from the decision must accept the burden of proof."

response, individually and collectively, morally and politically, unless and until it is clear that the choice of war is a necessary one.[49]

Wolf's point is surely well taken. When groups within the government and citizens at large debate the issue of war and peace, it would seem to be a sign of a healthy society if those advocating war assumed the burden of proof. The difficulty with Wolf's argument is that he fails to give any moral weight to the decision *precisely because it is a decision of government*. It seems that the man who opposes the war is in the same position both before and after the decision. He bears a different label—"dissenter" rather than "opponent"—but *morally* his position has not changed; he still indulges a presumption against a war *that is now underway*. Perhaps this is Wolf's intention, for in the same article he maintains that it is "doubtful whether the presumption in favor of authority is still an adequate criterion in our form of democracy." [50] If so, the failure to distinguish the moral situation before and after the authoritative decision has been made limits the value of Wolf's case for a presumption against war. We can travel half the way with Wolf and accept a presumption against war before the decision is made. But the fact that the decision has been made "by the State as a moral and political agent," assumes that the presumption against the war has been rebutted by those responsible for the decision. The presumption must now be for the war, not because it is a war but because it is a decision made by legitimate authority. If such a presumption is unwarranted, the role of the State as a moral agent is rendered meaningless.

If we focus our attention on the moment of decision as the suitable time for shifting presumptions, we can reconcile the innate moral revulsion toward war (by presuming against it before the decision) with the demand for public order in times of difficult decisions (by presuming for the government after the decision).[51]

The present discussion of the just war theory and selective conscientious objection has emphasized the presumption of justice the citizen owes his government. If SCO should ever become public policy, one can only hope that the importance of this presumption will not be overlooked. Because it is only a presumption and not a definitive judgment, there would be no danger of the presumption rendering the right of selective objection ineffective. On the other hand the complex nature of international affairs would

[49] The quotation I have cited appears in a draft of Wolf's article which the author kindly gave me; this section does not appear in the condensed version, "Vietnam Morality: Who Judges What, When, How?" appearing in *The Catholic World*, CCVII (June, 1968), 108-9.

[50] See preceding note.

[51] See Paul Ramsey, *The Just War*, pp. 275-76; and Quentin L. Quade, "Civil Disobedience and the State," *Worldview* (November, 1967), 4-9.

enable the presumption to act as a check against the irresponsible use of SCO. If a citizen felt he had to assume the burden of proof before he could honestly claim an exemption from military service, it would be less likely that men of integrity would confuse conscientious objection with personal convenience.

Even if the present state of the law does not change, the presumption of justice principle could be very helpful for selective objectors. At present the SCO must go to jail for his beliefs. No responsible citizen can fail to be concerned about the talented young men now languishing in federal prisons for their refusal to "step forward." Many of them are there because they were faithful to the just war doctrine *as they understood it*. Perhaps had they paid as much attention to the presumption of justice as they did to the other principles of the just war doctrine, they might have found a way to justify "stepping forward" without sacrificing their integrity.

Finally, the presumption of justice principle must be underscored to safeguard the survival of the just war doctrine itself. This doctrine has, over the centuries, provided a viable alternative to the extremes of pacifism on the one hand and moral abdication on the other. If the presumption of justice is ignored, the just war doctrine could become a surrogate for pacifism by forbidding participation in *all* wars one by one on the grounds that the government failed to prove the justice of its cause. To prove that a war is just is, after all, no small task.

The adherents of the just war doctrine who cannot accept the presumption of justice principle would do well to reflect on whether they are not actually pacifists. Is their demand that the government prove its case tantamount to the rejection of force as a licit means of settling international disputes? If so, it might be advisable for such persons to abandon the just war doctrine altogether in favor of pacifism. They certainly do not "purify" the just war doctrine by constantly escalating the moral demands a government must meet before it can count on the support of its citizens. Such escalation seems to forget that war is always a matter of marginal morality at best; in this awareness lies the attractiveness of the pacifist position. If the just war doctrine becomes too "pure," it will cease to be relevant. Its realism is the key to its relevance. Unlike pacifism, it does not tell men what they ought to be; it is content to tell them what they ought *not* to be. This is not a counsel of perfection, but over the centuries it has helped to contain and control man's perennial resort to violence. It would not be wise to sacrifice this modest achievement on the altar of nonviolence.

In summary, then, it seems quite unlikely that many Catholics could claim that the just war doctrine *obliges* them to refuse to serve in a particular war. To do so they would have to get around the traditional position that excuses ordinary soldiers from concerning themselves with

122

such questions. To do this they would have to "update" the tradition in light of the responsibilities of citizenship in a democratic republic. In this very process of "updating" they would have to reinterpret the traditional norms of the just war doctrine in terms of the particularly savage style of warfare practiced today. Before they could claim an *obligation* to refuse to serve, they would have to arrive at a moral *certitude* that the war is unjust. All this they would have to accomplish in the face of a presumption in favor of the government's decision.

Vatican II

In the previous section my main concern was the extent to which adherence to the just war theory would oblige a Roman Catholic to refuse to serve in a particular war. In this section I shall consider the second major support in the Catholic case for SCO—the teachings of the Second Vatican Council. In their appeals to Vatican II the proponents of SCO do not neglect the question of personal obligation,[52] but their emphasis is primarily on the argument that the teaching of Vatican II requires that a well-ordered society make some provision for selective objection.

No one contends, of course, that the government of the United States has any obligation to insure that its laws reflect the values of any church. It is no secret, however, that such values are frequently reflected in public policy. A decade ago, when Roman Catholics provided a united front on the issue of birth control, the question whether public agencies should issue contraceptive devices was profoundly affected by the church's condemnation.[53] Legislators involved in the issue of liberalizing the laws regulating divorce and abortion need no reminders of the church's impact in these areas. As we stated above,[54] public policy cannot ignore questions of orthodoxy—at least where major religious bodies are concerned. For this reason it is important to investigate the statements of Vatican II to see to what extent, if at all, the Catholic Church at its highest authoritative level has supported the principle of selective objection.

CONSTITUTION ON THE CHURCH IN THE MODERN WORLD. One of the most significant statements of the Second Vatican Council was its *Pastoral Constitution on the Church in the Modern World.* In this document the bishops attempted to articulate the role of the church in such vital areas as marriage, education, labor relations, and international affairs. The

[52] See, for example, the depositions of Bishop James P. Shannon, the Rev. Peter J. Riga, and James McFadden in *McFadden.*
[53] See John A. Rohr, "Birth Control in Illinois: A Study in Church-State Relations," *Chicago Studies,* IV (Spring, 1965), 31-51.
[54] See above, p. 105.

document evidences a profound concern for world peace, especially in light of the development of nuclear technology. Perhaps it is the bishops' strong demand for peace among the nations that has led many Catholics to the conclusion that the document supports SCO. In an article entitled "Must Conscientious Objectors Be Pacifists," John Sheerin, editor of *The Catholic World,* maintains that "the problem for Catholics is this: the [U.S.] draft law in its implementation is radically at variance with the *Constitution on the Church in the Modern World.*" [55] "Must we keep silent?" he asks.[56]

There are three texts from the "Pastoral Constitution" which are most frequently cited by those who feel the Council has spoken in favor of SCO:

(1) Moreover, it seems right that laws make humane provisions for the case of those who for reasons of conscience refuse to bear arms, provided, however, that they accept some other form of service to the human community.[57]

(2) Contemplating this melancholy state of humanity, the Council wishes to recall first of all the permanent binding force of universal natural law and its all-embracing principles. Man's conscience itself gives ever more emphatic voice to these principles. Therefore, actions which deliberately conflict with these same principles, as well as orders commanding such actions, are criminal. Blind obedience cannot excuse those who yield to them. Among such must first be counted those actions designed for the methodical extermination of an entire people, nation, or ethnic minority. These actions must be vehemently condemned as horrendous crimes. The courage of those who openly and fearlessly resist men who issue such commands merits supreme commendation.[58]

(3) Any act of war aimed indiscriminately at the destruction of entire cities or of extensive areas along with their population is a crime against God and man himself. It merits unequivocal and unhesitating condemnation.[59]

A close look at these texts indicates that their connection with SCO is extremely tenuous. There is no reason to read *selective* objection into the Council's plea for "humane provisions for the case of those who for reasons

---

[55] CCVI (January, 1968), 147.   [56] *Ibid.*

[57] *Vatican II,* p. 292 cited by James Sheerin. Cited also in "The Selective Conscientious Objector," *America,* CXVII, No. 4 (July 22, 1967), 73; Riga, "Selective Conscientious Objection," p. 111; depositions in *McFadden* of Bishop James Shannon, p. 2; Msgr. John T. Ellis, p. 1; the Rev. Francis Baur (Exhibit B-1); the Rev. Terence O'Shaughessy, p. 1; and letter of James McFadden to Local Board No. 40, also in *McFadden.*

[58] *Vatican II.* p. 292. This text has been cited by Protestants as well as Catholics to support SCO. See Alan Geyer, "The Just War and the Selective Objector," *The Christian Century,* LXXXIII (February 16, 1966), 199-201, and Roger L. Shinn, "The SCO Again," *Christianity and Crisis,* XXVII (April 3, 1967), 61-63. See also Riga, "Selective Conscientious Objection," p. 112; and depositions of Bishop Shannon, pp. 1-2; the Rev. William J. O'Donnell, p. 2; the Rev. Dominic Domenico, p. 2; the Rev. Francis Baur (Exhibit B-1); and Letter of James McFadden to Local Board No. 40, all in *McFadden.*

[59] *Vatican II,* p. 294. See Riga, "Selective Conscientious Objection," p. 112; depositions of Bishop Shannon, p. 3; the Rev. William J. O'Donnell, p. 4; and the Rev. Francis Baur (Exhibit B-2) in *McFadden.*

of conscience refuse to bear arms." Some of the bishops come from countries which, at the time of Vatican II, had no provision for total objectors. It seems only reasonable to presume that if the Council's intention were to break new ground by advocating *selective* objection, it would have spelled out its intention more explicitly.[60]

The second statement disallows blind obedience as a justification for carrying out immoral orders. The statement appears in the context of a discussion of permissible military action.[61] It prescinds from the justice or injustice of war and insists that there are certain acts which can never be justified under any circumstances. The only specific example is that of genocide.[62] As far as Americans are concerned, such a crime is already forbidden by the regulations of the Army *Field Manual*.[63] Thus, if American soldiers were ever issued orders to carry out "the methodical extermination of an entire people," their refusal would not have to be based on moral revulsion alone. They could refuse to carry out such an order on the basis of Army regulations as well. The activities condemned by the *Field Manual* are broad enough to include anything else the Council may have intended when it "vehemently condemned" certain actions as "horrendous crimes." [64]

The Council's praise, then, for those who courageously resist immoral commands does not really deal with the question of the selective objector. Its thrust is to uphold the principle that even in warfare a man does not cease to be a morally responsible agent. Richard McCormick gives an accurate statement of the relevance of these texts for SCO:

Vatican II's endorsement of laws which "make humane provisions for the case of those who for reasons of conscience refuse to bear arms" is probably too general to apply clearly to the selective conscientious objector. However, its teaching clearly supposes personal moral decisions and responsibility.[65]

McCormick's statement is helpful because it brings out a distinction that is sometimes overlooked in debates over SCO—the distinction between selective objection and personal responsibility for actions commanded by law. Long

[60] This is the position of Donald Campion, an outstanding authority on the text of this Constitution (telephone conversation of May 1, 1969). Paul Ramsey maintains that the Council failed to address the problem of the "just war objector." Ramsey, *The Just War*, p. 385. Richard McCormick, a prominent Roman Catholic moral theologian, maintains the text in question "is probably too general to apply clearly to the selective conscientious objector." "Notes on Moral Theology: January-June, 1967," *Theological Studies*, XXVIII (December, 1967), 788.

[61] *Vatican II*, pp. 291-92.

[62] *Ibid.*, p. 292, note 255.

[63] Department of the Army, *Field Manual*, No. 27-10 (Washington, D.C.: Government Printing Office, July 18, 1956), pp. 17; 25-30; 78-99.

[64] *Ibid.*

[65] McCormick, p. 788.

before Vatican II, Western man (if not all mankind) has known there are limits on what the law may command him to do.[66] The Council's condemnation of blind obedience merely reaffirms this tradition. Given the dreadful experiences of World War II, the Council has done well to recall to man his heritage of personal responsibility. This, however, is an entirely different question from that of SCO. The latter concerns *the response of the state* to the citizen who rejects an authoritative decision on moral grounds. The traditional question has been under what circumstances the individual may (or must) disobey the law. The Council's condemnation of blind obedience speaks from this tradition. Its focus is the conscience of the person. SCO raises a new question—to what degree can the state accommodate the man who will not obey? Its focus is the *state,* not the individual.

The third text condemns the indiscriminate slaughter of innocent civilians. It has been used to support SCO on the basis of U.S. counterinsurgency warfare in South Vietnam, which, it is argued, involves the sort of indiscriminate slaughter the Council has condemned.[67] This is a very weak argument because a fleeting glance at the context of the statement makes it obvious that the Council is talking about indiscriminate slaughter resulting from the use of *nuclear* weapons in *total* war.[68] One may have good reason for strong moral objections to the high number of civilian deaths in Vietnam, but such objections cannot be based on *this* text of *Vatican II.*

If we confine our analysis, then, to the three texts cited most frequently by proponents of SCO, we find no support for John Sheerin's observation that "the draft law in its implementation is radically at variance with *The Pastoral Constitution on the Church in the Modern World*" in regard to the rights of conscientious objectors.[69]

Elsewhere in the same document the Council offers a directive that would

---

[66] Cf. Sophocles' *Antigone,* lines 70-77, 450-70, and the Acts of the Apostles 4:19.
[67] Riga, "Selective Conscientious Objection," p. 112.
[68] The paragraphs preceding the text in question read as follows:

"The horror and perversity of war are immensely magnified by the multiplication of scientific weapons. For acts of war involving these weapons can inflict massive and indiscriminate destruction, far exceeding the bounds of legitimate defense. Indeed, if the kind of instruments which can now be found in the armories of the great nations were to be employed to their fullest, an almost total and altogether reciprocal slaughter of each side by the other would follow, not to mention the widespread devastation which would be spawned by the use of such weapons.

"All these considerations compel us to undertake an evaluation of war with an entirely new attitude. The men of our time must realize that they will have to give a somber reckoning for their deeds of war. For the course of the future will depend largely on the decisions they make today.

"With these truths in mind, this most holy Synod makes its own the condemnation of total war already pronounced by recent Popes, and issues the following declaration:

"Any act of war. . . ."
[69] See p. 124, above.

seem to advise any citizen who would dissent from the laws of his country to do so only with great caution.

Where public authority oversteps its competence and oppresses the people, these people should nevertheless obey to the extent that the objective common good demands. Still it is lawful for them to defend their own rights and those of their fellow citizens against any abuse of this authority, provided that in so doing they observe the limits imposed by natural law and the gospel.[70]

Thus, while the Council upholds the citizen's right to defend himself and others against the abuse of authority, it does not hesitate to remind the citizen that at times "the objective common good" may require him to obey a law that "oversteps" the competence of public authority and "oppresses the people." This is an important text for it brings out the gravity involved in any violation of law. It certainly calls into question any "automatic" application of the just war doctrine—"the war is unjust; therefore I will not serve." [71]

Before a citizen can ignore an authoritative decision on grounds of conscience, he must do more than be certain that the law is unjust. He must also be careful that his disobedience will not harm the common good. Thus, the potential objector must ask two questions: (1) Is the policy decision unjust; and (2) shall I obey? An affirmative answer to the first does not *demand* a negative to the second.

DECLARATION ON RELIGIOUS FREEDOM. Although *The Pastoral Constitution on the Church in the Modern World* was the only document that touched explicitly the question of conscientious objection, the Council's *Declaration on Religious Freedom* took up some principles of government which pertain to our inquiry. The latter document is of particular interest because it was the only conciliar statement in which American bishops and theologians took the leading role.[72] This was because the "Declaration" addressed the difficulties occasioned by several nineteenth-century papal statements on the question of the legal establishment of the Roman Catholic

[70] *Vatican II*, pp. 284-85.
[71] For an example of the "automatic" mentality, see the statement of the Rev. Victor Balke in *U.S.* v. *Kuebrich*:

"Judge Hoffman: Civil disobedience meant that there was a law that those who were disobeying it didn't approve of, their conscience wouldn't permit them to obey it, so they in a non-violent way disobeyed the law.

"Fr. Balke: Yes, as a result of conscience, your Honor. I mean, if I violate my conscience, if I act against Roman Catholic terminology, I am committing a sin. Simply, if it comes to a choice between committing sin and violating a civil statute, I simply have to follow my conscience."
[72] John C. Murray, "The Problem of Religious Freedom," *Theological Studies,* XXV (December, 1964), 510-12.

Church. Certain statements of Gregory XVI, Pius IX, and Leo XIII led to the conclusion that the church was committed to the position that Catholics were obliged to try to bring about the "establishment" of their religion whenever this was possible. This conclusion had always been an embarrassment to American Catholics.[73] More than a decade before Vatican II, John Courtney Murray challenged this conclusion in a series of widely read articles in *Theological Studies*.[74] The thrust of Murray's argument was to show that the offensive statements were historically conditioned and that the real objects of papal displeasure were certain overtly anticlerical regimes in France and Italy. Vatican II presented an opportunity to affirm the church's unqualified approval of regimes in which the Roman Catholic Church was not "established." There was strong resistance to the statement by a small but powerful group of bishops—mostly Italians and Spaniards. After several postponements, the "Declaration" won the overwhelming approval of the Council.[75]

Among those supporting the "Declaration" there were two competing views on how to present the case for religious liberty. One approach was known commonly, but perhaps inaccurately, as the "French View." [76] Its starting point was the dignity and freedom of the human person. It proceeded *deductively* to arrive at conclusions concerning man's life in society—viz., his right to worship in accordance with his conscience. A second approach was advanced by Murray and many American bishops. They tried to keep two principles operative simultaneously—the dignity and freedom of the person and the nature of limited government. For Murray, these two principles worked in tandem to ground the right to religious freedom. He described the difference between the two schools in an article written during the Council:

One school [the "French View"] regards religious freedom as formally a theological-moral concept which has juridical consequences, *scil.*, within the order of constitutional law. The other school [the "American View"] regards religious freedom as formally a juridical or constitutional concept, which has foundations in theology, ethics, political philosophy, and jurisprudence. The first school begins

[73] Paul Blanshard, *The Irish and Catholic Power* (Boston: Beacon Press, 1953) and *Freedom and Catholic Power in Spain and Portugal* (Boston: Beacon Press, 1962).
[74] The following articles by John C. Murray appeared in *Theological Studies:*
"Freedom of Religion: The Ethical Problem," VI, 229-86.
"St. Robert Bellarmine on the Indirect Power," IX, 491-535.
"On Religious Freedom," X, 409-32.
"The Problem of State Religion," XII, 155-78.
"Leo XIII on Church and State," XIV, 1-30.
"Leo XIII: Separation of Church and State," XIV, 145-214.
[75] The best study available on the conciliar history of the "Declaration on Religious Liberty" is Richard J. Regan, *Conflict and Consensus* (New York: Macmillan, 1967).
[76] *Ibid.*, p. 118.

with a single insight—the exigence of the free human person for religious freedom. Only in the second instance does it raise what we have called the constitutional question. Consequently, within this structure of argument the political-juridical argument for religious freedom is secondary and subordinate to the theological-ethical argument. In contrast, the second school begins with a complex insight— the free human person under a government of limited powers. The constitutional question is raised at the outset; it is equally as primary as the theological-moral question. Consequently, the political-juridical argument for religious freedom is co-ordinate with the theological-moral argument. In other words, both religious freedom, as a legal institution and constitutional government, as a form of polity, emerge with equal immediacy as exigencies of the personal consciousness in its inseparable correlation with the political consciousness.[77]

It is the question of limited government that concerns us in our study of SCO. Government is forbidden to tell men how to worship not only because of the freedom of the person, but also because of the nature of government itself. This is a question in which government simply has no competence. In Murray's words:

The public powers are not competent to judge whether conscience be erroneous or not. The good faith or bad faith, the truth or falsity of conscience are not matters for adjudication by the civil magistrate, upon whom public care of religion devolves.[78]

The question of the state's *incompetence* in determining religious truth is important in our consideration of SCO—at least to the extent that its proponents appeal to Vatican II.[79] If the Council had rested its case for religious liberty exclusively on the dignity and freedom of the person, its argument could be applied convincingly to SCO. A man is just as free and dignified when he decides he will not fight in a particular war as he is when he decides he will not worship in a particular church. Perhaps it is because the "Declaration" did not rest its argument on the nature of man *alone* that the proponents of SCO have, for the most part, ignored this document in their appeals to Vatican II.[80]

When human dignity is combined with the principle of the state's incompetence in religious affairs, we have solid grounds for affirming religious liberty and denying selective objection. The key to the argument is, of course, that the state is incompetent in the first area but not in the second. The

[77] Murray, "The Problem of Religious Freedom," pp. 514-15.
[78] *Ibid.*, p. 516.
[79] Most of the appeals are directed to *The Pastoral Constitution on the Church in the Modern World*. Those who appeal to the authority of the Council to support SCO cannot complain when the same authority is invoked against SCO.
[80] Peter Riga is an exception. See p. 132.

state has no competence to discern religious truth, but it is certainly competent to decide whether the nation should go to war.[81]

Even if we muddy the waters by calling selective objection "religious," the question of competence is still controlling.[82] We need only rearrange our labels to point out that in the judgment of the Council there are certain "religious" questions over which the state has competence (e.g., war and peace) [83] and other "religious" questions over which it has no competence (e.g., the right to worship as one chooses).

Murray's understanding of the Council's caution in appealing to the rights of conscience is clearly indicated in his commentary on the text:

It is worth noting that the Declaration does not base the right to the free exercise of religion on "freedom of conscience." Nowhere does this phrase occur. And the Declaration nowhere lends its authority to the theory for which the phrase frequently stands, namely, that I have the right to do what my conscience tells me to do, simply because my conscience tells me to do it. This is a perilous theory. Its particular peril is subjectivism—the notion that, in the end, it is my conscience, and not the objective truth, which determines what is right or wrong, true or false.[84]

It is because the state is competent to decide when a nation should go to war that the case for SCO is always in danger of slipping into the subjectivism Murray rightly deplores. Its incompetence, on the other hand, to discern religious truth enabled Murray to support religious liberty *on the objective grounds of the nature of limited government*.[85]

---

[81] *Vatican II*, p. 292. "Certainly, war has not been rooted out of human affairs. As long as the danger of war remains and there is no competent and sufficiently powerful authority at the international level, governments cannot be denied the right to legitimate defense once every means of peaceful settlement has been exhausted. Therefore, government authorities and others who share public responsibility have the duty to protect the welfare of the people entrusted to their care and to conduct such grave matters soberly."

[82] We raise the broader meaning of religion to make the argument relevant to the American scene. The Council itself, however, clearly understands religion in its confined and traditional sense: "For, of its very nature, the exercise of religion consists before all else in those internal voluntary, and free acts whereby man sets the course of his life directly toward God." "Declaration of Religious Freedom," *Vatican II*, p. 681.

[83] The fact that the state is competent to decide when to go to war does not mean it is always right. A citizen may still be morally obliged to refuse to serve, but this is a question of civil disobedience, not SCO.

[84] *Ibid.*, p. 679, note 5. As a member of the President's Advisory Commission on Selective Service (The Marshall Commission), Murray backed the minority report that supported SCO. It is interesting to note that in his only published statement on SCO he makes no reference to *Vatican II*. This would seem to suggest that if one is going to argue for SCO, one would do well to look elsewhere than in *Vatican II*.

[85] The "objective grounds," therefore, are political not religious. The substance of the religious claim may be blatantly subjective, but the citizen's right to worship in accordance with that belief rests on the objective grounds that the state, as such, is unable to judge between truth and error in religious matters. The state may quite

130

We have already observed that "The Declaration on Religious Freedom" had to accommodate both the "French" and the "American" points of view. For this reason, its line of argument is not always clear since it must smile in two directions. Nevertheless, the two principles of human dignity and limited government survived the five revisions the text underwent.

The opening paragraph of the "Declaration" speaks of a growing "sense of the dignity of the human person" and of contemporary demands "that constitutional limits should be set to the powers of government, in order that there may be no encroachment on the rightful freedom of the person and of association." [86] Thus, the first paragraph keynotes the theme of human dignity and limited government as the basis of religious liberty. This theme is developed throughout the document. After discussing those "internal, voluntary, and free acts whereby man sets the course of his life directly toward God," the Council insists that "no merely human power can either command or prohibit acts of this kind." [87] Indeed, the "Declaration" maintains that questions of religious worship "transcend by their very nature

---

properly regulate forms of religious worship as the needs of public order will dictate, but this does not alter the principle of the state's incompetence in religious affairs. For example, public authority may require snake handlers to meet extremely stringent demands on the times and places of worship. Such regulations would not mean that the state seriously doubts whether snake handling is the way God intends man to worship. It would simply mean that the state recognizes the dangers some snakes present to the life and health of its citizens. It is the same principle that permits the state to demand that more conventional religious groups obey local fire prevention ordinances. This principle, like all principles, can be abused. "Public order" may simply be the camel's nose that enables the government to harass unpopular religious minorities. But when this happens, it is the government, not the principle of state incompetence in discerning religious truth, that is discredited.

SCO, unlike the case for religious liberty, has no such objective principle to which it can appeal. The fact that the selective objector must rely on the subjective norm of his own conscience does not, of course, mean that he is always wrong. The government may really be waging an immoral war. The Germans who resisted Hitler's war efforts relied on the subjective norm of conscience; they did not say the *Reich* was morally incompetent to decide whether or not Germany should go to war. They simply concluded that their government had made an immoral decision and refused to have anything to do with it. Had Hitler required every German citizen to take an oath denying that Jesus was a Jew, conscientious men would have resisted not on the grounds that the policy represented a decision that was morally wrong but, rather, because the policy represented a decision in an area that did not concern the government at all.

The "Declaration" does not call into question the traditional teaching that in the final analysis the *individual* must follow his conscience. Its focus, however, is public policy, not personal decisions. It insists upon a *public policy* that recognizes freedom of conscience in matters of religious worship. It does not call for a public policy that would recognize every claim of conscience. And wisely so, for, unfortunately, there are many people— e.g., racists of all creeds and colors—who go about their ugly business with a sincere but perverted conscience.

[86] *Vatican II*, p. 675.
[87] *Ibid.*, p. 681.

the order of terrestrial and temporal affairs." [88] A moment's reflection on the tone and substance of these statements reveals how wide of the mark are those who appeal to the "Declaration" to support SCO. The "Declaration" is concerned with government policy that inhibits freedom of worship. It does not uphold this freedom simply because it involves a question of conscience, but, rather, because it involves a question of conscience in an area in which the state is incompetent.

In light of the overall purpose of the document (freedom of religious worship) and its emphasis upon the incompetence of the state in religious affairs, it seems fair to conclude that proponents of SCO err when they summarize the intent of the "Declaration" in the following manner:

Thus, the Church enjoins upon all who exercise government over men to recognize and protect the sacred right of all men to weigh moral values with an upright conscience, and not to be hindered in leading their lives in accordance with their conscience.[89]

The Council does not enjoin "upon all who exercise government over men" a general obligation to see to it that citizens are not "hindered in leading their lives in accordance with their conscience." If it did, it would have endorsed not only the principle of selective objection, but the right of every extremist from the Black Panthers to the KKK to "follow his conscience" untrammelled by the power of the state. The Council never said, "My conscience right or wrong, my conscience." Its *Declaration on Religious Freedom* was far more responsible. It never failed to balance its affirmations of human freedom with a concern for public order.[90] More importantly, it restricted its injunction upon "all who exercise government over men" to those issues in which government has no competence. For this reason, the document cannot be cited in support of SCO.

Conclusion

The purpose of this chapter has been to "demythologize" the case for SCO. Regardless of the merits of the Quakers' argument for the statutory recognition of total objection, the prudent legislator knows the Quaker community would be "up in arms" if such a provision were ever repealed. Even those most insensitive to the rights of conscience would hesitate to repeal this provision. Surely it is no small part of political wisdom to avoid alienating one's fellow citizens unnecessarily.

[88] *Ibid.*

[89] Deposition of Peter J. Riga in *McFadden,* p. 9.

[90] See Section 2, p. 679, and p. 689; Section 3, p. 681; Section 4, p. 682; and Section 8, p. 687 of the "Declaration of Religious Freedom," in *Vatican II.*

Can Catholics do for SCO what the Quakers have done for total objection? To answer this question we had to look at Catholic doctrine to see how deeply the Catholic Church is committed to SCO. The fact that the American bishops have supported it suggests that there is more than marginal interest in this question within the Catholic community.

Our sources were the twin pillars of the "Catholic Case for SCO"— the just war doctrine and *Vatican II*. In both cases we have criticized the "selective perception" of the proponents of SCO. If we look at the just war doctrine as a whole and go beyond a few ambiguous texts of *Vatican II,* it seems clear that Catholics cannot, in the light of their tradition, maintain that the absence of SCO discriminates against them.

Thus, we are now in a position to "secularize" the argument and investigate the merits of SCO in the more familiar terms of political discourse.

VII
Theoretical Foundations of SCO

The public debate over SCO raises fundamental questions of political theory. Since the debate takes place in journals of opinion, it is not surprising that these theoretical questions seldom receive more than passing attention. The participants in the debate are advocates of a specific policy recommendation. Their failure to address basic theoretical considerations is understandable. In our attempt to elevate the level of public debate, however, we cannot gloss over these fundamental issues. The arguments for SCO must be analyzed in terms of basic philosophical considerations before we can determine the theoretical soundness of selective objection as public policy. The purpose of this chapter, therefore, is to make *explicit* the underlying principles of the case for SCO.

The first two sections of this chapter will examine these theoretical foundations. The third section will present a brief statement of my response to the theoretical issues raised in the earlier sections. The first section is entitled "Politics and Morality"; it has two subdivisions—"The Dichotomy" and "The Aftermath." The former refers to the dangerous tendency of some proponents of SCO to consider the individual's judgment as "moral," while dismissing the government's decision as "mere politics." In the "Aftermath" I shall examine the consequences of dichotomizing politics and morality.

The second section is called "The Slippery Slope." [1] Here we shall look for a *principle* that would allow selective objection to military service without

[1] The expression is borrowed from Jeff Greenfield, "The Selective C.O.," *The New Republic*, CLIX (July 6, 1968), 15-16.

at the same time committing Congress to support selective objection to other forms of government policy—e.g., taxes, public health regulations, and racial integration. That is, can we have selective objection to military service without putting Congress on a "slippery slope" that would demand recognition of conscientious objection in other areas as well? This section, like the first, has two subsections—"Where Does It Stop?" and "The National Interest." The first subsection looks at the "slippery slope" from the citizens' point of view—what Congress does for the conscience of citizen A it should also do for the conscience of citizen B. The second considers "the slope" from the government's point of view—if SCO to military service cannot be distinguished from other forms of selective objection *in principle,* are there pragmatic considerations of national interest that would warrant Congressional approval of SCO to military service while ignoring other forms of selective objection?

Politics and Morality

THE DICHOTOMY. A fundamental assumption in the case for SCO is the moral nature of political life. A dichotomy of morals and politics would be fatal to SCO, for the state could then turn a deaf ear to pleas for accommodating conscientious scruples on the grounds that moral issues were not its proper concern. Before the argument for SCO can be taken seriously one must first acknowledge the connection between morals and politics. That is, some moral questions concern business practices, others deal with sexual behavior, while still others deal with life in the *polis.* Not all political questions are of equal moral significance. Some are quite marginal—e.g., if the Federal Power Commission permits gas and electric companies to raise their rates, its decision would have only the slightest impact on fundamental human values. As long as there was no bribery or any other irregularity in the decision, it would have minimal moral significance. In questions of war and peace, however, the impact on human values is immediate and obvious.

It is not surprising that *opponents* of SCO should flirt with a dichotomy of morals and politics in an effort to simplify their task. Thus, the *Report of the National Advisory Commission on Selective Service* maintained "so-called selective pacifism is essentially a political question of support or non-support of a war and cannot be judged in terms of special moral imperatives." [2] It is surprising, however, to see *proponents* of selective objection indulging the same tendency. The reason for this is that they yield to the temptation to take a shortcut to SCO by disregarding concerns of public interest. In separating politics and morality they hope to base an argument

[2] *Report of the National Advisory Commission on Selective Service;* Chairman, Burke Marshall (Washington, D.C.: Government Printing Office, 1967), p. 50.

for SCO on "moral" (i.e., individual) grounds alone. Government policy should prevail against objections that are "merely political," but not against those that are "moral." Roger L. Shinn provides a good example of this line of reasoning:

Everybody finds himself as the minority on some public questions, but he conforms. We are asking for the right to reject governmental policy on the grounds not simply of opinion but of conscience.

We think it is possible to make some distinctions between moral and political judgments. If a man says, "I think this war is not the most effective way to serve the national interest," he would not be a conscientious objector. If he says, "I profoundly believe that this war is morally evil," he probably is a conscientious objector.[3]

This simplistic argument belies the considerable political sophistication Shinn has shown elsewhere.[4] Distinguishing political and moral judgments by putting a "national interest" label on one and a "morally evil" label on the other simply will not do. A war that is not in the national interest cannot be moral. This does not mean that "national interest" is the ultimate norm of political morality. A war is not justified simply because it serves the nation's interest. But if it is not in the nation's interest, it cannot be justified. Warfare unrelated to national interests is simply military adventuring. The national interest, therefore, is a *necessary but insufficient* condition for a just war. Its absence renders a war unjust, while its presence does not necessarily justify a war.[5] In Shinn's hypothetical case, the man who refused

[3] Roger L. Shinn, "The Selective Conscientious Objector Again," *Christianity and Crisis,* XXVII (April 3, 1967), 63.

[4] Roger L. Shinn, "How Free Can a Society Be?" *Christianity and Crisis,* XXV (November 1, 1965), 224-25.

[5] One might object that if a nation went to war simply to help another nation—with no self-interest of its own at stake—it would not be acting unjustly. Hence, national interest is not a necessary condition for a just war. In reply, I would suggest that in such an unlikely event we would not have a just war but a "crusade." In a nation state system I do not see how a government can morally require its citizens to give their lives for a cause unrelated to the interest of the nation. One might appeal to the Evangelical principle that praises men who lay down their lives for their neighbor. This principle, however, would seem to apply to individuals, not to governments. It would require an exegetical tour de force to show that the Sermon on the Mount was really a major foreign policy address. Further, the morality of imposing a specifically Christian ethic upon a secular society would seem to be rather dubious; especially when secular men would be required to give their lives. "As He died to make men holy, let us die to make them free"; so sang the soldiers of Lincoln's armies. This theological position could not *in itself* have justified the Civil War—any more than it would justify today a nuclear crusade to "free" Red China. Christian principles undoubtedly helped to make the men of 1861 sensitive to the evils of slavery. But in the absence of serious national interests, the war would not have been justified. This need to consider national interests accounts for the difference between John Brown and Abraham Lincoln. Among those interests were the preservation of the Union and fidelity to the

military service on grounds of national interest has already made a moral judgment.

Shinn recognizes that in distinguishing morals and politics "the difference is not always clear cut." Nevertheless he supports his original distinction by appealing to the fact that "we can tell a hot day from a cold day even if we are not certain about every day." [6] The image is interesting because, at first, it seems to blur his sharp distinction between the political and the moral. A closer look at Shinn's thermometer, however, reveals how serious he is in distinguishing politics and morality. The two come together only when the mercury is near the middle. *Real* politics and *real* morality are as different as hot and cold. This kind of thinking is fatal for SCO.

An article by Peter Riga in *Modern Society* reveals the same tendency to separate morals and politics. Riga's position is particularly interesting because he emphatically denounces this separation as "something absolutely abhorrent to the whole of Christian tradition." [7] However, in his zeal to uphold the autonomy of the individual's conscience he seems to succumb to the tendency he had wisely deplored. Consider the following paragraph:

The hoary argument that the government knows more than the citizen and that somehow he must "trust" the public authority is as obscene as it is historically unfounded. Morally, no one can make decisions for a free man if he is to remain truly free. In the momentous decision that a man must make in regard to killing, this responsibility revolves directly upon him as a free agent, not on a Church or government.[8]

The second sentence in this statement invites several interpretations. It may mean that no man should surrender his sense of moral responsibility in the name of civic virtue. If this is all that is meant, the statement can pass unchallenged. A different interpretation, however, is quite possible. If it is true that "morally no one can make decisions for a free man if he is to remain truly free," does this not imply that moral activity takes place only when the *individual* decides whether or not he will obey? In other

---

principles upon which the nation was founded. To be sure, there were economic considerations as well, but it would be a mistake to consider national interests exclusively in terms of markets and natural resources. Fidelity to the character of the regime is a national interest of the highest order. For further discussion of the meaning of "national interest," see Vol. XLVI of *The American Political Science Review* (1952), viz., Robert Tucker, "Professor Morgenthau's Theory of Political Realism"; Thomas Cook and Malcolm Moos, "The Realism of Idealism"; and Hans J. Morgenthau, "The National Interest of the U.S." See also Wolf's article, pp. 107-9. For a cogent criticism of Shinn's position, see Quentin Quade, "Selective Conscientious Objection and Political Obligation," in James Finn (ed.), *A Conflict of Loyalties: The Case for Selective Conscientious Objection,* pp. 197-98.

[6] Shinn, "The Selective Conscientious Objector Again," p. 63.

[7] Riga, "Selective Conscientious Objection," p. 115.

[8] *Ibid.,* p. 111.

words, the state's action is without moral significance. Its decisions are amoral because "morally no one can make decisions. . . ." For Riga, the man who takes the decisions of government as normative has lost his freedom. Moral values come into play only in the *citizen's response* to government policy. There is no presumption that the government's policy is moral until proved otherwise.

The inadequacy of this sort of reasoning becomes apparent when we consider concrete examples. Let us take the case of a citizen who feels it would be just if the government demanded twenty-five percent of his taxable income. Surely, he has no moral obligation to surrender this sum until the government enacts a law taxing him at that rate. Or, if the government should take only twenty percent of his taxable income, he would have no moral obligation to give twenty-five percent. We cannot say that such a citizen has lost his freedom because he allowed his government to make a moral decision for him.

Again, consider the case of a soldier participating in a war that is clearly just—e.g., a British soldier in World War II. Let us assume this soldier is Jewish and harbors deep resentment against the Hitler regime. Let us further assume he kills a German soldier at Dunkirk and receives a medal for bravery. Had the same man been visiting Berlin in 1938 and killed a storm trooper, he would be a murderer. The reason one act of killing is virtue and the other vice is because an act of government has intervened to legitimate activity that would otherwise be morally wrong. In a word, the soldier has let someone else make a moral decision for him.

In the light of this analysis, it would seem that Riga's statement must be qualified. If we are to avoid a dichotomy of politics and morality—which Riga wisely deplores—we must acknowledge that there are times when a man must look to his government to determine right and wrong. This does not mean that the government's decisions will always be morally sound. There may be times when a man will have to refuse compliance. This is the meaning of the principle that gives the government only a *"presumption* of justice." As we saw in the previous chapter, a presumption is not a blind commitment to do the government's bidding. It means that the citizen must obey unless he is *certain* that the government's policy is immoral. In this way the moral character of public policy is preserved without destroying the individual's sense of responsibility. In the examples we have just considered the citizen makes the moral judgment that his government has the right to prescribe specific conduct for him in the areas of taxation and warfare. When the government passes *this* tax law or declares *that* particular war, he must obey unless he is certain that the government has acted unjustly. If, as Riga says, this kind of trust in one's government is "obscene," then we cannot avoid the conclusion that governmental activity

138

is of itself amoral—i.e., the mere fact a government has adopted a policy says nothing about the morality of that policy—it enjoys no presumption of justice. If this is the case, then the moral problem focuses on the individual alone. The political is what governments do; the moral is what citizens do.[9]

Gordon Zahn suggests a separation of politics and morals when, in supporting SCO, he writes: "A moral issue is not one that is susceptible to 'majority rule' but, rather, must be decided by each person himself and alone." [10]

This statement could pass without comment if Zahn were writing about total pacifists. Obviously, no human law can undo an *absolute* moral commitment. A man who thinks adultery, warfare, or card-playing is always wrong for all men at all times will not change his mind simply because his government has "legalized" the offensive behavior. But Zahn writes in support of selective objection where by definition the objection is not absolute. In this context one cannot say as readily that a moral issue is not "susceptible" to majority rule without implying that positive law carries no moral authority. This does not mean the government is always right or that the citizen can never dissent from "majority rule" or public policy. It does mean that if the state is the agent of a moral community, its decisions cannot be void of moral significance. Zahn certainly suggests an amoral view of the state when he insists that "a moral issue must be decided by each person himself and alone." As the previous chapter has shown, this same amoral view of politics prompts Zahn to withhold from the state "the presumption of justice" traditionally associated with the just war theory.[11]

The tendency of proponents of SCO to separate politics and morality is difficult to explain since the effectiveness of their position requires a state sensitive to moral values. Perhaps their attention is fixed so rigidly on the alleged injustices of the Vietnam war that they have lost sight of the broader question of the nature of authority. There is no need here to defend the proposition that political authority is not mere coercion. It will suffice to point out that legal positivism is fatal to SCO. If politics is not included within the broader concept of morality, the state in the name of politics can ignore moral arguments.

[9] For a related discussion see Ramsey, *The Just War*, pp. 274-75, esp. notes 15 and 16.

[10] Gordon Zahn, "An Explosive Principle," *Worldview*, X (March, 1967), 5.

[11] For other examples of the tendency of SCO proponents to separate morals and politics, see Congressman Edward I. Koch's letter to President Nixon, printed in *Congressional Record*, February 17, 1969, H.R. 897, and Howard Zinn, *Disobedience and Democracy: Nine Fallacies on Law and Order* (New York: Random House, 1968), pp. 8-15. In the pages I have cited, Zinn develops his basic jurisprudence which differs radically from mine. His explicit treatment of SCO (pp. 96-99) follows quite clearly from his jurisprudence.

A more fundamental objection to the politics-morality approach to SCO, however, is that even if the moral character of politics is acknowledged, the case for selective objection is still in trouble. If the state is a moral agent, why should the individual's moral claim enjoy a priority over the moral claim of the state? A man may well argue that his personal integrity is of greater moral value to him than any consideration of public order. This, however, at the very most would justify violating the offending statute. It would not make a claim upon the state to abdicate its moral character by yielding to the "higher morality" of the individual's conscience. But this is precisely what SCO demands, for not only does it justify disobedience, but it requires *that the state support the citizen in his disobedience.* In the question of war and peace, the state arrives at its decision on moral grounds. The fact that the decision is political does not mean it is not moral. It merely tells us what *kind* of *morality* is involved—viz., not business morality or sexual morality, but political morality, the morality concerned with promoting the common good of the community. Under SCO the government would allow the citizen to make the same decision the government itself has just made on behalf of all the people. If a government cannot be permitted to make an effective decision binding all citizens in a matter as crucial as war or peace, we may well ask why we should have governments at all. Since the heart of the SCO argument is to allow the citizen to undo what the government has already done for him, one might turn the argument on its head and demand the right to organize paramilitary vigilantes to combat a hostile nation when one's government has chosen peace instead of war. For example, had the Lincoln administration chosen not to react to the capture of Fort Sumter, would not the logic of SCO have justified individual citizens taking up arms on their own to suppress a rebellion which they might quite reasonably oppose on grounds of conscience? As we saw in the previous chapter, the reason the just war theory demands a declaration of war is precisely to avoid such military adventuring.

THE AFTERMATH. A hidden assumption behind the tendency to separate politics and morality is a univocal concept of morality. The only real moral situation is that of the individual determining the sort of man he will be. This tendency ignores or denies that the decisions of government have moral value simply because they are governmental decisions. It becomes manifest in "moral" arguments for SCO in which considerations of public order are gently laid to rest. In this section we shall consider three such arguments. The first is called "the leap of faith," because it is an argument frequently found in theological circles—i.e., the "leap" from the conscience of the person to public policy without concern for the public interest. The second is the very common attempt to assimilate the position

140

of the selective objector to that of the pacifist. The third argument would deduce SCO from the "logic of democracy."

"THE LEAP OF FAITH." The leap of faith describes a type of argument to which some clergymen and theologians are especially prone. The essence of the argument is to affirm what few would deny—the duty to follow one's conscience—and, then, to deduce public policy from this affirmation. Unlike the "Declaration on Religious Freedom," the leap of faith fails to take into consideration the "just requirements of public order" as one of the considerations that must go into any moral judgment. Perhaps it is their role as counselors and confessors that prompts the clergy to see public policy in terms of its moral impact on the conscience of the individual. Whatever the reason for this tendency may be, the religious press offers abundant examples of its occurrence.

An editorial in *America,* for example, opened with the statement that "every man is obliged to follow his conscience." [12] After noting the absence of SCO, the writer proceeded *deductively* to the conclusion that we must have "new legislation that will respect the selective objector's freedom of conscience." [13] The editorial was innocent of even the slightest concern that SCO might inhibit the government's effectiveness in executing a decision to go to war and that such a decision might be morally correct.

In a letter to the editors of *The Christian Century,* the Rev. James Fleck argues for SCO as an obvious corollary of the just war doctrine. He maintains "there is an immediate need to implement in statutory law this right which God gave man through nature and divine revelation." [14] This sort of reasoning is a good example of what Quentin Quade has criticized as the presumption "that the individual's need to follow his conscience is equivalent to a directive to society to enact a selective conscientious objection provision." [15]

The leap of faith appeared in its purest form in the following statement of the World Council of Churches:

Protection of conscience demands that the churches should give spiritual care and support not only to those serving in the armed forces, but also to those who, especially in the light of the nature of modern warfare, object to participation in particular wars they feel bound in conscience to oppose, or who find themselves

[12] "The Selective Conscientious Objector," p. 73.
[13] *Ibid.*
[14] *The Christian Century,* LXXXIII (March 30, 1966), 404.
[15] Quade, pp. 201-2. For further examples of the tendency to deduce the desirability of SCO from the just war doctrine, see "Selective Objectors and the Court," *America,* CXXIII (July 11, 1970), 6. See also Robert McAfee Brown's "Vietnam: Crisis of Conscience," in Martin E. Marty and Dean G. Peerman (eds.), *New Theology No. 6.* (New York: Macmillan, 1969).

unable to bear arms or to enter the military service of their nation for reasons of conscience. Such support should include pressure to have the law changed where required.[16]

Again, the focus of the statement is on the individual alone. There is concern for the spiritual welfare of military personnel as well as for the integrity of selective objectors. But the concern is exclusively pastoral. The implications for the various nations that might attempt to follow the Council's recommendations are ignored. For example, the United States government could not establish its corps of military chaplains *simply* because military personnel need religious guidance. Congress would first have to be sure the military chaplaincy did not violate the establishment clause of the first amendment. Such a concern is part of the American public interest and cannot be disregarded simply because of the spiritual needs of the men in uniform. Likewise, SCO should not be enacted simply because its absence creates problems of conscience for certain young men. As Harry R. Davis has observed, "Even in Christian perspective, individual moral rights are not automatically or fully translatable into legal rights." [17] The leap of faith ignores the wisdom of Davis' comment.

"CO AND SCO." The relation of the pacifist to the selective objector presents serious difficulties for those who approach moral questions from the viewpoint of the individual alone. One need not dichotomize politics and morality to encounter this problem. One need only conceive of public morality in terms of the individual's *response* to public policy rather than in terms of the policy itself. With such an attitude the difference between selective objection and total objection grows dim. Both involve personal moral decisions against war, but one is respected and the other rejected. Can this be right?

Here I wish to scrutinize three attempts to assimilate the position of the selective objector to that of the total objector. The first of these is the following statement of Arnold Kaufman:

Assume that one arrives, by some route or other, at the conviction that human life is specially sacred. Belief in the sacredness of life would quite naturally be expressed as commitment to the right to life. Assume also that this right is accorded high priority in the moral scheme of things. Finally, assume that conscientious thought and conduct are among the central values of civilized society. I have described my own deep convictions. But they are important here only

[16] *New York Times,* July 17, 1968, p. 1.

[17] Harry R. Davis, "Christian Neglect of Political Values," *The Christian Century,* LXXXVI (November 26, 1969), 1511.

because they are premises that are widely accepted, and on the basis of which legal exemption of absolute pacifists can plausibly be defended. Given these assumptions, the strongest kind of case against forcing anyone to kill against his will, can be made. If these assumptions are effectively challenged, the case for legal recognition of absolute pacifists cannot help but be weakened. If they are sustained, the case for extending recognition to selective conscientious objectors cannot help but be strengthened. I can think of no plausible defense of one that does not support the other; no plausible attack on one that does not throw doubt on the other.[18]

The strength of Kaufman's argument rests on its preoccupation with the individual. What the government does for one conscience, it must do for every conscience. If, however, we compare selective and total objectors from the government's point of view, the situation is quite different. The total objector presents no embarrassment to the government. He bases his judgment on principles that transcend the political process. He does not single out his own government as morally delinquent. He would refuse to support any government that rallies its citizens to arms. The selective objector, however, presents a different problem. He challenges *his own government* in an area in which it professes some competence. Governments do well when they leave to exegetes and theologians the meaning of the Decalogue's prohibition on killing, but they cannot abdicate their responsibility for the pursuit of justice and for resort to military force.

Furthermore, there is a dynamism in selective objection that any government would find distressing. If there is selective objection to participation in war, why can there not be other forms of selective objection—a point we shall consider in detail later. The position of the total objector is static. It is based on a divine command or (in recent times) on reverence for life. Such a position is far less likely to spill over into other areas, for, aside from warfare, there are few instances in which a government would command a citizen to take the life of another man.

Finally, there is the element of predictability. Before the guns sound, the government knows how many pacifists it must accommodate and can plan accordingly. Under SCO long-range military planning would be seriously impaired. The news of an atrocity perpetrated by a handful of soldiers could cause a wave of moral revulsion against an otherwise just war. This could lead to widespread claims for SCO status with disastrous foreign policy consequences.

None of these considerations, of course, is sufficient to defeat the case for SCO. But they do suffice to show the inadequacy of Kaufman's contention

[18] Arnold S. Kaufman, "The Selective Service System: Actualities and Alternatives," in James Finn (ed.), *A Conflict of Loyalties: The Case for Selective Conscientious Objection*, pp. 224-25.

that in comparing total and selective objection there is "no plausible defense of one that does not support the other." [19]

John M. Swomley, writing in *The Christian Century*, assimilates selective and total objection by arguing that "in principle, a man's conscience should be respected for objecting to a specific act quite as much as for objecting to a whole range of specific acts." [20] The description of the CO as one who objects "to a whole range of specific acts" misrepresents the position of the total objector. He does not object to a series of specific acts, but to war as such. Here is a case where the whole does not equal the sum of the parts. A *different type of judgment* is involved. Those who object to specific wars do what governments do. They go through the same process of weighing pro's and con's, the good that will be accomplished and the evil that will be endured. The total objector operates on a different level. He does not soil his hands with the messy empirical data involved in balancing advantages and disadvantages. No matter what might be accomplished, he will have none of it. The pacifist does not object to the total number of wars that have ever been or will be fought. He objects to war as such.

Carl Cohen, writing in *The Nation*, offers a third approach to the relation between total and selective objection. He describes the present state of the law as allowing conscientious objection to *means* (killing) but disallowing objection to ends (the purpose for which the war is fought). He complains that the conscientious objector

is not permitted effectively to ask, "Is this means justified by this end?" He is permitted to say, "I *never* kill," and (if he says that truly) he will be excused. But let him once admit that under certain circumstances he will kill, it must then be presumed that he is not able to judge where or when it is appropriate for him to do so in matters of national concern. [21]

In reply to Cohen one might question the accuracy of his attempt to distinguish CO and SCO on the basis of objection to means and ends respectively. Selective objection could be based on means alone. A selective objector might think the American goals in Vietnam—whatever they may be—are entirely praiseworthy, but he could still object in conscience to the war because of certain means he believes are being used in prosecuting those goals—e.g., the alleged torturing of prisoners of war, violations of civilian immunity, the My Lai incident, etc. Or he might believe that the

[19] For further discussion of the difference between CO and SCO, see Jeff Greenfield, "The Selective C.O.," *The New Republic*, CLIX (July 6, 1968), 15-16.

[20] John M. Swomley, "The Limited Objectors," *The Christian Century*, LXXXII (December 15, 1965), 1542.

[21] Carl Cohen, "The Case for Selective Pacifism," *The Nation*, CCXLVII (July 8, 1968), 12.

goals are justifiable but that the scale of violence is disproportionate to whatever value the goals might represent.

For our purposes, however, Cohen's most interesting point comes in his last sentence—"But let him once admit that under certain circumstances he will kill, it must then be presumed that he is not able to judge where or when it is appropriate for him to do so in matters of national concern."

This point is well taken. Cohen is upset with this sort of reasoning, but we might suggest that it is a mark of a civilized community that it does *not* allow the individual to decide when and where it is appropriate for him to kill other human beings in matters of national concern. If this liberty were given to the individual, the late Congressman Rivers might have deployed nuclear weapons against North Korea for the seizure of the *Pueblo*. We can be reasonably sure that Cohen would not have applauded this sort of freedom for that particular individual. Political communities have wisely taken to themselves as a whole the right to decide when and where massive acts of violence will take place. The selective objector does not differ from the total objector because one judges ends and the other means. The difference is that the selective objector is one of us. He participates in the political process and judges issues of war and peace as a member of political society. If he disagrees with the final results of that process, the community will not let him have his way any more than it will let those have their way who would "send in the Marines" whenever a developing nation expropriates an American oil company. If wars are too important to be left to the generals, they are surely too important to be left to the consciences of individuals.

The total objector is, in the area of war and peace, a political dropout. His dissent is politically irrelevant, though he may be a salutary witness in a society too eager to use violence to support its interests. The crux of his case rests on principles that transcend space and time. The government is incompetent in such questions. It wisely avoids punishing such a man for, unlike the SCO, he presents no threat to the regime's understanding of its own integrity.

"THE LOGIC OF DEMOCRACY." The nature of democratic government provides the third opportunity to support SCO on the basis of an individualistic understanding of morality. Two arguments are involved: (1) Personal freedom is an important value in a democratic society. SCO broadens the scope of personal freedom and therefore expands democratic values. (2) Democracy requires the consent of the governed. SCO would excuse a man from fighting in a war to which he did not "consent" and therefore would reinforce that democratic value.[22]

[22] For examples of this sort of reasoning, see the articles by Riga and Zahn cited

The first argument presupposes that whatever increases personal freedom in a democracy is good because of the need for freedom in a democratic society. This supposition is challenged in Aristotle's *Politics*.

Aristotle recognized that "the underlying idea of the democratic type of constitution is liberty," [23] but he was quite emphatic in denying the principle behind "the logic of democracy"—i.e., that whatever furthers liberty is good for democracy. In his treatment on how to preserve a regime, he advises the statesman to check the dominant tendency in a regime lest it be destroyed by an excess of its own principle. Thus he maintains that "many of the measures which are reckoned democratic really undermine democracies; many which are reckoned oligarchical actually undermine oligarchies." [24] For this reason he advises caution in moving a regime further in the direction to which it naturally tends. Those who would preserve an oligarchic regime must not ignore the interests of the poor. Likewise, the partisans of a democracy must show concern for the wealthy. Finally, in educating a citizen for participation in public life one should not encourage "actions in which the partisans of oligarchy, or the adherents of democracy, delight." [25] Rather the emphasis should be on "actions by which an oligarchy, or a democracy, will be enabled to survive." [26]

Aristotle's observations on regime maintenance do not undermine the case for SCO. If it is true that liberty is the underlying principle of a democracy, SCO might be a sound way of reinforcing this principle. It *might* be, but it doesn't have to be. Proponents of SCO err when they argue *deductively* from the nature of democracy to the wisdom of SCO. A democratic regime is not committed *in principle* to SCO any more than it is committed to any other *specific* policy that expands the citizens' freedom. It is committed in principle to as many freedom-expanding policies as are necessary to preserve its democratic character. Whether SCO should be among these policies is a question that can be solved only by a prudential judgment and not by proceeding deductively from the nature of democracy. A prudent democratic government might reject SCO to check the dominant tendency of the regime. Conversely, an enlightened authoritarian government might approve SCO as a prudent way of checking *its* dominant tendency.

The second argument for SCO based on "the logic of democracy" touches

---

above. See also Everett Gendler, "As Freedom Is a Fantasy," *Worldview*, X (February, 1967), 7, and Ellery Haskell, "Fortas and Selective Objection," *Christianity and Crisis*, XXVII (October 30, 1968), 1373. Obviously there is more to democracy than consent of the governed. For example, see Yves Simon, *The Philosophy of Democratic Government* (Chicago: University of Chicago Press, 1951). I have emphasized consent because this is the argument made by the proponents of SCO—it is undemocratic to make men fight in a war to which they have not consented.

[23] Aristotle, *Politics* VI. ii.   [24] *Ibid.*, V. ix.
[25] *Ibid.*   [26] *Ibid.*

the meaning of consent of the governed. The argument presumes that whatever expands the consent of the governed contributes to the development of democratic values. In examining the presumption two considerations are involved: (1) What is the *object* of the consent of the governed? (2) How many of the governed must consent?

"Consent of the governed" ordinarily means that a legitimate *government* is one that is based on the consent of the governed. It does not mean that every *policy* of that government should reflect the consent of the governed. The existence of representative institutions suggests that the governed consent to let certain *men* make authoritative decisions for them. Once elected, these men are expected to pursue the public interest to the best of their ability. While they should keep in touch with their constituents, they are not expected to "re-present" automatically the majority sentiments of their district. Thus the immediate object of the consent of the governed is government, not policy. If the government's policies are unsatisfactory, the governing personnel can be changed. Thus an argument for SCO based on consent of the governed misses the mark. It implies that this principle requires the governed to consent to every policy decision of the government. If this were true, representative institutions would be meaningless.

The second consideration is how many of the governed must consent. In a regime based on the equality of the citizens, fifty percent plus one would seem to be the most reasonable norm—at least as far as formal elections are concerned. Although, as we have just seen, the consent of the governed is not required for every policy decision, no government can long ignore popular sentiment with impunity. This does not mean a government should abandon a given course if at any time it fails to rally a majority to its side. It does mean it cannot habitually pursue policies that seriously alienate a significant number of the people. This is especially true when a nation goes to war for then a great deal of cooperation and sacrifice will be necessary to achieve the military objectives. A wise government, therefore, ordinarily will not risk war unless it is assured of massive support. Some might choose to call this support "consent of the governed," thereby expanding the phrase to include policy (as well as government) as the object of consent. Even if this more generous interpretation is accepted, the case for SCO is not thereby strengthened. To the extent that the case for SCO rests on the integrity of the individual conscience, the argument based on consent of the governed is irrelevant. The proponents of SCO are not concerned with the number of selective objectors to a particular war. They are outraged at the prospect of even one man's conscience being compromised in a question so important as that of participating in an unjust war. The government can be satisfied that it is meeting the criterion of "consent of the governed" as long as (1) it has been duly elected and

147

(2) it enjoys widespread support for its policies. "Consent of the governed" could support SCO only if it is interpreted to mean that *every* citizen must consent to the government's efforts. This would be a bold innovation to the traditional meaning of government by consent of the governed.

The Slippery Slope

In this section we shall examine the response of the proponents of SCO to a common objection—wouldn't the enactment of SCO as public policy put the government on a "slippery slope" leading to demands for the right of selective objection in areas other than military service? In the first subsection, "Where Does It Stop?" we shall investigate the problem from the point of view of the citizen. First, we will show that many proponents of SCO would not be content with the enactment of this policy alone. Then we shall look for a *principle* that might convince a citizen with conscientious objections to the use of his tax dollars (or any other form of conscientious objection) that his position is different *in principle* from that of the selective objector to military service. That is, by enacting SCO to military service, does the government commit itself to other forms of SCO as well? If there is such a principle, the case for SCO would be considerably strengthened. For the government would then be able to give a principled reply in defense of SCO to citizens with more extreme claims of conscience who cry "me too." We touched on this point earlier when we contrasted total and selective conscientious objection.[27] One of the reasons the law can accommodate total objectors is that their position has a *limiting* principle built into it.[28] The writ of government indulgence runs no further than the area of military life because of the nature of the pacifist position. Does SCO to military service enjoy a similar limiting principle, or would the logic of SCO require more exemptions in the name of conscience?

While the presence of such a limiting principle would considerably strengthen the case for SCO, its absence would not necessarily be fatal. If the question is approached from the point of view of government (rather than the citizen), SCO could be rescued from the "slippery slope" on grounds of public interest. This will be the point at issue in the second subsection—"The National Interest." Sound public policy should always be based on reason rather than whim. Nevertheless, it is impossible to avoid some arbitrary decisions in enacting public policy. As a nation we have

---

[27] See pp. 142-45, above.

[28] The limiting principle is, as we saw above, that the total objector does not single out his own government for being morally delinquent. His position transcends the political process. For an excellent treatment of pacifism, see Roland Bainton, *Christian Attitudes Toward War and Peace* (Nashville: Abingdon Press, 1960).

always been committed in principle to the equality of all men. However, there have been times in our history when considerations of public interest made it impossible to put fully into practice this principle to which we were already committed. Even if SCO in principle commits Congress to uphold all claims of conscience against public policy, there might still be sound considerations of national interest that would justify Congress in refusing to apply the principle across the board.[29] Such a prudential judgment, of course, would not satisfy selective objectors to racial integration or to certain taxes, but their complaints, even if quite sound in principle, would not necessarily mean Congress had blundered. Good government does not demand that whenever Congress grants a privilege it must grant any other privilege that would be logically consistent with the initial grant.[30]

In this section, then, we shall consider two questions: (1) Is there a *principled* distinction between SCO to military service and other forms of selective conscientious objection, and (2), in the absence of such a distinction, to what extent could SCO to military service alone be justified on grounds of national interest?

WHERE DOES IT STOP? For the proponents of SCO, taxation is perhaps the area most akin to war and peace. We have it on good authority that taxation without representation violates a basic American principle, but what about taxation for purposes the taxpayer considers immoral? The Marshall Commission saw little difference between conscientious objection to participating in a particular war and paying a particular tax. It feared that approval of SCO would "open the door to a general theory of selective disobedience to law, which could quickly tear down the fabric of government." [31] *Commonweal* ridiculed this fear as a "hoary conservative bugaboo," but the literature supporting SCO suggests that, while the Commission's argument may be hoary and conservative, it certainly is not a "bugaboo." [32] Among the proponents of SCO, a vigorous intramural debate has arisen over the issue of taxation. The editors of *Commonweal* have no difficulty separat-

---

[29] Obviously there are limits to the degree of arbitrariness people would tolerate. Congress could not grant Veterans' Benefits to those who served in Europe in World War II, but not to the veterans of the Pacific Theatre. It might be true that Hitler was a greater threat to the U.S. than were the Japanese, but such a judgment would not justify neglecting those who fought in the Pacific. In a word, good government can be somewhat arbitrary but not too arbitrary. Putting content into this formula is part of political wisdom and statesmanship.

[30] As we saw in Chapter II, however, there are *constitutional* limitations on how far Congress can go in conferring privileges on one group and withholding them from another. Strictly speaking, however, this limitation does not raise a theoretical question; it deals with a provision peculiar to the American regime.

[31] *Report of the National Advisory Commission . . . ,* p. 50.

[32] "Editorial," *Commonweal,* LXXXVI (April 21, 1967), 140.

ing selective objection to war and selective objection to taxes.[33] Gordon Zahn, however, challenges any facile distinctions between these two issues. He grants that President Johnson's surtax did not involve much money for the individual taxpayer, but for those opposing the war on grounds of conscience even this little was too much—"certainly much more than that little pinch of incense on a pagan altar that has to be the parallel governing their decision." Zahn goes on to call for recognition of "conscientious objection to taxation" complete with a system of "alternative payments" by which the taxpayer could be assured that his money would not be spent on programs he considered immoral.[34]

Walter Arnold favors a similar program. He faces the issue of how one can support selective objection to paying taxes for an unjust war without putting public policy on a "slippery slope" that would demand recognition of every claim of conscience. Unfortunately, he resolves the problem by simply asserting that "the line can be clearly drawn" between conscientious objection to taxes for an immoral war and other forms of taxation.[35] He fails to offer any principle that would assure the government that its recognition of selective objection would not create further demands for exemption from civic responsibilities in the name of conscience.

Michael Harrington, also a proponent of SCO, recognizes the danger in extending selective objection into the area of taxation. He fears that "Gordon Zahn's principle of 'conscientious objection to taxation' [could be] put to the most reactionary use."[36] For example, he sees no reason why Zahn's principle would not support those whose consciences do not approve of certain government welfare programs. Harrington singles out the government's attempt to abolish poverty, but even less ambitious programs would be vulnerable to the conscientious scruples of fundamentalists who might sincerely object to most welfare programs. They could offer the following biblical text as the basis of their objection: "For even when we were with you, this we commanded you, that if any would not work, neither should he eat."[37] Nor would there be wanting numerous citizens who would object to any part of their taxes being used for the dissemination of birth-control information and devices, to say nothing of abortions performed in public hospitals.

The principles behind SCO extend into areas other than taxation. Francis

[33] *Ibid.*

[34] Zahn, "An Explosive Principle," p. 5. For details about the "War Tax Resistance," a nationwide campaign to encourage the refusal to pay the surtax, see *The National Catholic Reporter* (February 4, 1970), p. 1.

[35] Walter Arnold, "Selective Objection and the Public Interest," *The Christian Century,* LXXXIV (December 27, 1967), 1220.

[36] Michael Harrington, "Politics, Morality and Selective Dissent," in James Finn (ed.), *A Conflict of Loyalties: The Case of Selective Conscientious Objection,* p. 232.

[37] 2 Thess. 3:10, AV.

Heisler developed this point in his sympathetic treatment of "The New Conscientious Objector"—the title of a recent article in *Liberation*. For Heisler the new breed of CO's are men who feel "the state will become tyrannical both at home and abroad unless its thinking citizens refuse to submit just because submission represents compliance with the law." [38] On the contrary they feel obliged to oppose any law that does not "advance society morally and ethically." [39] To meet the demands of the new CO, Heisler maintains, the government must show that its laws do not work "to the disadvantage of the masses." [40] The new CO's are not impressed with the tradition of majority rule. They prefer to return "to the original idea of the Encyclopedists who wrote the American constitution"—that the constitution and laws of the United States "ought to protect the minority and not the majority, since a majority can take care of itself without any law." [41] If Heisler's view of the new CO enjoys any accuracy at all, the worst fears of the Marshall Commission would seem to be justified. Men who are committed to resist any law that does not, in their opinion, "advance society morally and ethically" will not be satisfied with SCO. This would be mere tokenism as far as their objectives are concerned. In giving this "token," however, the government would be vulnerable to the argument that if it honors the conscientious imperatives of selective pacifists, why should it not do the same for the "neo-Enclyclopedists" described by Heisler.

One need not turn to the pages of *Liberation,* however, for examples of the far-reaching implications of SCO. Consider the case of Joseph Mulligan, a Jesuit seminarian serving a prison sentence for burning draft records in Chicago. [42] Although he enjoys an exemption from military service because of his status as a seminarian, Mulligan is, nevertheless, an ardent supporter of SCO. He was not satisfied with the assurance that he would not be forced to kill other men in a war he considers unjust. He saw a need to give "some kind of moral leadership" and hit upon the plan of returning his draft card to his local board. He was reclassified 1-A and was ready to refuse induction so that he could go to prison with the just war objectors who did not enjoy a seminarian's exemption. [43]

When the Supreme Court declared punitive reclassification unconstitutional in the *Oesterreich* case, it looked as though Mulligan would not go to jail after all. But then the chance to destroy Selective Service records presented

[38] Francis Heisler, "The New Conscientious Objector," *Liberation,* XI (January, 1967), 25.

[39] *Ibid.*   [40] *Ibid.*   [41] *Ibid.*

[42] I have a personal interest in Joseph Mulligan's case. I taught him when he was a boy in high school. As the reader may guess, Mulligan did not learn his present political philosophy in my Cicero classes. Despite our political differences, we have maintained our friendship over the years.

[43] From a mimeographed letter circulated by Mulligan dated Christmas, 1968.

itself. Mulligan looked upon this as an opportunity for a symbolic protest against the war. He participated in this illegal action and is now in prison.

Joseph Mulligan is an intelligent, sensitive, and courageous man. He was not content with cheering on selective objectors from the sidelines. Quite literally, he practiced what he preached and abandoned the safety of his clerical exemption. Men of diverse political persuasions may well admire Mulligan's integrity, but how does *government* deal with such a citizen? He was given an exemption from military service because of his calling, but this was not enough. He felt his calling to moral leadership was not satisfied until he had broken the law, and when the Supreme Court upset his expectations he soon found another law to break. Mulligan's case, of course, is not typical of those supporting SCO. Nevertheless, we cannot help wondering just how many like him there are in the ranks of those supporting selective objection. If SCO became public policy, would they be satisfied or would they make real the fears of the Marshall Commission and look upon SCO as an invitation to unravel the fabric of government in the name of conscience and moral leadership? Could they not argue that in recognizing SCO, the government was already committed *in principle* to the recognition of other forms of selective conscientious objection?

David Kuebrich's approach to SCO suggests a problem similar to that presented by Joseph Mulligan. Like Mulligan, Kuebrich is a very competent and winning person. During the course of his trial it was obvious that Judge Hoffman was eager to avoid sending him to prison. At one point in the trial Hoffman even suggested he would try to get the defendant a CO exemption, but Kuebrich would have none of it.[44]

His position was that he would not accept a CO exemption unless selective objection was recognized in principle. In telling his own story in court he said:

> I think it was during the winter of '67 that I decided that the proper thing for me to do—excuse me, the winter of '66, or '66-'67, with the beliefs I had that I could not and, in fact, never would participate in this war, and that, in fact, I couldn't even continue to participate with the Selective Service System, but I was not willing to sever my relationship at that time and I had a privileged deferment and it seemed like to me a rather bizarre thing to do in a way.
>
> And then things just intensified in my own mind until I finally decided that I no longer wanted a student deferment, because I thought it was participation in an unjust law and so during the summer of '67, I decided that I would no longer participate with the Selective Service.[45]

This statement makes it clear that Kuebrich's conscientious objections go beyond the Vietnam war. He is not concerned with merely avoiding the

---

[44] *U.S. v. Kuebrich, T.R.,* p. 37.   [45] *Ibid.,* pp. 43-44.

moral difficulties he would encounter if he had to kill a man in combat in an unjust war. He will not participate in an unjust *law*. Would Kuebrich refuse to cooperate only with those "unjust" laws that concern "unjust" wars or would he refuse cooperation with any law that did not meet his moral standards?

In an interview at the federal penitentiary in Springfield, Missouri, Kuebrich told me that his objective in life is to build a world of justice and love. His selective objection to the Vietnam war was part of this larger plan. When asked why he did not leave America rather than go to prison, he replied, "America is everywhere. What bugs me here will bug me wherever I go." [46] He feels the United States is the biggest obstacle to this world of justice and love. The United States must be changed if the world is to change. Draft resistance is just one way to bring about this new world. While he is eager to have the war come to an end as quickly a possible, he fears that "the movement" may disband after the war is over. His big hope is that new causes will arise to keep the movement together.

The desire to build a world of justice and love can only be applauded, but, again, Kuebrich's apparent willingness to break the laws of the United States to bring this about presents a serious political problem. To incarcerate a citizen of Kuebrich's talent and ambition is an unpleasant prospect for any regime to contemplate. But would SCO really solve the sort of problem Kuebrich presents or, as we mentioned above, would it merely tempt him to escalate his demands on the system until he went to jail anyway?

Finally, we might note that some of the sources quoted to buttress the case for SCO offer little hope of limiting selective objection to war alone. Thus, in an affidavit in support of SCO, John T. Ellis offers the biblical principle that it is better to obey God than man.[47] Few religious men would deny this, but such an open-ended principle offers no way of confining selective objection to war and peace. The same criticism can be brought against James McFadden's reference to Pope John's *Pacem in Terris* to support SCO. The Encyclical repeated the traditional teaching that no one is obliged to obey a law that violates the moral order.[48] In offering this doctrine as an argument for SCO, McFadden only reinforces the fears of those who

---

[46] From notes taken during an interview with Kuebrich in the federal penitentiary, Springfield, Missouri, December 22, 1968. For an enlightening account of the mentality of "the movement," see Philip Nobile's "The Priest Who Stayed Out in the Cold," *New York Times Magazine* (June 28, 1970), pp. 9 ff.

[47] Deposition of John T. Ellis in *McFadden*.

[48] The section McFadden cited reads as follows: "Since the right to command is required by the moral order and has its source in God, it follows that, if civil authorities legislate for or allow anything that is contrary to that order and therefore contrary to the will of God, neither the laws made nor the authorizations granted can be binding on the consciences of the citizens, since God has more right to be obeyed than man."

wonder: Where will it stop? The principle Pope John reaffirmed pertains to the conscience of the individual, not to public policy. The principle applies to any law, not just to questions of war and peace. If the principle—that no one is obliged to obey an immoral law—is used to support SCO, there is no reason to restrict SCO to questions of war and peace. McFadden has confused the principle behind civil disobedience (no obligation to obey an immoral law) with the principle underlying SCO (government should endow conscientious dissent with legal status). That proponents of SCO would confuse these principles is most disturbing. If SCO became public policy for the reason given in *Pacem in Terris,* the government would, in principle, be defenseless against conscientious claims for exemption from any law.

Our consideration of the far-reaching implications of SCO, as evidenced in the statements supporting that policy, are relevant to a study of public policy. We are not discussing selective objection in the abstract order; we are discussing it as a possibility for the United States in the final third of the twentieth century. For this reason we had to point out that at least some supporters of SCO are quite willing to jump on the "slippery slope" that could lead to serious instability in our republic. Since, however, our main concern in this chapter is the theoretical case for SCO, we must resume our search for a *principle* that might allow us to distinguish selective objection to war from selective objection to other policies and thereby avoid the "slippery slope."

Richard McCormick offers the following consideration:

There is a rather sharp distinction between a tax law, for example, and draft laws which could involve one in killing. Contributing to a war by my taxes is one thing; killing in a war is another. The difference is that between more or less remote cooperation toward and direct participation in. Just as the common good strongly suggests that the government respect sincere selective conscientious objection to a particular war, so it is the same common good which will strongly suggest to the individual that rights in society (here legal protection of conscience claims) must be limited. A government can respect every conscience claim against any law only at the price of its own disappearance. The community consensus has affirmed in the past the reasonableness of a limitation on rights. I believe it will continue to do so. Hence it will admit the reasonableness of a distinction between more or less remote forms of co-operation in a cause one regards as unjust, and direct participation in this cause. And even if certain citizens fail to honor this distinction, serious thinkers and more sensitive citizens will, precisely because it is necessary for the preservation of that social stability which alone guarantees any freedom.[49]

[49] McCormick, "Notes on Moral Theology," p. 787.

154

McCormick's approach would seem to meet the problem of paying taxes in an unjust war. The distinction between remote cooperation and direct participation is the same distinction that would have eased the conscience of an abolitionist before the Civil War. There is certainly a significant moral difference between owning slaves and being a citizen (and therefore participating) in a society that permitted slavery. Gordon Zahn might be unhappy with McCormick's distinction, but, perhaps, many selective objectors would find it persuasive. If so, McCormick would have rendered signal service to the cause of SCO.

While McCormick's distinction is helpful in solving the problem of distinguishing the payment of unjust war taxes from fighting in an unjust war, he is not entirely successful in keeping SCO off the "slippery slope." His operative principle is that government should not so force a man's conscience that he must *directly participate* in an activity he considers gravely immoral. It may however demand *remote cooperation.* If we apply this distinction to race relations we find it less helpful. The government does not hesitate to demand that parents send their children to integrated schools even though some parents may find such mingling of blacks and whites offensive to their consciences. This would certainly be an example of government compelling direct participation in activity considered gravely immoral. The entire area of compulsory blood transfusions and vaccinations would present a similar problem.

In these questions the participation-cooperation distinction is not enough to keep SCO off the "slippery slope." If direct participation in morally offensive activity is the norm justifying SCO, the same norm could be applied to permit selective objection to compulsory integration, vaccinations, and blood transfusions.

The most common method for distinguishing the objector to warfare from objectors to other policy decisions is that war involves the killing of other human beings and is therefore *qualitatively* different from all other decisions of government. Many decisions of government touch upon questions of life and death. Inadequate safety standards for air and highway travel are examples that come readily to mind. But war is different from these questions because in war we directly intend the death of other men, whereas deaths on the highway are tolerated as a "lesser evil." [50]

The difficulty with the position that would isolate decisions for war from all other decisions of government is that it ignores the subjective element in the argument for SCO. The essence of the case for selective objection is the dignity of the human conscience, not the horrors of war. If it were the latter, proponents of SCO would have to show that a decision for war

[50] The "greater evil" we avoid is the inconvenience we should suffer if we had a 25 m.p.h. speed limit.

is qualitatively different from every other decision a government makes. To mobilize a nation for acts of massive violence may well be—at least morally—the most important decision a government can make.[51] But does its importance *reduce* the government's right to expect compliance and, if so, why? At the heart of the argument for isolating war from all other decisions is the unexamined assumption that such a reduction in expected compliance is entirely warranted. Such an assumption suggests a reluctance to believe that we elect governments to make difficult decisions as well as easy ones.

THE NATIONAL INTEREST. As mentioned above,[52] the absence of a distinction *in principle* between selective objection to particular wars and other forms of selective objection is embarrassing, but not fatal to the case for SCO. Selective conscientious objection to particular wars could be preferred over other forms of selective objection on the grounds that it is the only form of SCO that is in the national interest. Before discussing this possibility, however, let us briefly review the relationship between "national interest" and the previous question—"where does it stop."

In raising the question, "where does it stop," we considered a common objection to SCO. The objection is that once the government inserts a provision for SCO in the Selective Service Act, it has *in principle* recognized the supremacy of the individual's conscience over the need for universal conformity to public policy. How can the government, then, refuse to accommodate the most bizarre claims made in the name of conscience—or "where does it stop?" The objection looks at SCO from the viewpoint of the citizen with a bizarre claim of conscience, who will argue that *his* conscience is as sacred as that of the just warrior. In attempting to answer the objection we looked for a *principle* that would distinguish the just war SCO from the selective objector to policies in other areas—e.g., taxes and racial integration.

The fruit of our search was McCormick's helpful distinction between direct participation and remote cooperation in a policy one considers morally offensive. If this distinction is meaningful, it would enable the government to give a principled reply to those who objected on grounds of conscience to paying taxes for purposes they consider immoral. The government's position, then, would be that it does not recognize the supremacy of claims of conscience in *every case,* but only when the objector would be forced to *participate directly* in the allegedly immoral behavior. This distinction would

---

[51] This need not always be the case. Not all wars are equally severe. The Federal Government's support of the "separate but equal" doctrine for over half a century may have been of greater moral significance than the decision to go to war with Spain.

[52] See pp. 148-49.

handle the tax question, but it would not solve the problem of conscientious objection in such areas as racial integration or compulsory vaccination.

In our consideration of "national interest" we will shift our viewpoint from the citizen's conscience to that of the legislator. The latter might want to resist just war SCO because of its implications for racial integration and other government policies. Nevertheless, the *nation's* need for SCO to military service might be so compelling that he would be willing to support it while arbitrarily refusing to apply the principles behind SCO to other areas of government policy. Thus SCO would be public policy not because the government accepted its underlying principle, but because it was vital to the national interest.

Proponents of SCO have little to say about the national interest. This may be because the expression was so overworked when General Hershey presided over the Selective Service System. At times Hershey seemed to equate the national interest with military policy. Such rhetoric was not likely to win the hearts and minds of a generation vulnerable to compulsory military service in an unpopular war. Nevertheless, the tendency to ignore considerations of national interest is a weak point in the case for SCO, for it leaves SCO open to the objection that it disregards man's social nature and the civic duties based on life in society. By this time we are well aware that most arguments for SCO are structured in terms of the individual *versus* the state. Here we shall investigate the possibilities of making an argument for SCO on the basis of the *harmony* between the demands of the individual's conscience and the public interest. This is an important step in the case for SCO because the conscience of the legislator must be attuned to the public interest. It is the conscience of the legislator, not that of the individual, that is the primary concern in the question of SCO. This is because the debate over SCO *presupposes* the citizen has already decided that he will not participate in a particular war. On the basis of that presupposition, the debate is structured in terms of how the government should handle the dissenter. Since the fate of SCO rests ultimately with the conscience of the legislator—a man whose vocation it is to promote the public interest— the proponents of SCO ignore considerations of public interest only at their peril.[53]

Despite the importance of public interest considerations for SCO, the literature supporting selective objection virtually ignores this entire dimension. The few authors that raise the question do so only in passing. Walter Arnold and Michael Harrington see in SCO a means of reducing the "bitterness and mistrust which this war occasions at home,"[54] while Carl Cohen

[53] For a sound criticism of this tendency, see Davis, "Christian Neglect of Political Values." See also Peter J. Riga, "Selective Conscientious Objection Progress Report," p. 163.
[54] Arnold, p. 66; Harrington, p. 226.

thinks it is "a mark of sophistication and self-restraint" [55] for a government to avoid forcing moral dilemmas upon its citizens. The most common national interest consideration, however, is the argument that SCO would develop the citizen's sense of personal responsibility and thereby strengthen the moral fabric of society. *Commonweal,* for example, supports SCO in the hope that we will raise individual responsibility to the level of other national goals.[56] Roger Shinn maintains that "courageous conscience is not in such oversupply that we can afford to consign it to penitentiaries." [57] And the Lutheran Church in America supports SCO because the ethical sensitivity and human concern of conscientious objectors "can have a salutary effect upon a nation." [58] These national interest considerations are incidental to the thrust of the arguments the authors propose in support of SCO. It would be unfair to attempt an extensive criticism of these points because they were never intended to carry a significant share of the burden of the argument for SCO. But since public interest considerations are so important in the case for SCO, a brief analysis of these positions is in order.

Of the arguments we have cited the pragmatism of Arnold and Harrington is the most persuasive. If Congress could be assured that the approval of selective objection would substantially reduce the level of domestic unrest, this would be a powerful, if not a compelling, reason for making SCO public policy. Such an argument is questionable for three reasons: (1) It assumes that the antiwar protests are motivated by the desire to avoid military participation in an unjust war. This assumption would surely be challenged by many protesters who would consider the war itself and not their possible participation in it as the main focus of their protest. (2) The argument may underestimate the extent of antiwar sentiment in the nation. If SCO were public policy, how do we know we would be able to raise an army of sufficient size to prosecute the war effectively without extending the tours of duty of those already in the service? If serving in the army were a legal duty only for those who consider the Vietnam war just, would there not be a danger that conscience and self-interest would conspire to find ways to take from the war whatever justification it might possess? In other words, the passage of SCO might make conscientious objectors of many men who are now "borderline" cases. The almost universal lack of enthusiasm for the Vietnam war suggests that many young men may well be "borderline" cases who resolve their scruples in favor of the government only because

[55] Cohen, p. 11.

[56] *Commonweal,* LXXXVI (April 21, 1968), 140.

[57] Roger L. Shinn, "The Trial of Captain Dale E. Noyd," *Christianity and Crisis,* LXXXV (April 1, 1968), 66.

[58] *Social Statements of the LCA,* Fourth Biennial Convention, June 19-27, 1968, Atlanta, Georgia.

they consider it their duty to respond to the government's decisions and do what this requires of them. (3) The pragmatic argument is tied so closely to the Vietnam situation, rather than to SCO in general, that we cannot ignore the question of timing. If SCO were passed *now*, how would it be interpreted by the international community in general and "the other side" in particular? Would it be considered as a liberal gesture by an enlightened government or would it be taken as a formal recognition at the highest level of government of that government's misgivings about the justice of its own cause?

We have already mentioned Carl Cohen's opinion that it is a mark of political sophistication for a government to avoid forcing moral dilemmas on its citizens.[59] This argument is not particularly helpful, however, because sometimes the wise course is to do just the opposite. At times government must rely on its coercive power to place some citizens in a moral dilemma. Not a few citizens of this republic have looked upon freedom of contract and other private concerns as "sacred rights." The same is true of racial segregation. It was surely a sign of political wisdom that the government was willing to place such citizens in a dilemma in which they would have to surrender their principles or pay a severe penalty.

Finally, those who see an argument for SCO on the grounds that strengthening the rights of dissenters will strengthen the nation are vulnerable to two main objections.[60] The first is all too obvious. Dissent is not an unalloyed blessing; no nation can be based on dissent alone. The political problem is not to look for new ways in which to encourage dissent. It is rather to determine *to what extent* a government can encourage dissent without threatening its own survival. The second objection is that the argument confuses dissent and exemption from the law. The idea that some dissent strengthens a political society has deep roots in the American tradition. It is at the heart of the first amendment. While dissent, as we have just argued, cannot be the *basis* of a regime, it is extremely useful for correcting abuses. If SCO were merely a question of dissent, prudence might dictate its adoption. But SCO is not mere dissent. It does not ask that a law be passed or changed or repealed. It asks for an exemption from public policy. It is difficult to see with what relevance the American tradition of inviting public dissent can be applied to exempting dissenters from the burdens of citizenship in the name of strengthening our society.

Before a prudent legislator could support SCO on grounds of national interest he should have some idea of how it would work in practice. What good might it achieve; what risks would it run? Specifically, to what extent

[59] See pp. 157-58.
[60] See p. 158.

would it hinder Congress in fulfilling its constitutional mandate to "raise and maintain armies"? Freedom House has called SCO a fantasy[61] and the Marshall Commission said it will tear the fabric of government.[62] A newspaper columnist has, perhaps, come even closer to describing the reaction of many citizens to SCO when he said it was "a helluva way to run a railroad." [63] The British experience in World War II is frequently put forth as a rejoinder to these complaints.[64] It is true that England adopted a form of SCO during World War II and still managed to prosecute its military goals with considerable effectiveness.[65] This example, however, is of little relevance to the American situation today. One cannot isolate the simple fact that there were not enough SCO's to hinder the British war effort from the circumstances of World War II. Hitler was the enemy. The *Luftwaffe* was bombing London and there was no doubt that the stakes were no less than the survival of the United Kingdom. Under these circumstances, it is no wonder that there were few SCO's in *that* war.[66]

Hopefully, the United States will never have to face so obvious a threat to its survival. If we do not, it is likely that our military actions in the future will be limited wars fought in far-off places. Such wars would be far more likely to stimulate selective objection than the total war waged from 1941-1945. Since the patent need to avoid total war is at the heart of our foreign policy, the British experience in World War II is not particularly helpful in addressing the question of how SCO would work in practice.

Some proponents of selective objection maintain that the enactment of SCO would not threaten the national interest because so few citizens would take advantage of the provision. As Carl Cohen puts it: "When a nation goes to war, for whatever cause, the vast majority of its citizens rally to its flag." [67] Cohen does not think the passage of SCO could possibly endanger national security. Those who think it would create security problems "grossly underestimate the passion of our citizens (and that of the citizens of most countries) for their national welfare and their general readiness to respond, particularly in times of crisis, to the requests of their elected leaders." [68]

Cohen's argument requires a great deal of evidence. One wonders whether he has been unduly influenced by the American experience of World War II when the attack on Pearl Harbor united the nation in its determination to fight the Axis powers. He assumes that Vietnam is an exception to the American style of making war. A *prima facie* case against him can be made

[61] See "Freedom House Statement," *New York Times,* November 30, 1966, p. 37.
[62] *Report of the Advisory Commission . . .* , p. 50.
[63] Cited by James Finn, "Selective Service and Selective Objection," *Worldview,* X (February, 1967), 1.
[64] *Commonweal,* LXXXVI, 140. [65] *Ibid.*
[66] See Quade, pp. 204-5. [67] Cohen, p. 13.
[68] *Ibid.*

by simply recalling the substantial Tory sympathy in the Revolutionary War, the Hartford Convention in the War of 1812, and the Draft Riots of the Civil War. The resistance to President Polk's "manifest destiny" in the Mexican War and the sullen resentment of many German-Americans during World War I should not be overlooked. Perhaps there is more than flag-waving chauvinism in the assertion that we are a peace-loving people. Perhaps Staughton Lynd is correct when he sees in the tendency to demonstrate against the Vietnam war the expression of a venerable American tradition.[69] If we are seriously concerned about questions of national security, the American tradition of protesting against war is an argument against, not for, SCO.[70]

The problem of determining sincerity is another practical objection to SCO. How could SCO be administered in such a way that the privilege would be extended only to those who objected on grounds of conscience but not to those whose objection was based on personal convenience or cowardice? Under the present system dreadful injustices are perpetrated by local draft boards that grant or withhold CO status on seemingly arbitrary grounds. The problems of letting "Little Groups of Neighbors" determine sincerity is severe enough; under SCO it would only be worse because the discretion of local boards would be increased.[71]

A final practical consideration in the case for SCO is Quentin Quade's suggestion that a "scientific" survey be taken to determine just what effect selective objection would have on the stability of our institutions. He deplores "the American tradition of non-political discourse about politics" [72] that leads participants in the SCO debate to see the issue as one of freedom *versus* stability. Rather than shout slogans on the relative value of freedom and stability, Quade would have the participants in the SCO debate gather factual information to see if we cannot have both.

What needs to be done, accordingly, is to probe empirically these various possibilities, to better ascertain the likely costs in order to better judge the real costs of such a program. The tools exist: public opinion surveys have considerable utility for identifying future actions. Within the national pool of service-eligible men, surveys could seek answers to such broad questions as these: how many young men would be likely to apply for selective objector status; more important, what would be the impact (in terms of morale or esprit) of such a provision on those in service and those likely to serve in the future? With this kind of data available, one could judge more rationally whether selective objection would have a seriously

[69] Staughton Lynd, "Notes on a Tradition," *Worldview*, X (February, 1967), 4-6.
[70] Lynd interprets this tradition as an argument for SCO, but his article confuses the case for civil disobedience with that for SCO.
[71] James W. Davis and Kenneth M. Dolbeare, *Little Groups of Neighbors* (Chicago: Markham, 1968), *passim*.
[72] Quade, pp. 195 and 215.

debilitating impact on the services, and whether it would impair the capacity of the services to perform their functions.[73]

Quade's suggestion introduces a welcome element of common sense into the SCO debate. Such a survey would undoubtedly be helpful for the Vietnam conflict, but it would not offer any useful guidelines for adopting SCO as a general policy. If SCO were public policy, it would apply to objectors to wars other than the current intervention in Southeast Asia. The survey would then have to consider such questions as whether one would object on grounds of conscience if the United States would go to war with North Korea should another Pueblo incident take place. Presumably, a selective objector could not answer such a question until events were actually upon us. The assurance that most Americans support the war in Vietnam—if, indeed, such is the case—tells us nothing about how our people would respond to an intervention on behalf of Israel, or a U.N. police action in Northern Ireland, or Rhodesia. In each of these cases one's judgment might be influenced and even determined by racial or religious prejudices. In the name of conscience we would encourage our citizens to give vent to the ugliest passions in the American spirit.

Regime Character

This final section will suggest a response to the basic problem SCO addresses. We have criticized at some length the failure of the proponents of SCO to take seriously the moral dimensions of public life, a failure that explains many of the unsatisfactory reasons advanced for SCO. It accounts for the tendency to dichotomize morals and politics, which, in turn, leads to confusing the nature of total and selective objection, the "leap of faith," [74] and an excessively individualistic view of democracy. The same failure leads these proponents to ignore the moral problems created by the absence of a limiting principle in SCO—"where does it stop?" Finally, this failure leads to moral arguments for SCO that ignore the conscience of the legislator and the public interest to which he is committed by his calling.

Even those who readily acknowledge the moral character of positive law and public life cannot gainsay the fact that governments at times disregard their moral commitments and declare wars for base reasons. This massive fact is the starting point for SCO. There may be, however, a more fruitful way

---

[73] *Ibid.*, p. 216.

[74] For a discussion of "the leap of faith," p. pp. 141-42. The expression refers to the tendency in theological circles to deduce public policy from the conscientious scruples of the individual.

to approach this question than by trodding the path of politics, morality, and selective objection. This would be the method of considering regime character. Rather than decide on an *ad hoc* basis which laws one should obey or disobey, one might look at the regime as a whole and make one fundamental decision on whether or not one should commit oneself to this regime. This decision would be political and therefore moral. Its guidelines would be such considerations as whether it offered a reasonable hope for a virtuous life, whether its institutions promoted civic harmony and friendship, and whether its structure embraced the means for improving the undesirable aspects that accompany any regime. Once a man has decided in favor of a particular regime, he would look upon his citizenship as a moral commitment to promote the common good by upholding the laws of the regime. It is, of course, conceivable that the regime may disappoint him and pass laws which his conscience would never permit him to obey. Then he would have to reconsider his commitment and perhaps go elsewhere, especially if such laws seemed to be part of a general pattern. Or perhaps, he could even justify disobeying the offensive law and *accept the consequences of his action.*

Under this method he would never do what the proponents of SCO suggest; he would never demand that the regime prefer his moral choices to its own. For he would see in the moral character of the regime's policies an important area of his own moral growth. He would never sacrifice this part of his moral development by reducing the decisions of government to "mere politics." He would see in his conformity to law a necessary condition for his full development as a social being. If the moral content of the laws became so offensive that he could no longer obey, he would seek another regime whose laws would further the harmony between being a good citizen and good man.

The principles of regime character might clarify the difficulites James McFadden encountered when he wrote his draft board:

Sir,

I believe that I *alone* am responsible for the actions of my life—not the government. I refuse to surrender my moral responsibility in the name of patriotism. For our government to ask such a course of action reveals a deep-seated sickness and hypocrisy within the core of our nation. This "my country right or wrong" sentiment held by our government leaders and docile followers is starkly expressed by Adolf Eichmann: "It wasn't I who persecuted the Jews. That was done by the government. . . . I accuse the rulers of abusing my obedience. Obedience has always been praised as virtue. Therefore permit me to request that this fact should be considered." [75]

[75] *McFadden*, Exhibit A.

If McFadden really means what he says, he has fallen into the separation of politics and morality which he deplored elsewhere.[76] For if he *alone* is responsible for the moral quality of his life, then the government bears no responsibility in this area. Why should it make SCO public policy if McFadden alone is responsible for the kind of man he becomes? A sounder view of political life would acknowledge that the government shares with the citizen the responsibility for the moral quality of the life he leads. This is why politics is so important, for the character of the regime in which we spend our days will have no small effect on the kind of men we will be. From this point of view the Eichmann argument can be easily defeated. Eichmann's problem was not that he obeyed; it was rather that he obeyed the commands of an evil regime. It is useless to discuss obedience in the abstract. It is the character of the regime that determines whether obedience is vice or virtue.

The superiority of regime character over selective objection as a method of confronting the problem of the abuse of authority can be seen from considering the moral problems concerned with the official harassment of American citizens of Japanese extraction on the West Coast during World War II. Let us consider the position of the administrators responsible for putting the curfew and relocation program into practice. Let us suppose they knew these Japanese-Americans were being treated unjustly. What should they do? Selective objectors, like McFadden, would seem to demand that they resign, for they *alone* are responsible for the moral quality of their actions. The principles behind "regime character" would ask such questions as: (1) How unjust is the treatment these people must undergo? (2) Is there any chance of stopping or mitigating it by appealing "through channels?" (3) Would resigning help the victims of the injustice? (4) Is this kind of injustice part of a larger pattern of injustice or a temporary aberration? (5) Will the good this country is doing through its war effort be hindered by my resignation and if so, how much?

Such an examination of conscience might lead a man to resign,[77] but if he chose to stay he could not be considered a poor man's Eichmann. Like Eichmann, he would have obeyed unjust orders, but unlike Eichmann's orders, they would not have come from a thoroughly corrupt regime committed in principle to the systematic extermination of the persons it was treating unjustly.[78]

[76] *Ibid.*, Exhibit B.

[77] A similar example would be the conscience of a state official in Alabama or Mississippi who felt he was part of a system that was thoroughly corrupted by racism. See also the statement of Vatican II that at times the greater good demands that one obey unjust laws (see p. 127, above).

[78] Perhaps it is the failure to consider regime character that leads Gordon Zahn to think that many people would find the following statement a "shocking proposal":

This principle of regime character could be quite valuable for contemporary Americans. The opportunities for travel, the miracles of modern communication, and the affluence of our society enable interested Americans to acquire considerable knowledge of other countries. Romeo could say, "there is no world outside Verona," but to say there is no world outside America is blatant chauvinism. The position of world leadership that has been thrust upon the United States has surely had some adverse effects on the American dream of a peace-loving republic. One might well conclude that the Vietnam enterprise is not an aberration, but the wave of the future.[79] Perhaps for many generations Americans will have to fight limited wars in far-off places for goals not as clear as those symbolized by Sumter or Pearl Harbor. Undoubtedly, many citizens would find such a future intolerable. Should they, then, continue to enjoy the benefits of world leadership during peace and languish in prison during war? Or would the wiser course be to look elsewhere in the hope of spending their days in a land not burdened with the painful and sometimes tragic responsibilities of power?

We have all seen the red-white-and-blue bumper stickers that say, "America! Love It or Leave It!" Unfortunately, the owners of these stickers often reveal a degenerate form of patriotism. In a very un-American way they confuse dissent with disloyalty. If we refine the meaning of "loving America," the statement can be redeemed. To love America one need not accept uncritically every cause to which the nation is committed. Martin Luther King, Jr. was merciless in exposing the sham and hypocrisy in our society, but he never lost his dream for America. No one would say he did not love his country. The citizen who cannot find within himself this sort of love of his country might do well to consider whether he does not owe it to himself and to his fellow citizens to look elsewhere for a political society whose values he can support in good conscience.

"There are times when obedience is not a virtue, times when, in fact, obedience would be a vice" ("An Explosive Principle," p. 6). The principle of regime character reduces this "shocking proposal" to a truism.

[79] See, for example, the following statement of former Secretary of Defense, Robert McNamara: "The greatest contribution Vietnam is making—right or wrong beside the point—is that it is developing an ability in the U.S. to fight a limited war, to go to war without the necessity of rousing the public ire. In that sense Vietnam is also a necessity in our history because it is the kind of war we'll most likely be facing for the next fifty years." Cited in Finn (ed.), *A Conflict of Loyalties* . . . p. xiii.

VIII
The Worldly Theologians

The title of this chapter calls for a word of explanation. In the two previous chapters many arguments for SCO from representatives of the theological community have been cited. The value of their contribution has been somewhat questionable. For the most part this has been due to a failure to take seriously the needs of a political society. Stable government has been looked upon as a "given" rather than as an achievement. This may be an occupational hazard for theologians. In fairness to the "queen of the sciences," however, we must hasten to add that her court is not bereft of men with profound political insight. This final chapter will consider the arguments for SCO brought forward by three politically sophisticated theologians—John Courtney Murray, Ralph Potter, and Paul Ramsey.

Students of government will find congenial the terms in which these "worldly theologians" structure their discourse. They accept the moral character of positive law. They studiously avoid the temptation to deduce policy from the conscientious scruples of the individual. They recognize that the selective objector presents a far greater threat to his government than the total objector. In a word, they advocate SCO without taking the shortcuts that avoid the difficult questions of public interest. For this reason the argument of the worldly theologians may well be described as "the last best chance" for SCO.

John Courtney Murray

The untimely death of John Courtney Murray in the summer of 1967 was a severe blow to the SCO cause. Murray had dissented from the

166

Marshall Commission's recommendation against broadening the CO category to include selective objectors.[1] Just a few months before he died he outlined his main arguments for SCO at a commencement address at Western Maryland College. There he stated, "I advocate selective conscientious objection in the name of the traditional moral doctrine and also in the name of the traditional American political doctrine on the rights of conscience." [2]

Despite his advocacy of SCO, the thrust of Murray's address was one of caution and concern lest the principle of SCO be abused. So cautious were Murray's remarks that at times they seemed to suggest the opposite conclusion from the one he drew. For example, he simply notes without further comment "the enormous difficulty of administering a statute that would provide for selective conscientious objection." [3] If there is any truth to Woodrow Wilson's dictum that administration is the heart of modern government, "enormous" administrative difficulties may well be reason enough to abandon a program which might otherwise be quite appealing. The administrative process provides a link between political theory and public policy. That a legislative proposal be based on sound theoretical considerations is a condition for public policy that is necessary but not sufficient. No matter what theoretical merits a proposal may enjoy, no legislator can support it unless there is some assurance that it will work in practice. Perhaps Murray had some concrete proposals on how the administrative details could be handled, but, unfortunately, there is nothing in his writings to help us along these lines.

Another of Murray's misgivings in advocating SCO was "the perennial problem of the erroneous conscience."

Suppose a young man comes forward and says: "I refuse to serve in this war on grounds of the Nuremberg principle." Conversation discloses that he has not the foggiest idea what the Nuremberg principle really is. Or suppose he understands the principle and says: "I refuse to serve because in this war the United States is committing war crimes." The fact may be, as it is in South Vietnam, that this allegation is false. Or suppose he says, "I refuse to serve because the United States is the aggressor in this war." This reason again may be demonstrably false. What then is the tribunal to do?

Here perhaps we come to the heart of the difficulty and I have only two things to say. First, unless the right to selective objection is granted to possibly erroneous consciences it will not be granted at all. The State will have to abide by the principle of the Seeger case, which does not require that the objection be the truth but that it be truly held. One must follow the logic of an argument wherever it

[1] *Report of the National Advisory Commission* . . . , pp. 48-51.
[2] Murray, "War and Conscience," pp. 22-23.
[3] *Ibid.*, p. 29.

leads. On the other hand, the political community cannot be blamed for harboring the fear that if the right to selective objection is acknowledged in these sweeping terms, it might possibly lead to anarchy, to the breakdown of society, and to the paralysis of public policy.[4]

If Murray's comment was intended as a response to the problem of the "erroneous conscience," it certainly is not satisfactory. It is no answer to say that "unless the right to selective objection is granted to possibly erroneous consciences it will not be granted at all." The point at issue is precisely whether SCO should be granted at all. The probability that SCO will be abused (i.e., the case of the erroneous conscience) is a *prima facie* argument for scuttling SCO. This objection is not answered by saying the likely abuse of SCO is part of the risk one must accept in supporting SCO. The crucial question is: Why run the risk?

The remainder of Murray's response to the problem of the "erroneous conscience" reveals a further hesitancy in his support for SCO. He sympathized with the fears of the political community that SCO "might possibly lead to anarchy, to the breakdown of society, and to the paralysis of public policy." If the political community cannot be blamed for harboring this fear, then it would seem that it could not be blamed for rejecting SCO in the face of such fears. It would seem that only the most compelling reason could justify a legislator in supporting a proposal in which, by Murray's own admission, he could blamelessly fear the possibility of anarchy.

In the light of these misgivings, why did Murray support SCO? He felt it might be possible for selective objection to be exercised in a responsible manner that would avoid the worst fears of its critics.

The solution can only be the cultivation of political discretion throughout the populace, not least in the student and academic community. A manifold work of moral and political intelligence is called for. No political society can be founded on the principle that absolute rights are to be accorded to the individual conscience, and to all individual consciences, even when they are in error. This is *rank individualism* and to hold it would reveal a misunderstanding of the very nature of the political community. On the other hand, the political community is bound to respect conscience. But the fulfillment of this obligation supposes that the consciences of the citizens are themselves formed and informed.

Therefore, the final question may be whether there is abroad in the land a sufficient measure of moral and political discretion, in such wise that the Congress could, under safeguard of the national security, acknowledge the right of discretionary armed service. To cultivate this power of discretion is a task for all of us.[5]

[4] *Ibid.*, pp. 29-30.
[5] *Ibid.*, p. 30.

With these words Murray concluded his address. It is surely significant that he closed with a question—the question of whether there is today "a sufficient measure of moral and political discretion" to warrant Congressional support for SCO. Thus Murray's advocacy of SCO is qualified by his questioning attitude toward the political maturity of his fellow citizens.

Earlier in the Western Maryland address Murray had expressed his doubts about the measure of political discretion abroad in the land. The context was one in which he was explaining his reasons for supporting SCO before the National Advisory Commission on Selective Service.

I was also following the suggestion of Ralph Potter that the concession of status to the selective objector might help to upgrade the level of moral and political discourse in this country. It is presently lamentably low. On the other hand, Paul Ramsey has recently suggested that the matter works the other way round. "A considerable upgrading of the level of political discourse in America is among the conditions of the possibility of granting selective conscientious objection. At least the two things can and must go together." He adds rather sadly: "The signs of the times are not propitious for either." I agree.[6]

The last sentence in this paragraph is quite important. Does Murray's "I agree" refer only to the immediately preceding statement—the signs of the times are not propitious for either—or does it refer to Ramsey's contention that elevated political debate must precede or at least accompany SCO? If it refers to the second of these alternatives, the pieces of our puzzle begin to fall in place. It would mean that between the time he served on the Marshall Commission and the time of the Western Maryland address, he abandoned Potter's position in favor of Ramsey's. That is, he originally looked upon SCO as a means of elevating public debate. Judging from Murray's political writings, this consideration alone would give SCO a tremendous appeal in his eyes.[7] If later he became convinced that Ramsey and not Potter had the correct order of priorities—that SCO must follow or at least accompany, but not precede, more elevated debate—his caution in supporting SCO by the time of the Western Maryland address would be quite reasonable. His state of mind might then be described as one of favoring SCO as a long-range objective. This would seem to be consistent with his insistence that the current debate over the Vietnam war should not be confused with the issue of selective objection.

The issue of selective conscientious objection must be argued on its own merits. It is not a question of whether one is for or against the war in Vietnam, for or

[6] *Ibid.*, p. 28.
[7] John Courtney Murray, *We Hold These Truths* (Garden City, N.Y.: Doubleday, 1964), *passim.*

against selective service, much less for or against killing other people. The worst thing that could happen would be to use the issue of conscientious objection as a tactical weapon for political opposition to the war in Vietnam or to the general course of American foreign policy. This would not be good morality and it would be worse politics. Perhaps the central practical question might be put this way: Do the conditions exist which make possible the responsible exercise of a right of selective conscientious objection? The existence of these conditions is the prerequisite for granting legal status to the right itself.[8]

This passage suggests that Murray's support for SCO was only at the level of principle. The central *practical* question is whether the conditions exist which make possible the responsible exercise of a right of selective objection. His agreement with Ramsey on the dismal state of public debate would seem to imply a negative response to this practical question. This negative, in turn, explains the tone of the final paragraph of the address.[9] He does not exhort the graduates to lobby for SCO, but charges them with the task of cultivating the power of political discretion. This would seem to be the first step in making the world safe for SCO.

Ralph Potter

Ralph Potter, an assistant professor of social ethics at Harvard Divinity School, has written a lengthy essay on "Conscientious Objection to Particular Wars" [10] which Paul Ramsey has called "the best study I have seen on the subject." [11] Potter deserves this accolade. His approach is at once sensitive to the claims of conscience and alert to the need for political community and public order. His treatment of the history of conscientious objection and the just war doctrine, though exceptionally clear and concise, need not concern us here. For our purposes, the most interesting part of Potter's essay is the section he calls "Counterarguments." Here he attempts to answer objections to SCO with an argument based on considerations of public interest. Potter is of course not alone in this attempt.[12] The other authors, however, consider the public interest only obliquely and in passing. While Potter does not ignore the benefits SCO would bring to the individual, he emphasizes its public appeal in reply to the objection that

an individual has no right to arrogate to himself the power to define the conditions under which he will participate in the common actions undertaken by decision of

[8] Murray, "War and Conscience," pp. 25-26. See also p. 22.
[9] See p. 168, above.
[10] Ralph Potter, "Conscientious Objection to Particular Wars," in Donald Giannella (ed.), *Religion and the Public Order* (Ithaca, N.Y.: Cornell University Press, 1968).
[11] Ramsey, *The Just War*, p. 95.
[12] See the preceding chapter, pp. 156-62.

the citizens of the state. To admit an absolute right of an individual to withdraw with utter impunity from participation in actions obnoxious to his political, moral, or religious sensitivities would be to invite anarchy.[13]

Potter maintains this objection can be answered "without trying to settle, once and for all, the boundary issue of political philosophy by making a forced choice between anarchy and totalitarianism."[14] He then appeals to the American tradition of respecting the individual conscience, "a tradition buttressed by the belief that such respect serves the best interest of the state as well as the individual."[15] Potter would include the claim of the selective objector within the protected "sphere of life" that Americans have always recognized as being beyond the reach of the state. Thus, SCO could "be recognized as an idiosyncracy that can be tolerated by the state, indeed even prized as a peculiar expression of the integrity which is the ground of other civic virtues."[16]

Potter is not altogether happy with his own argument. He calls it "philosophical 'muddling through,'"[17] and "a pragmatic evasion of an abstract puzzle."[18] He should not be embarrassed, however, because the art of governing does not aim at solving abstract puzzles. It is eminently practical. There are times when "pragmatic evasion" and "muddling through" may be the highest wisdom. The strength of a public interest argument is that it could enable a legislator to favor SCO without stepping on the "slippery slope" we have discussed earlier.[19] It is only if the argument for SCO is based exclusively on the rights of the individual that it is vulnerable to the rejoinder—"where does it stop?" that is, why favor the conscience of the selective objector rather than that of the Klansman or the Black Panther? It is the element of arbitrariness in the public interest argument that delivers it from the slippery slope. As long as the national interest is the basis of the decision, we can live with a certain amount of arbitrariness. Many of us may be unhappy that the poverty line was drawn at $3,000, but no one would base his complaint on the *principle* that whatever you do for a man making $2,900 you must do for a man making $3,100. Nor would those who favor a lower voting age in state elections argue that whatever we do for a twenty-one-year-old we must do for an eighteen-year-old. The argument against the $3,000 poverty line would be based on such considerations as the level of wages in certain poverty areas, the cost of living, etc., while an appeal for a lower voting age might maintain that a man old enough to fight

[13] Potter, p. 87.
[14] *Ibid.*
[15] *Ibid.*
[16] *Ibid.*
[17] *Ibid.*, p. 88.
[18] *Ibid.*, p. 87.
[19] See pp. 148 ff., above.

is old enough to vote.[20] Such arguments do not call into question the right of the government to draw lines that affect some citizens favorably and others adversely. They simply maintain the lines are drawn in the wrong place. In the same way, SCO based on considerations of national interest could be defended by the prudential judgment that this was the place to draw the line—i.e., that the government can go this far but no further in accommodating claims of conscience.

If SCO were passed on grounds of public interest, its proponents might consider it a Pyrrhic victory. If their objective in proposing SCO is to establish the *principle* of the supremacy of the individual's conscience over the laws of the city *as a matter of public policy,* an SCO provision based on national interest would be a hollow triumph indeed. If, however, the objective is SCO itself, national interest considerations should not create any difficulty. Such considerations would be seen as the only basis on which a legislator could support SCO without leaving himself vulnerable to the claims of any extremist group that invoked the name of conscience.

Thus far we have concentrated on Potter's suggestion that selective objection might be justified on the basis of its contribution to the public interest. We have agreed with Potter that this is, indeed, a sound way to approach SCO. The question remains, however, whether SCO is in the public interest. An answer cannot be given to this question at the level of principle alone. We must look at how SCO would work in practice. This Potter attempts to do in the closing pages of his essay:

There are three types of "practical" arguments against recognition of the selective objector which deserve more extensive consideration than can be given here. They are, first, that "slackers" might evade military duty by posing as selective objectors; second, that evaluation and accommodation of the highly particular objections of the selective objector is administratively impossible; third, that implementation of national policy might be impaired if great numbers assumed the status of selective objectors.[21]

Potter is correct in stating that these objections "deserve more extensive consideration" than he gives them. The previous objection—that SCO would lead to anarchy—was speculative. It was turned aside by Potter's willingness to support SCO on grounds of public interest. These three objections are "practical," as Potter says, but are no less important than the theoretical consideration. He responds to the first objection as follows:

For a would-be slacker to submit to the rigors of establishing a claim to classification as a selective conscientious objector would surely amount to "doing it the

[20] This argument is cited because it is typical, not because it is persuasive. The very qualities that make an eighteen-year-old a good soldier might disqualify him as a voter.
[21] Potter, p. 92.

hard way." Under the most liberalized program conceivable there would be the tests of seriousness mentioned above, investigations of character presently provided for, and requests for coherent explications of the grounds for objection to a particular war, that is (whether the title is used or not), a well-reasoned discussion of the norms of the just or unjust war. Stringent procedures would remain that would either deter or detect those who might feign conscientious scruples against a particular war.[22]

This response is inadequate. One of the most common criticisms of the Selective Service System is its lack of uniform standards in processing CO claims.[23] "Tests of seriousness" and "stringent procedures" will have very little meaning as long as the administration of the Selective Service System is kept in local hands. To broaden the bases of conscientious objection would only increase the already excessive discretion of local boards. If Congress would insist on a more highly centralized Selective Service Administration, the problem of "the slacker" could be reduced. But such a change would probably meet more congressional resistance than SCO itself.[24] Without such a change, however, SCO would only reinforce the erratic and uneven norms that exist within the same draft board and among different draft boards.

Potter takes the second and third objections together:

The argument that recognition of selective objection, if taken seriously and carried far would raise exceedingly difficult administrative problems cannot be so quickly dismissed. The moral strength of the selective objector position—its precision, timeliness, and contextual relevance—contributes to its practical weakness. The thoroughgoing pacifist can declare ahead of time, once and for all, that he is opposed to participation in all forms of war. With regard to administrative processes, his rejection is stable, total, and tidy. But the non-pacifist presents a "threshold problem." He must constantly reassess a changing situation and his position with it. Only the norms by which he shall judge can be specified prior to the moment in which the input of certain information leads to the conclusion that he can no longer participate in the activity in which he is already engaged. Compared to the pacifist, his decision is more unpredictable in time and more disruptive in effect since, prior to his claim, he had been counted upon to perform precisely the duties now morally obnoxious to him.

Even a rickety administrative apparatus could process claims with reasonable dispatch and equity if selective objections were posed by only a few civilians in peacetime. But what if the stance were assumed by many soldiers in wartime? The

[22] Ibid.
[23] Davis and Dolbeare, passim, and Charles H. Wilson, Jr., "The Selective Service System: An Administrative Obstacle Course," California Law Review, LIV (December, 1966), 2123-2179.
[24] Davis and Dolbeare, passim.

second argument concerning administrative feasibility is interlocked with the third, based upon the fear that there might be so many selective objectors that national policy decisions could not be carried out.

Those who take selective objection seriously should also take this counterargument seriously. It should be made clear that in admitting the right of selective objection to participation in particular wars, we would be doing something more than making a marginal concession to a small, strange group afflicted with an unusually squeamish conscience. The state would voluntarily be making itself vulnerable to a *de facto* referendum, to a form of influence upon policy decisions which, whether intended as such or not, could be a potent means of political action. Such a step requires considerable confidence in the sobriety and balanced intelligence of the citizenry.[25]

In these paragraphs Potter does not attempt to dispose of the "counterarguments." He simply explains them and wisely counsels supporters of SCO to take them seriously.

It is not enough, however, merely to take these objections seriously. If SCO is to be public policy, they must be met and answered. Potter is undoubtedly correct when he says SCO "requires considerable confidence in the sobriety and balanced intelligence of the citizenry." But what basis is there for thinking this confidence is warranted? Potter seems to have misgivings along these lines:

It also creates a demand for a considerable upgrading of the level of political discourse in America. Recognition of the selective objector might contribute to that goal. There would be an educational benefit from the attempt to counter his arguments, for the only way to counteract the presentation of a well-informed selective objector is to meet his points head on with thoughtful analysis of the nature of political existence, the role of force in public affairs, and the relationship of ethical norms to policy-making processes. Pressure would be put upon his judges to ask questions more edifying than, "What would you do if your grandmother were attacked by . . . ?" If conscientious objection could be debated within the framework of the just-war doctrine rather than exclusively in terms of pacifist conscience, public discussion of the issues of war and peace might become less moralistic, increasingly precise, and more direct in its bearing upon decisions actually pending.[26]

We have already seen that Paul Ramsey and, perhaps, John Courtney Murray think Potter has confused the order of priority. Their criticism would seem to be well founded. Potter maintains that SCO demands that we up-

[25] Potter, pp. 93-94.
[26] *Ibid.*, p. 94.

grade the level of political discourse. And how are we to do this? By passing SCO! [27]

Paul Ramsey

Paul Ramsey is the third of our worldly theologians. Like Murray and Potter he arrives at a qualified acceptance of SCO only after prolonged soul searching. He feels an argument can be made for SCO because "the case for this is an intrinsic moral one while the obstacles are in the empirical order, however deeply embedded these are in our culture and law." [28]

He discusses these obstacles at great length. The obstacles to SCO arising from our culture are the absence of a sense of political community and the low level of public debate. Before SCO could be approved we would have to decide whether our citizens are more like Socrates, "who while suffering imprisonment and death for conscience's sake still effectively acknowledged 'the conscience of the laws'" or "like Sophists putting in individualistic claims that their own subjective opinion is the measure of truth." [29]

Ramsey maintains that SCO requires a common universe of moral discourse in which citizens could agree on how to go about deciding whether a particular war is just or unjust.

Its acceptability depends first of all upon whether there exists in the ethos of this country a moral consensus or doctrine on the uses of military force that could be used in determining the statutory grounds for conscientious objection, in contrast to the time-honored doctrine that all uses of military force are inherently immoral. Unless this is the case, it would seem that the proposal for particular war objection is at bottom a plea for individualistic consciences, all sincerely moral no doubt, each to be able not simply to make his own determination of justice within some minimal agreement about everyone's political responsibilities, but rather free to *determine how he is going to determine* what is just or unjust for him to do, with *whatever degree* of recognition he may *choose* to give to the claims of his nation upon him. [30]

The following paragraph presents the clearest statement of the obstacles Ramsey sees arising from our culture.

The truth is that every time we endorse or propose selective conscientious objection to our fellow countrymen, we are mainly making a proposal to ourselves, and

---

[27] I regret closing this section on such a sour note. Potter deserves better treatment. Indeed, his argument "deserves more extensive consideration than can be given here." I have presented only one small section of Potter's essay. His analysis of the just war doctrine, the *Seeger* case, and the history of CO are exceptionally well done and have been most helpful to me in thinking through the problems of SCO.

[28] Ramsey, *The Just War*, p. 124.

[29] *Ibid.*, p. 91.   [30] *Ibid.*, p. 100.

delivering a judgment upon ourselves. This self-incriminating judgment can be summed up in the obvious fact that we who are the vocal voices in church and in academic community have done very little to articulate and transmit an adequate political philosophy in the present day. It may be exhilarating to get behind this reform. But it is another thing again to create the conditions of its possible enact-ment—or, for that matter, even to imagine how we are going to do this. To raise the level of public debate in any nation of the modern world so that there could be a *proper* adoption of selective objection seems insurmountably difficult. We ought not to think we have made any advance if we succeed simply because modern weapons eliminate the need for many men in order for force to be used, and eliminate in some measure also the need for integral, purposive political community, because opposition to national policy can be shrewdly accommodated by exemption from particular wars. Nor should we rejoice if this proposal commends itself to our contemporaries simply because it is one more step in the erosion of imperative political obligation by an omnivorous individualism and by apolitical optimism about the trustworthiness of men's moral sensibilities.[31]

The obstacles to SCO arising from our law come from the broad under-standing of religion in *Torcaso* and *Seeger*.[32] Ramsey holds that the more generous the Court is in defining religion, the more difficult is the case for SCO. That is, the broader the sphere of religion, the more difficult is the task of distinguishing a religious belief from a political belief. But this distinction is, for Ramsey, crucial to the case for SCO:

We must face the fact, in other words, that no political society can allow exemption for purely political objection to its uses of military force, and we must find a way to distinguish between this and refusals to participate on moral grounds if we are ever to legislate exemption for selective conscientious objection. Without the manifold intellectual work that is needed to wrestle successfully with this distinction, the proposal of selective objection will remain an ideological protest—or else one that is based on the optimistic faith of philosophical anarchism that out of the self-determining freedom of individual consciences political community can be com-posed and its energies effectively disposed one way rather than another in the course of its history.[33]

Ramsey returns again and again to the need to distinguish political and moral judgments if we are to support SCO. His own commitment to the moral character of political life would seem to predestine his search to frustration. For Ramsey this distinction *"is the sticking point,* and one which in my judgment Father Murray too quickly assumes would be solved by a greater degree of common, articulated, moral and political discourse."[34]

[31] *Ibid.,* p. 126.
[32] 367 U.S. 488, and 380 U.S. 163.
[33] Ramsey, *The Just War,* p. 101.
[34] *Ibid.,* p. 126.

He sees two difficulties in assuming that political education would enable us to draw "an acceptable line between conscientious moral and conscientious political objection to particular wars." [35]

One difficulty is simply the fact that we are morally a pluralistic political community no less than we are religiously a pluralistic people, and are apt to remain so. Can we come to agreement on what is to count as conscientious moral objection any more than on what counts as a religious belief? The other, and a deeper, obstacle may lie in the fact that moral reasons and political reasons (which are admittedly inseparable) may intrinsically not be distinguishable enough for this to be a foundation of the proposed system. [36]

The last sentence in the paragraph just quoted indicates Ramsey's difficulties with SCO go beyond "empirical" obstacles arising from law and culture. In suggesting that moral and political reasons "may intrinsically not be distinguishable enough for this to be a foundation of the proposed system," he is, in effect, sounding the alarm to abandon the argument for SCO as a moral claim. This is so because, as we have seen, Ramsey is quite emphatic in his insistence that this distinction must be made before we can get on with the case for SCO.

Even if the morals-politics question could be solved in a satisfactory manner, there would remain another problem to which Ramsey gives insufficient attention. This is the question we have already discussed at some length—how to isolate war from other policy decisions in a way that would enable the government to permit selective objection to military service without allowing selective objection to other laws as well.

Ramsey concludes his essay with a proposal for a modified form of SCO. He cautions the reader that he puts "this suggestion forward only as one long question." [37] His proposal rests on the distinction in just-war literature between *jus ad bellum* and *jus in bello*. The former refers to the question of whether it is right for a nation to go to war, while the latter refers to what sort of actions are legitimate once a nation has opted for war. Ramsey proposes that selective objection be granted on the basis of the second criterion but not the first. He would have us look

to where the claims of humanity have, in the matter of war, been largely registered and given some shape or form not wholly subject to the passions and strongly-held opinions of the moment, namely, in *jus gentium,* in international law, in agreements and treaties and conventions expressing men's agreements as to justice and governing the conduct of men and nations in war. . . . The proposal is,

[35] *Ibid.,* p. 127.
[36] *Ibid.*
[37] *Ibid.,* p. 126.

therefore, that the class of exemptible conscientious objection to participation in particular wars shall be based on opposition to the war because of the claimant's conscientious belief that the war is in violation of international conventions and the "laws of war" and in violation of agreements to which his nation was and is a party. Other sorts of objection to particular wars, which are also, of course, moral appeals and claim moral warrant (as do the opposing and prevailing opinion), shall nevertheless be regarded as falling wholly within the legitimate due processes of democratic society, from the burdens and outcome of which no participant can claim exemption.[38]

He explains his proposal more fully:

We should distinguish between what is stupid and therefore morally wrong and what is inherently wrong (even if not stupid). It is one thing to determine whether and when a war is rightful, another thing to determine in *prohibitiva* what is rightful or wrongful in war. It is one thing to determine that the overall "cause" of war is just, another to determine whether the war is conducted unjustly. And between these two tests of just conduct of war, it is one thing to determine whether the mode of warfare is excessive in terms of what is at stake (or is likely to lead to proportionately greater evil than the evil prevented), and it is another thing to determine or conscientiously to believe that acts of war are being "aimed indiscriminately" and are in direct violation of the moral immunity of non-combatants from direct, intended attack. In all these cases, my proposal is that the *second* in these pairs be recognized as a possible basis of a creditable claim to conscientious objection to participation in a particular war, because in these respects the claimant would state his belief that something is unjust no matter what are the good policy-consequences alleged by others or by the government. These policy-consequences, in his own case or that of any other citizen, would not be allowed as bases of a claim to exemption because, while equally a moral claim, such judgments would not be distinguishable from merely political opposition to a particular war or from disagreement with the general course of the nation's foreign policy.[39]

Ramsey's suggestion is a refreshing addition to the debate on SCO. It seems to make the best of both worlds. It fosters sensitivity to the claims of conscience on the one hand, without undermining political authority on the other. By restricting SCO to *jus in bello,* Ramsey avoids the objection that SCO lets the citizen veto the decisions of his government on whether a given situation calls for war. Also, the international acceptance of certain norms of what is permissible in warfare provides the common moral doctrine that is absent in questions of *jus ad bellum.* Finally, the *jus in bello* selective objector can more readily assimilate his position to that of the total objector. We have already discussed the difference between the total

[38] *Ibid.,* p. 128.　　　　　　　　　[39] *Ibid.,* p. 129.

pacifist and the selective objector. The latter singles out his own government for his moral displeasure, whereas the pacifist objects to war as such. The *in bello* objector is like the pacifist in that for both men certain objective actions are intrinsically wrong no matter what nation performs them. He does not ask exemption from any of his nation's policy decisions. He asks exemption only from certain behavior which his nation as a member of the community of nations is pledged to avoid.

The proposal, however, is not without difficulties. First of all, there is the difficult theoretical question of the binding character of international law in a nation state system. A sanctimonious appeal to international law can be a facade enabling the more advanced nations to keep the developing nations "in their place." Terrorist raiding on peace-loving peasants is despicable indeed. The reason for such raids, however, is not always the moral degeneracy of the terrorists. If they had the technological means at their disposal, one can assume they would not hesitate to conform to the demands of international law and protect their interests by stockpiling a nuclear arsenal.

Secondly, there is the question of accurate information. Was the bombing of North Vietnam the reasoned, measured "counterforce" strategy the Pentagon advertised? Or was it instead the "systematic slaughter," or "genocide," or "bloodbath," or "mass murder of countless women and children" that the protesters would have us believe? The celebrated Green Beret case is a most interesting example of this problem. The news media tell us the Green Berets murdered a South Vietnamese national they mistakenly thought was a double agent. Colonel Rheault maintained nothing of the sort ever happened. Whom do we believe? More importantly, whom is the draft board to believe? The board members might think Colonel Rheault is a liar, but can they let their belief influence their official behavior and agree with a young man who shares their belief? If so, the fate of an *in bello* objector would be favorable in areas whose draft boards questioned the colonel's veracity and unfavorable where they did not.

Thirdly, it would be necessary to distinguish isolated acts from patterns of behavior. This distinction should govern our attitude toward the alleged massacre at My Lai. One fall from grace cannot condemn the entire military establishment. Before the *in bello* selective objector could be excused from military service, there would have to be some reasonable grounds for thinking he might be told to perform similar actions. But, again, to whom do the draftee and his board turn to find out if there are systematic violations of the laws of war? Isolated violations could not suffice to keep a man out of the army. Under the present status of military law a soldier may refuse to carry out a command contrary to the laws of war.[40] In this way *in bello* SCO is already recognized. To use the *in bello* argument to stay out of the army, it would seem that a man would have to show that his refusal to carry out a command contrary to the laws of war would not be upheld by military courts.

Finally, let us conclude by observing that Ramsey brings himself to support SCO only by shifting the grounds of the discussion. The shift is a contribution to the literature that is both welcome and long overdue. In denying, however, the right to *ad bellum* SCO Ramsey has put himself on the side of the opponents of selective objection as that term is commonly used.[41]

[40] *Field Manual* (No. 27-10), Department of the Army, pp. 182-83. The outcome of the current trials of military personnel accused of murdering civilians at My Lai will be instructive. It will be interesting to see what punishments—if any—are given to draftees. The question of SCO is relevant only to men who have been *drafted*—not to officers or enlisted men who have volunteered for military service.

[41] For a critical review of Ramsey's work on SCO, see Marvin M. Karpatkin's review of *A Conflict of Loyalties* (James Finn, ed.) in *New York Times Book Review* (November 2, 1969), pp. 10-16. A rejoinder by Professor Richard W. Day in defense of Ramsey and a further statement by Karpatkin appear in *New York Times Book Review* (November 30, 1969), p. 62. Ramsey gave his own comments in a letter to the editor of the same publication (February 1, 1970), p. 24.

Conclusion

It will come as no surprise to the reader who has persevered this far that I have serious reservations about the wisdom of SCO as public policy. At times, I fear, I may have lost the sense of detachment that usually characterizes an academic investigation. It was not my intention to assume the role of advocate—devil's or otherwise—in this question. This role at times, however, was cast upon me because of the one-sided character of the debate. Nearly all the literature on SCO favors its enactment. The authors may have serious reservations about it, but in the end they are willing to run the risks it entails. One cannot dismiss such arguments with the flippant, though perhaps rather shrewd, observation that SCO is a "helluva way to run a railroad." This may well be the feeling of the "silent majority," but this feeling will not suffice to answer the thoughtful arguments for SCO that have been brought forward by nearly everyone who has taken the trouble to write on this topic.

In trying to give a worthy response to the arguments for SCO, I could not afford the luxury of nicely balanced sentences starting "on the one hand" and ending "on the other." The reason, of course, was that all the arguments were on *one* hand. It was impossible to state the relevant points at issue without criticizing the proponents of SCO. To have done otherwise would have meant approving SCO by default. Nor could I state the case against SCO by simply repeating the impoverished arguments of the Marshall Commission and the Freedom House advertisement. With friends such as these, the case against SCO would need no enemies. Thus, in the interests of elevating the level of public debate over SCO I had to stress the forgotten side of a hitherto one-sided argument.

Looking back over the arguments for SCO, I am convinced that a major defect in the friends of selective objection is their failure to take seriously the conscientious obligations of the legislator. It cannot be stressed strongly enough that SCO, unlike civil disobedience, ultimately concerns a decision of government, not of the citizen. To be sure, the case for civil disobedience is not without its difficulties,[1] but its advocates are concerned with a question of individual behavior. The point at issue is whether there are times when a citizen may break the law. SCO asks an entirely different question: Should the law accommodate the conscientious scruples of those who consider a particular war unjust? The paeans to conscience that dominate SCO literature miss the mark. In SCO the crucial conscientious judgment is that of the legislator, the man whose vocation it is to excel in promoting the common good. Can he, in good conscience, favor SCO without compromising his responsibilities to society as a whole?[2]

It is my concern with the conscience of the legislator that has prompted me to argue that if we must have SCO, we should have it for reasons of national interest. Such reasons may not be hard to find. One need look no further than the federal penitentiaries where many SCO's are imprisoned. No one will deny that some of these young men are among the most promising citizens of our republic. In happier times they would have spent these years launching careers that would be of considerable benefit to society. Their alienation from American society and its values is a serious loss for our nation. I can see how a legislator might favor SCO to avoid a repetition of this tragedy. But if he does so, he should make it clear that his decision is an act of statesmanship aimed at promoting the public interest and not an act of abject surrender by a government that has lost its moral vigor.

Personally, I do not think SCO would contribute significantly to the public interest. In the present climate of public debate I feel it would only reinforce popular misunderstandings of the moral nature of political life. It is unfortunate indeed that calls for "law and order" have become identified with increased police activity. If a society is to remain free, there must be respect for the law. The citizen must ordinarily obey spontaneously and willingly; police action must always be the exception. To achieve this desirable state, the moral character of law must be upheld. I fear that SCO would have just the opposite effect. I fear it would suggest that law deals with

---

[1] See Herbert J. Storing, "The Case Against Civil Disobedience," and Abe Fortas, *Concerning Dissent and Civil Disobedience* (New York: Signet, 1968).

[2] John A. Rohr, "The Mature Conscience," in William C. Bier (ed.), *Conscience: Its Freedom and Limitations* (New York: Fordham University Press, 1970).

"political" matters where "power" and "special interests" hold sway, whereas the "moral" sphere is that of the individual and his conscience. Would it not be difficult to take seriously the excellence of a government that exalts private opinion above its own on *moral* grounds?

But should we not make one exception—just in the case of war? I do not think we should. We have already been through the problem of the "slippery slope." Behind the pleas of those who say "just this once" there is, I am afraid, an attitude that cannot take seriously the moral dimensions of public life. When they say "just this once," are they not implying that they will accept the moral character of public policy in every case except that in which the highest moral values are at stake?

The case for SCO demands recognition of the moral character of political decisions. Otherwise, the state could reject the plea for SCO on the straight-forward grounds that moral questions are purely private concerns. But once the moral character of public policy is acknowledged, it cannot be mitigated just because the policy in question is of considerable moral significance.

Finally, let us reflect briefly on the title of this essay, *Prophets Without Honor*. I do believe that many SCO's offer an authentic contemporary expression of the prophetic tradition. They speak out boldly against the folly of those in power. They have also been treated in a manner consistent with that tradition. Jerusalem stoned her prophets, while we merely incarcerate ours. This may be "progress," but I am sure it will bring small comfort to those in prison for conscience' sake. The traditional manner of disposing of prophets testifies to the perennial problem they present to any government. It also underscores the wisdom of the Evangelical observation that it is only in his own country that the prophet goes without honor. Indeed, the prophet may be honored even in his own country once the events that inspired his prophecy have passed. Jerusalem built monuments to the prophets her fathers had killed, and our historians will surely do the same for the SCO's we have imprisoned. Nevertheless at the moment of prophecy, the prophet is an acute embarrassment to his government. The more convincing the prophet is, the greater the embarrassment. The Vietnam war has been such an unmitigated disaster that few reasonable men will dismiss the SCO as a fanatic or a Communist sympathizer.

In the United States we have tried to institutionalize the right to dissent through the first amendment. When this does not suffice, we pass from the problem of the dissenter to that of the prophet—the man who is willing to break the law rather than participate in what he feels is morally wrong. Underlying his position is the principle "my conscience right or wrong, my conscience"—a principle every bit as dangerous as "my country right or wrong, my country." The conscientious legislator is thus faced with a cruel dilemma. Will he vote against selective objection (thereby stoning our prophets) or risk the apotheosis of autonomous conscience by supporting it? There is, as I have already suggested, a way out of the dilemma. He could support SCO on grounds of national interest rather than the rights of conscience, but my personal opinion is that such reasoning would fall on deaf ears today. Perhaps I take too seriously the rhetoric of those who see the war as merely a "symptom" of much deeper problems in our society—fascism, racism, imperialism, etc. I think their analysis is mistaken, but I am convinced they believe what they say. If so, they will never be persuaded by the protestations of legislators who insist they voted for SCO for reasons of national interest. SCO will be looked upon as a "symptom" of the moral insecurity of the system and a harbinger of its collapse under stern moral pressure. I fear it will only invite further demands for exemptions for those who break the law for reasons of conscience. I do not believe that SCO would be in the national interest because I think it would be interpreted as only the first in a series of domestic "dominoes" which, I fear, would not prove as illusory as their international counterpart. For this reason my personal opinion is that the wise legislator should not vote for selective objection at this point in our history. Given the present level of public debate on Vietnam, I do not think SCO would be handled in a responsible manner. I would therefore invoke the principle of "the lesser evil" to justify the painful course of stoning our prophets now and building our monuments in happier times.

SELECT BIBLIOGRAPHY

General

Arnold, Walter. "Selective Objection and the Public Interest," *The Christian Century*, Vol. LXXXIV (December 27, 1967).

Cohen, Carl. "The Case for Selective Pacifism," *The Nation*, Vol. CCXLVII (July 8, 1968).

Conklin, Francis J. "Conscientious Objector Provisions," *Georgetown Law Journal*, Vol. LI, No. 2 (Winter, 1963).

Conscientious Objection. Selective Service Monograph No. 11. Washington, D.C.: Government Printing Office, 1950.

Davis, Harry R. "Christian Neglect of Political Values," *The Christian Century*, Vol. LXXXVI (November 26, 1969).

"The Draft and Conscience," *Commonweal*, Vol. LXXXVI (April 21, 1967).

Finn, James (ed.). *A Conflict of Loyalties: The Case for Selective Conscientious Objection*. New York: Pegasus, 1969.

————. "Selective Service and Selective Objection," *Worldview*, Vol. X (February, 1967).

Fortas, Abe. *Concerning Dissent and Civil Disobedience*. New York: Signet, 1968.

"Freedom House Statement," *New York Times*, November 30, 1966, p. 37.

Gaylin, Willard. *In the Service of Their Country: War Resisters in Prison*. New York: The Viking Press, 1970.

Gendler, Everett. "As Freedom Is a Fantasy," *Worldview*, Vol. X (February, 1967).

————. "War and the Jewish Tradition," in James Finn (ed.), *A Conflict of Loyalties: The Case for Selective Conscientious Objection*. New York: Pegasus, 1969.

Geyer, Allen. "The Just War and the Selective Objector," *The Christian Century*, Vol. LXXXIII (February 16, 1966).

Greenfield, Jeff. "The Selective C.O.," *The New Republic*, Vol. CLIX (July 6, 1968).

Harrington, Michael. "Politics, Morality and Selective Dissent," in James Finn (ed.), *A Conflict of Loyalties: The Case for Selective Conscientious Objection*. New York: Pegasus, 1969.

185

Haskell, Ellery. "Fortas and Selective Objection," *Christianity and Crisis,* Vol. XXVIII (October 30, 1968).

Heisler, Francis. "The New Conscientious Objector," *Liberation,* Vol. XI (January, 1967).

Hochstadt, Theodore. "The Right to Exemption from Military Service of a Conscientious Objector to a Particular War," *Harvard Civil Rights-Civil Liberties Law Review,* Vol. III, No. 1 (Fall, 1967).

Karpatkin, Marvin M. Review of *A Conflict of Loyalties* (James Finn, ed.). *New York Times Book Review* (November 2, 1969). With rejoinders by Richard W. Day (November 30, 1969) and Paul Ramsey (February 1, 1970).

Kaufman, Arnold S. "The Selective Service System: Actualities and Alternatives," in James Finn (ed.), *A Conflict of Loyalties: The Case for Selective Conscientious Objection,* New York: Pegasus, 1969.

Lutheran Church of America. *Social Statements of the LCA.* Fourth Biennial Convention, June 19-27, 1968, Atlanta, Georgia.

Lynd, Staughton. "Notes on a Tradition," *Worldview,* Vol. X (February, 1967).

Macgill, H. C. "Selective Conscientious Objection: Divine Will and Legislative Grace," *Virginia Law Review,* Vol. LIV (November, 1968).

Mansfield, John H. "Conscientious Objection, 1964 Term," in Donald A. Giannella (ed.), *Religion and the Public Order.* Chicago: University of Chicago Press, 1965.

McCormick, Richard A. "Notes on Moral Theology: January-June, 1967," *Theological Studies,* Vol. XXVIII (December, 1967).

Murray, John Courtney. "War and Conscience," in James Finn (ed.), *A Conflict of Loyalties: The Case for Selective Conscientious Objection.* New York: Pegasus, 1969.

———. *We Hold These Truths.* Garden City, N. Y.: Doubleday, 1964.

Orr, Eston Wycliffe. "*Mens Rea* and the Selective Conscientious Objector," *Tennessee Law Review,* Vol. XXXVII (Spring, 1970).

"Pastoral Constitution on the Church in the Modern World" (*Gaudium et Spes*), No. 79, *The Documents of Vatican II.* Edited by Walter M. Abbott. New York: Guild Press, 1966.

Peck, Harry F., Jr. "Selective Service—Right to Counsel, Due Process and the First Amendment," *Marquette Law Review,* Vol. LI, No. 4 (Spring, 1968).

Potter, Ralph. "Conscientious Objection to Particular Wars," in Donald A. Giannella (ed.), *Religion and the Public Order.* Ithaca, N. Y.: Cornell University Press, 1968.

Quade, Quentin. "Selective Conscientious Objection and Political Obligation," in James Finn (ed.), *A Conflict of Loyalties: The Case for Selective Conscientious Objection.* New York: Pegasus, 1969.

Ramsey, Paul. *The Just War.* New York: Charles Scribner's Sons, 1968.

———. *War and the Christian Conscience.* Durham: Duke University Press, 1961.

Redlich, Norman, and Kenneth R. Feinberg. "Individual Conscience and the Selective Conscientious Objector: The Right Not to Kill," *New York University Law Review,* Vol. XLIV (November, 1969).

Report of the National Advisory Commission on Selective Service. Chairman, Burke Marshall. Washington, D.C. Government Printing Office, 1967.

Riga, Peter J. "Selective Conscientious Objection: Progress Report," *The Catholic World,* Vol. CCXI (July, 1970).

Rohr, John A. "Judge Wyzanski and Selective Conscientious Objection," *America,* Vol. CXXII (February 21, 1970).

———. "The Mature Conscience," in William C. Bier (ed.), *Conscience: Its Freedom and Limitations.* New York: Fordham University Press, 1970.

———. "The Selective Conscientious Objector," *America,* Vol. CXVII, No. 4 (July 22, 1967).

Sheerin, James. "Must Conscientious Objectors Be Pacifists?" *The Catholic World,* Vol. CCVI (January, 1968).

Shinn, Roger L. "How Free Can a Society Be?" *Christianity and Crisis,* Vol. XXV (November 1, 1965).

———. "The Selective Conscientious Objector Again," *Christianity and Crisis,* Vol. XXVII (April 3, 1967).

———. "The Trial of Captain Dale E. Noyd," *Christianity and Crisis,* Vol. XXVIII (April 1, 1968).

Silver, Isidore. "Sisson's Complaint, Wyzanski's Ploy," *Commonweal,* Vol. XC, No. 14 (June 20, 1969).

Storing, Herbert J. "The Case Against Civil Disobedience," in Robert Goldwyn (ed.), *Essays on Civil Disobedience.* Chicago: Rand McNally and Company, 1969.

Swomley, John M. "The Limited Objectors," *The Christian Century,* Vol. LXXXIII (December 15, 1965).

Taylor, Telford. *Nuremberg and Vietnam: An American Tragedy,* Chicago: Quadrangle Books, 1970.

Trillin, Calvin. "U.S. Journal: Clovis—No Sir, I Can't Go," *New Yorker,* Vol. XLIV (March 30, 1969).

Vanderpol, Alfred. *La doctrine scolastique du droit de guerre.* Paris: Desclée et cie., 1919.

Wolf, Donald. "Vietnam Morality: Who Judges What, When, How?" *The Catholic World,* Vol. CCVII (June, 1968).

Zahn, Gordon. "An Explosive Principle," *Worldview,* Vol. X (March, 1967).

———. *War, Conscience and Dissent.* New York: Hawthorn Books, 1967.

Zinn, Howard. *Disobedience and Democracy: Nine Fallacies on Law and Order.* New York: Random House, 1968.

Legal Citations

Berman v. *U.S.,* 156 F 2d 377.

Engle v. *Vitale,* 370 U.S. 421.

Everson v. *Board of Education,* 330 U.S. 1.

Hamilton v. *Regents of the University of California,* 293 U.S. 245.

In re Summers, 325 U.S. 561.

McFadden et al. v. *Selective Service System Local Board No. 40,* 423 F 2d 1291.

Negre v. *Larsen*, 418 F 2d 908.

Noyd v. *Bond*, 393 U.S. 1048.

Schempp v. *Pennsylvania*, 374 U.S. 244.

Sheldon v. *Fannin*, 221 F. Supp. 775.

Sherbert v. *Verner*, 374 U.S. 398.

Sicurella v. *U.S.*, 348 U.S. 385.

Torcaso v. *Watkins*, 367 U.S. 488.

U.S. v. *Bland*, 283 U.S. 636.

U.S. v. *Estep*, 327 U.S. 114.

U.S. v. *Gillette*, 420 F 2d 298.

U.S. v. *Kauten*, 133 F 2d 703.

U.S. v. *Kuebrich* (unreported).

U.S. v. *Kurki*, 255 F. Supp. 161; 384 F 2d 905.

U.S. v. *Macintosh*, 283 U.S. 605.

U.S. v. *McFadden*, 309 F. Supp. 502.

U.S. v. *Mitchell*, 369 F 2d 323; 386 U.S. 972.

U.S. v. *O'Brien*, 391 U.S. 367.

U.S. v. *Reynolds*, 98 U.S. 145.

U.S. v. *Schwimmer*, 279 U.S. 644.

U.S. v. *Seeger*, 380 U.S. 163.

U.S. v. *Sisson*, 294 F. Supp. 511; 297 F. Supp. 907; 399 U.S. 267.

U.S. v. *Spiro*, 384 F 2d 159; 390 U.S. 956.

U.S. v. *Taffs*, 208 F 2d 329.

U.S. v. *Welsh*, 399 U.S. 333.

Supplemental Sources

Annals of Congress, Vol. XXVIII (1814).

Congressional Globe, February 16, 1863; January 14, 1864.

Congressional Record, Vols. LV (1917), LXXXVI (1940), XCIV (1948).

Hearings Before the Senate Subcommittee on Administrative Practice and Procedure of the Senate Committee on the Judiciary: 91st Congress, 1st Session; Washington, D.C.: Government Printing Office, 1969.

Report of the Senate Subcommittee on Administrative Practice and Procedure to the Senate Committee on the Judiciary. Washington, D.C.: Government Printing Office, 1970.

U.S. Code: Title 28, section 2282.

U.S. Code: Appendix, Title 50, section 462 (a), (b), (3).

U.S. Code Annotated: Appendix, title 50, section 456 (j) (both the 1951 edition and the revised 1968 edition).

U.S. Code of Federal Regulations: Vol. XXXII, sections 1622.11, 1622.14, 1622.43, 1622.44, 1622.50, and 1631.7.

U.S., Department of the Army. *Field Manual No. 27-10.* Washington, D.C.: Government Printing Office, July 18, 1956.

INDEX OF NAMES AND SUBJECTS

INDEX OF LEADING CASES